Sonic Signatures

Sonic Signatures

Music, Migration and the City at Night

EDITED BY

Derek Pardue, Ailbhe Kenny and Katie Young

intellect

Bristol, UK / Chicago, USA

First published in the UK in 2023 by
Intellect, The Mill, Parnall Road, Fishponds, Bristol, BS16 3JG, UK

First published in the USA in 2023 by
Intellect, The University of Chicago Press, 1427 E. 60th Street,
Chicago, IL 60637, USA

A catalogue record for this book is available from the British Library.

Copy editor: MPS Limited
Cover designer: Tanya Montefusco
Frontispiece image: Artwork by Fay-Orion Antar
Production manager: Sophia Munyengeterwa
Typesetter: MPS Limited

Hardback ISBN 978-1-78938-696-7
Paperback ISBN 978-1-78938-699-8
ePDF ISBN 978-1-78938-697-4
ePUB ISBN 978-1-78938-698-1

To find out about all our publications, please visit our website.
There you can subscribe to our e-newsletter, browse or download our current catalogue and buy any titles that are in print.

www.intellectbooks.com

This is a peer-reviewed publication.

Contents

Figures

1

Sensorial Belonging and Urban Migration: An Introduction to *Sonic Signatures*

Derek Pardue

During a period, when I was in my twenties, I lived in Austin, TX. My best friends and eventual housemates were two migrants turned locals, one originally from South Texas, the borderland region near Brownsville and Matamoros, México on the Gulf coast, and the other from Vietnam via Fort Worth, near Dallas. I had arrived from San Francisco, where I had only spent two years and was also an obvious outsider to this hip university, post-punk, alternative rock town. Richard Linklater's film *Slacker* had just been released.

During one particular summer (or was it an entire year?), our rhythms of work and play grew out of sync. There was a long stretch when Hung and Austin (yeah, my friend's name is Austin, like the city) never saw the light of day. Literally. They woke up at 5:00 p.m. or 6:00 p.m. and drifted off around the time my alarm sounded at 7:00 a.m. They were film buffs and musicians; they had studio eyes. Darkness was the normal background of everything. It was *everynight*. And, sure, we had fun and laughs, we made music in our living room and we searched for bats under urban bridges in the spring. The night and darkness didn't 'fall' onto the city or cover up the day. For Austin and Hung, it was quite the opposite. The day blotted out the steady comfort of blackness. The day *happened* against a mundane nocturne. It took me years to appreciate that the human condition is not necessarily day-centric and that the production of the city is importantly (and not just frivolously) nocturnal.

Sonic Signatures is a collaborative attempt to engage darkness and the night as epistemologies of the city, cultural production and the human condition. The night consists of a set of dynamic ecologies that constitutes the city. Such ecologies are generally referred to as 'nightlife', a marketing category based on leisure and informal economies, which scholars have discussed critically as part of the human 'colonization' of the night.[1] The night as a productive frame of urban experience is an easy enough paradigm to accept, but how can we represent this perspective in a way that approximates the sensorial nature of the night and the urban? The scholarly literature tends to parallel this general perspective on the night, i.e., darkness is about control, rebel joy or fear. Yet, these approaches reinforce the notion that the night's significance is solely related to a lack of light and human vision. The night is multi-sensorial[2] and the contributors of this volume have focused on the sonic, including music, as a formative imprint on the city.

The elements of agency and representation, embedded in the term 'signature', are also fundamental to this project. *Who* makes their mark on the city through sound? Do authors/composers sign their work as routine or is it improvisational? Or both? Given the intensification of human mobility, forced or voluntary, physical or virtual, 'the migrant' has emerged as a fundamental player in the sonic constitution of the city. Many of the contributors of this volume identify as migrants and are sensitive to the complex process of creating a presence in the city as a way of legitimizing and possibly popularizing our existence as that which makes Berlin, Detroit, Galway, Lisbon, Montreal and São Paulo, for example, the cities that they are. Migration is a 'sonic process' (Kun 2016; Western 2020) that mixes experiences with representations.[3] Contributors' positionalities as racialized, gendered, classed actors ebb and flow but are always in play.[4]

The sonic signature as an expression is a combination of content and form; therefore, the issue of representational genre is significant. Recently, scholar Shahram Khosravi (2021) confessed that he has felt a sense of failure and implied a certain limitation of scholarship as an idiom in translating the phenomenon of 'waiting' as it relates to migration into academic prose. Ethnomusicologist Martin Stokes (2020) intimated similar sentiments when he underscored the ethical and intellectual *tensions* between migrant creativity and survival, between migrant identification and political struggles. In my own work on contemporary African migration in the city of São Paulo, I have also been frustrated by conventional academic textual genres and have opted for fiction as a closer register to the variable experiences of precarity and façade. In *Sonic Signatures* we have taken a cue from Khosavi and others in so far as we have designed this book as a multi-modal conversation among scholars and artists, made manifest in a curated mixture of textual genres, visual representations and sonic imprints.

Baselines and lines of flight

Sonic Signatures is transdisciplinary in that contributors represent a variety of academic disciplines in the humanities and social sciences as well as several non-academic professions, and, most importantly, have moved across these disciplinary boundaries to produce innovative perspectives on sound, the city and migrancy (a short-hand for migrant agency). The volume coheres around a set of assumptions that anchor the approach to the empirical material (baselines) and savours the departures of thought and association (lines of flight) that the night affords and that urban migrant sounds represent.

With so much intellectual and professional diversity among the contributors to this volume, I, as principal editor, proposed a methodological experiment. Our baselines, that which might facilitate cohesion, would emerge from a set of readings including ethnomusicology, geography, philosophy and fiction. Implicit and explicit notions of music, the night, migrancy and urban space emerged. For example, the idea that darkness and the night change our outlook on ourselves and surroundings pervades the texts. People tend to explore more venues of intimacy, sensorial experiences and reflection at night. Such engagements have an effect on belonging or a kind of *sensorial citizenship*.[5] Thus, it stands to reason that sound would be more salient, as people have greater focal awareness towards sound and ultimately music at night. Music, itself, is best understood as a socio-cultural practice that expresses self, an 'auditory self' (Connor 1996) which is not easily mapped, and, for some, such ubiquitous yet unpredictable qualities indicate latent socio-political potentialities inherent in music (Kasinitz and Martiniello 2019). As Zora Neale Hurston (1928) once described, music provides situations or scenes when 'my color comes'.[6] Music-making, as a dynamic and contextual process of identification, should be understood as a dynamic interface, i.e., an ecological production. Making music, in particular, or engaging with sound, in general, help shape and thus construct the city.

Similarly, migrancy is an interactional and often interdependent practice of social relations. As Toynbee and Dueck (2011) describe, cities are *network nodes* for migrants, especially musicians. The experience of being a migrant, whether musician or not, is antithetical to autonomy; migrants depend, most assuredly more so than so-called 'natives', on others to perform basic tasks such as obtaining housing, education, health care and employment. These mundane activities do not occur in a void; they are essentially spatial. Migrancy is made manifest through occupation and presence, which is not limited to physical dwelling, the places of residence and leisure. It is also about memory, diasporic longing, chronotopic articulations to *over there* and *back then*, which constitute this scene *right here, right now*. In Marie Ndiaye's short story, 'The Death of Claude François', the collective memory of a working-class Parisian suburb, where immigrants go to get by, revolves around a voice and a hopelessly flawed heroic presence that no one can seem to remember exactly. That of 1970s Egyptian-French pop singer Claude François. Friendships and romantic bonds form from the sound of that popular voice and then as they wither away, the main characters struggle to recapture what had maintained their relationships alive. Signatures fade but never completely disappear.

Baselines, as grounded as they might be in social theory, historiography and personal experience, tend to drift off, splinter, meander and become other trails of thought and composition. We propose this book as a provocative 'line of flight'. This oft-quoted phrase from Deleuze and Guattari's *A Thousand Plateaus* emerged from their own attempt to explain their textual collaboration and 'the book' as an intellectual project in a more general sense. 'A book has neither object nor subject; it is made of variously for matters, and very different dates and speeds [...]. In a book, as in all things, there are lines of flight, movement deterritorialization and destratification' (Deleuze and Guattari 1987: 3). David Henderson articulates a similar perspective in his introductory essay on diasporic or 'scattered' kinds of music. 'Through music, people find a space for play in seeking to understand (diasporic) identity not as a fixed entity, but as an ever-changing relation (to the world around oneself)' (Sánchez and Henderson 2021: xii).

Sonic Signatures is a multi-modal movement; it's on the move. Sound as content; migration as method. While Deleuze and Guattari did not write about migration per se, their insistence on the primacy of encounters and associations, more spatially articulated as *deterritorizations* or 'scatterings', help us think with migrancy, sound and the urban in productive ways as we conjure the problematic format of 'the book'. Deleuze and Guattari continue,

> the book is not an image of the world. It forms a rhizome with the world, there is a parallel evolution of the book and the world; the book assures the deterritorialization of the world, but the world effects a reterritorialization of the book.
>
> (1987: 11)

Some contributions are like dispatches from abroad, from exile, from home or from somewhere in between, a third space (Bhabha 1994) where belonging is more complicated, a place from where increasingly many of us speak. I am reminded of a collaboration between anthropologist Erika Larkins and incarcerated criminal Joe Angelion. They co-authored a COVID-19 dispatch about Joe returning to his native city of Rio de Janeiro after almost a decade of confinement in maximum security prisons across Brazil. Joe returned 'home' just as the pandemic began to take hold in precarious sites such as prisons. He reflects, 'suffering is like the mortar that unites the bricks. *O sofrimento muitas vezes é a argamassa que une os tijolos*. I am Joe Angelion. This is my dispatch. This is Brazil' (Larkins and Angelion 2020: n.pag.). Migrancy is often not about being in control of the space that you occupy, but rather, it is an emotional, sensorial condition that requires frames of expression that signify differently than language. Sound and music appeal to the exile, who feels the limits of language and frustration of telegraphic symbols. Music, especially at night, encourages imagination that somehow gets at the core, or at least probes the existential self. Individual and collective.

The calls and responses continue. Representations circulate; the city changes. Rhizomes are not roots, Deleuze and Guattari tell us. The rhizome is the 'conjunctive' (Deleuze and Guattari 1987: 25) within the logic of 'and', rather than the appendage to a base of reality and truth and history. The 'book' is an intersection point, whose purpose is to provoke the reader to re-enter the world of associations, i.e., the unconscious. 'The issue is to *produce the unconscious* and, with it, new statements, different desires: the rhizome is precisely this production of the unconscious' (Deleuze and Guattari 1987: 18). We try to obliterate hierarchies of knowledge, subjects and objects, yet we can't help but project structure constricted by language and optics. The sentiment of ethnography is lacking. We are aware but still lacking.

In the following 'chapters' and 'interludes', contributors balance the unconscious with the 'state of the art' or a selected literature review. How have scholars understood the relationship between migrancy, sound and the nocturnal city? Our control is relative; slippage is expected.

For example, over the past years, a number of publications have appeared about music as constitutive of the city. For Giacomo Bottà and Geoff Stahl, editors of *Nocturnes: Popular Music and the Night*, music *animates* the city at night, because the time–space of 'the night' permits more public, albeit often commodified, displays of sounds, 'offering lines of flight away from the ordinary and the everyday' (2019: 2). In *Sounds and the City: Popular Music, Place and Globalization* (Lashua et al. 2014), the contributors make the important observation that sounds do not map clearly onto physical cities and, moreover, that landscapes themselves are not as tightly bounded as most representations suggest. Deena Weinstein's analysis of heavy metal through foundational bands, like Black Sabbath and Judas Priest, as reflective of the long durée of metallurgy in Birmingham, England is particularly cogent (Weinstein 2014). Earlier, Sara Cohen investigated critically the iconic coupling of The Beatles and the city of Liverpool to assess how sound/music reveals the city and vice versa (Cohen 1991). But, we don't need to rise to such heights of popularity and branding, nor do we need to relegate ourselves to local heroes to argue for the rich spatiality of music and the deep musicality of urban space. More in tune with the demographic realities of the current moment, the element of migrancy is essential to the ongoing conversation and performance of the urban in sound.

And, again, another line of flight springs forth. I become anxious about sound, music, language and representation. Bae Suah in her slim novel

A Greater Music employs a female narrator, a migrant faltering in life, unsure of how she feels about an aloof boyfriend and an intriguing female musician, friend and lover, referred to as 'M'. The narrator walks along a frozen pond on the outskirts of an unnamed German city and reflects on human engagement with the world through music and language. Music was around her as a child but she was not a musician.

> I imagined that this thing, music, was merely incidental to the world, a kind of garnish. In other words, I considered it on-par with overly embellished old-fashioned clothes, romantic poetry, my weekly art class, an intricately crafted dessert, the occasional trip to the theater as a reward for good grades.
>
> (Bae 2016: 8)

Languages swirl around Bae's narrator, as they are constitutive of any migrant navigation. For their part, musicologists have wondered about the relationship between music and language for close to a century. Beginning perhaps with Charles Seeger and later with ethnomusicologists, such as Susana Sardo, they concerned themselves with the gaps and disconnects between the two modes of representation (Seeger 1958; Sardo 2019). Semioticians have joined in to investigate this odd puzzle of how different human modalities of expression, identity and sociality make meaning.[7] Bae's narrator also ponders this relationship:

> [R]epresentation – this, after all, is what language and music have in common. Music, though, cannot say all; or even, in fact, anything. Its lips are sealed. Understanding music is not a gradual process. And yet, all of this gets collapsed into that trite expression 'listening to music'. As M said to me, that time in my rented flat with her own gaze holding me rapt, 'Music is the one thing which, of all human' so-called creations', will never belong to them.
>
> (2016: 106)

Music is 'out there'; it provokes creative reception and imprints itself on the city.

I become more anxious about the relationship between music and place. Even when the 'migrant story' is not about music-making, music often takes up space. Jhumpa Lahiri, the US-based writer and daughter of Bengali parents, uses the piano to contextualize one of the main characters in her short story, 'Third and Final Continent'. We learn that Mrs Croft taught piano to private students at her home for 40 years. 'It was how she raised us after my father died' (Jhumpa 1999: 96), Helen (Mrs Croft's daughter) said to the narrator, a Bengali man who moved to London and then to Boston for education and then employment. Music is made material in the narrative as the physicality of the piano is now used for other purposes (e.g. to place rent money for the occasional boarder in Mrs Croft's house). Music is a modest memory of livelihood and a routine of trying to move on after spousal death. Moreover, the piano is material support, a seat for Mala, the narrator's arranged wife, on her arrival to Boston and an introduction to her new husband's American world. It is at the centre of the scene when Mrs Croft finally declared, 'She [Mala] is a perfect lady!' (Jhumpa 1999: 100). Music fills in the frame even when there is no sound emitted. Sonic signatures fade but never entirely disappear.

Context, in its multiple facets, is obviously important to understand migrant resonance and imprint on the city. To this point, geographers have long emphasized that cities are not 'neutral containers' (Dunn 2016: 4), but are produced, often in a contested manner, by human and non-human inhabitants. The point here is that locality is not given but emerges from encounters or what I have referred to as 'interfaces'. Regarding sound, Tom Western writes,

> if we think specifically about ethnographic sound recording, and the kinds of work it can do in the current historical moment, all this prompts a shift away from archives of ethnicities and nations and toward an archive of encounters and relations.
>
> (2020: 303)

Many scholars have interpreted encounters as a way to discuss performativity and ultimately the formation of a 'scene' or 'scape'. For example, in *Shanghai Nightscapes: A Nocturnal Biography of a Global City*, the editors define 'nightscapes' as a 'series of urban stages upon which actors creatively improvise scripts as they create new lifestyles and identities for themselves in the context of larger social changes' (Farrer and Field 2015: 13). The scene is akin to Bourdieu's social field, where constellations of 'subcultural capital' form and percolate.

In fact, the keyword of *encounter* requires a bit more unpacking, because nocturnal soundscapes are not simply what happens when musicians get together and argue over which tune to play or negotiate contracts with nervous neoliberal club owners but also, more philosophically speaking, 'encounter' refers to the multi-faceted interfaces between humans and (built) environments. Nick Dunn explains it this way

> the city is not simply out there – a built construction separate from ourselves – but in the here of our bodies [...] particles inhaled and exhaled; its materiality and textures informing our gait and steadily reshaping our footwear; its smells, sights and sounds comforting us or perhaps causing concern. And, of course, pertinently the here of our mind where we reconstruct the city many times over, forging new maps and narratives in response to its restlessness [...]. During the nocturnal hours such cartography

> may be dramatically rescaled and retraced as daytime landmarks recede and new, often highly illuminated ones become signifiers instead.
>
> (2016: 7–8, 10)

Sonic Signatures is thus an attempt to address the heterogeneity of urban embodiment and embrace the nocturnal as sensorial knowledge that invites a range of sonic performances. The 'book', a coordinated but importantly untamed 'line of flight' constellation, is structured as a precarious balance between academic scholarship ('chapters') and reflexive, performative pieces ('interludes'). The interludes are multi-modal pieces involving sound and visual registers. Over the process of curating, common themes emerged among the contributions which help to bring chapters and interludes into relation.

Collaboration

Katie Young and Ailbhe Kenny's chapter, 'Music, memory, and migration at night: Relational ways of knowing through arts-based collaborations', explores four migrant musicians' memories of music and the urban night across two cities in Ireland: Galway and Cork. The discussion stems from a community project, 'Music, Memory and the Night', an audiovisual collaboration between four Black-Irish musicians and four Black-Irish visual artists. As part of the project, musicians narrated one nocturnal memory in their city, while four visual artists – each with their own experiences of migration – drew inspiration from these sonic memories for a commissioned artwork. While each transnational migration story varies temporally, regionally, and in purpose, this project offers a point of departure for exploring musical migration in the night through sonic means.

In her chapter, 'Resonating restrictions: Dreaming with EDM "in-between" Casablanca and Montreal', Jillian Fulton-Melanson writes an account of electronic dance music's (EDM's) physical and virtual migration between Casablanca and Montreal. Her collaborators consist of musicians, artists, DJs and dancers who frequent underground EDM scenes of various subgenres including house, techno and psytrance, and who use music as both a means for migration as well as a vehicle to drive political sentiments in booming nightclubs where words cannot be heard but melodic and percussive textures can be felt. It becomes clear that interlocutors use a creative agency to produce and perform music that explores the loneliness of displacement, the excitement for departure, the anxiety of returning and the indeterminacy of impasse. This chapter argues that EDM carves space for healing and interpersonal connection and that its position in the nocturnal city creates comfort for those experiencing both invisibility and hypervisibility during the daylight hours.

Interlude 1: Willians Santos and Derek Pardue – 'How "free" is the Free Africa Festival?'

This reflection emerges from the encounter between musicians of different nationalities on a night at Al Janiah, a Palestinian bar and cultural centre, located in the city of São Paulo, Brazil. The context is the Free Africa Festival, which was produced by musician Aboucabar Sidibé from Guinea-Conakry. There were performances from artists from Venezuela, Angola, Palestine, Haiti and the Democratic Republic of the Congo. There were two noteworthy musical performances, one from Togolese Edoh Amassize with Angolan Jéssica Areias, and one from the band Les Éitoles de Liberdade. The authors reflect upon the two themes of music as encounter and migrants' critique of local expressions of Blackness and Africanity.

Street sounds

In 'Nocturnal polyphony: Mobile music-making as urban composition', Nick Dunn asks the question: How does the night sound? More specifically, who provides the soundtrack? This chapter presents a soundscape walk of the urban night through the inner-city area of Cheetham Hill in Manchester, UK. The district is home to a multi-ethnic community, the result of several waves of immigration to Britain. In the mid nineteenth century, it drew Irish people fleeing the Great Famine, with Jews settling in the area in the late nineteenth and early twentieth centuries as they fled persecution in continental Europe. During the 1950s and 1960s, migrants from the Indian subcontinent and Caribbean established new communities in Cheetham Hill. More recently, it has become home for people from Africa, Eastern Europe and the Far East. It is immigration policy as urban landscape and its music is vibrant, discordant and ever-mutating. Of particular interest here is the way in which sounds bleed into one another, creating interstitial zones for the nightwalker where the city's music is unintentionally remixed. By moving through the place, the manifold tones and rhythms are recomposed in an improvisational way. This chapter discusses the mobile music of Cheetham Hill as an ongoing entanglement that occurs at the boundaries of body and urban landscape, sound and time, identity and place.

Interlude 2: Nick Prior – 'Tokyo After Hours'

The assembled nature of Tokyo is borne of its ceaseless movement: of capital, people, commodities, data and artefacts. This interlude is a reflection on the composition of a piece of music that explores the sonic world of the Akihabara area of Tokyo, known as electric city. It is a place where all kinds of voices congregate, coalesce and overlap to generate a vocal soundscape that can easily be mistaken for noise. In fact, when you pay attention to Akihabara's voices you hear a wonderfully rich, albeit fragmented, sonic tapestry, of things taking flight, assembling and disassembling. The aim of the interlude is to reflect on what digital flânerie (in this case, purposive drifting armed with a digital audio recorder) affords by way of insights into the sonic ecology of the city, and to demonstrate the way we hear particular zones of the city through their distinctive artefacts, spaces and commodities: from the electronic voice of children's toys, pachinko parlours and video games to auto-tuned singing voices, the street chants of festivals and misheard conversations.

Historicity

Pol Esteve Castelló, in his chapter 'Manolo D'Aro post-mortem: The eternal and the futurible in the musical landscapes of Francoist experiential capitalism', gives an account of the Platja d'Aro musical scene in relationship to nightclubs and discotheques between the 1960s and 1970s through the fictional memories of Manolo Escobar, one of the most popular folkloric Spanish singers of the second half of the twentieth century. It is in a sense a post-mortem because both Escobar and Platja d'Aro are currently 'dead'. We are once again reminded that signatures fade but never truly disappear. Escobar performed on several occasions in Platja d'Aro and publicly represents a conservative spirit loosely aligned with the Franco dictatorial regime (1939–75), and, yet, his sound and presence helped usher in a new youth culture around imported music and the phenomenon of the DJ and discotheque. The friction between the national figure of Escobar and new forms of cultural consumption related with tourism and international fluxes of people and music lies at the base of the piece.

Seger Kersbergen expands our dive into sonic memories through his analysis of a diasporic community of Cape Verdeans in 'Dancing down memory lane: (Re) experiences of Cape Verdean nightlife in Rotterdam'. Escaping poverty and political oppression at home from the Portuguese colonizers, Cape Verdeans in Rotterdam found in the night a way of bringing a group together, to educate, celebrate, raise money and have fun together. The histories of particular places and memories where Cape Verdeans used to meet and have fun together are appropriated in contemporary nightlife, as organizers draw on collective memories of historical nightlife events. These events are promoted through narratives of the nocturnal city, where both the community's and the city's past are reflected through practices of re-memory and re-experience and where an imagination of the nocturnal past is constructed. Drawing on a variety of materials – music, flyers, photos, promotional material and interviews – of several events and organizers, this chapter shows how current generations of nightlife organizers (and partygoers) imagine the city's different night scenes and the implications of this for diasporic identity and belonging.

Interlude 3: Masimba Hwati and Austin Richey – *Karingido*: Vigilante tricksters and feedback-loop approaches to a liberation struggle

Since 2017, interdisciplinary artist Masimba Hwati and musician/scholar Austin Richey have engaged in sonic, visual and written dialogues concerning critical nodal points across the Atlantic; as they tease out cultural resonances between Black cultural arts in Detroit and Harare, New York and London, the artists highlight the potent connectivities that performative cultures create. In their performances, Hwati and Richey utilize field-recordings, archival materials, self-made instruments, and choreography to construct a space that is distinct from, but wholly informed by, the interconnected Black Atlantic. Their collaboration centers the sonic expressions of cultural cohorts in post-colonial and post-Fordist spaces, and in the process, connects plural histories of migratory labor, covert resistance, and oral/aural memory into a call-and-response feedback loop.

Belonging

In 'Under construction: Lisbon's nocturnal stylings of *Batida do gueto*', Jacqueline Georgis maintains a focus on Luso-African musical formation by exploring notions of identity, race and space in Portugal's capital city. Based on ethnographic research into Lisbon's Afro-Portuguese electronic dance music scenes, this chapter considers how batida music and the music label Príncipe Discos are forging new expressions of cultural citizenship in the diaspora. As Portugal continues to wrestle with postcolonial questions of national belonging and identity, cultural hybridity and otherness, Lisbon's immigrant artists offer fresh constellations of localized, urban street culture and technologically driven modes of music production to create batida. She argues that batida's aesthetic and performative practices, which mirror the raw creativity of the neighbourhood, as well as the broader national and international arenas in which these artists move, construct and shape identities relational to these spaces.

Áine Mangaoang in '(Be)Longing: Irish musicking and place-making in Oslo, Norway' shows that demographic numbers certainly do not tell the whole story. In Oslo, the number of Irish-born immigrants registers at 0.05%, yet while this community may be small in numbers, their music-making plays an essential role in the city's soundscape, from 'trad' musicians in city pubs, solo troubadours singing cover songs on suburban stages and community choirs of Irish migrants who sing together every Thursday night. This chapter examines how various forms of 'musicking' are used by Irish migrants in the Norwegian capital in the production of a range of complex Irish cultural identities set against ongoing theorizations of multi-culturalism and superdiversity in contemporary Norway.

Interlude 4: Brendan Kibbee – 'New York Ne Dort Pas'

For drummers, dancers, praise singers and socialites in Senegal and its diaspora, a *tanebeer* is a type of event whose name simply means "darkness" (from French *tenebre*). Gathering well after midnight in a Harlem church basement, a few hundred party-goers assemble to recreate a context that regularly takes place on the streets of Dakar but only occasionally within New York's Senegalese community. After working during the day as cab drivers, hairdressers, restaurant workers, doormen or street hawkers, the artists at this event fuel several hours of pre-dawn excitement, most prominently highlighting the virtuosity of solo dancers, men and women, amateurs and professionals. They also praise. In eloquent sequences, singers praise patrons, drummers praise dancers (and vice versa), guests praise the host, and friends praise friends, usually accompanied by exchanges of cash but also establishing the groundwork for forms of solidarity that sustain urban life, whether in New York or Dakar. This interlude features an assemblage of praises sung and spoken in the Harlem church basement *tanebeer*. Presented in English and their original Wolof, these praises illustrate how a prominent New York City immigrant community coalesces through languages and rhythms of pleasure, solidarity, appreciation and admiration.

Discord

Sipho Sithole's chapter 'Urban outcasts and the defiant iSicathamiya music' explores how in an act of defiance, a subversive migrant community uses iSicathamiya music as a sonic or auditory cultural process to imagine new possibilities. Historically crafted in the middle of the night, far from the gaze of authorities, this music has earned its name *ngoma busuku* ('night music'). A call-and-response acapella style of music, sang in four-part harmony by male choral ensembles, iSicathamiya was developed by Zulu hostel dwellers who came to the cities as reluctant migrant workers. A cultural phenomenon which first came to life through Solomon Linda's Mbube (Mimoweh), and later popularized by Ladysmith Black Mambazo, iSicathamiya represents the sounds of migration – voices from the margins.

'Rooms for resistance: Migration and social markers of difference in Berlin queer underground electronic music scene' analyzes the role of migrants and the so-called 'expats' in the Berlin queer underground electronic music since 2010. Following the first moment of 'expats' creating new parties, such as Cocktail D'Amore and Homopatik, author Gibran Teixeira Braga posits that, since the recent migration wave of the mid 2010s, new migrants enter the scene, as in the case of the collective Room for Resistance, re-shaping the relations between politics of body, pleasure, sexuality, class, gender, race and nationality. Through the concepts of intersectionality and social markers of difference, Braga argues that the articulation of those elements raises new issues about integration and inequality in the vibrant scene.

Interlude 5: Emilie Amrein and André de Quadros – Sounding in, sounding out: Remembrance and resistance at the border

Emilie Amrein and André de Quadros experiment with literary forms to represent US-Mexico border realities. They present a narrative in the form of a short story located in their work in Common Ground Voices / La Frontera, a forced migration project on the Mexico-US border. When they crossed the border at San Ysidro, they intended to create a space for forced migrants to build community and find meaning in shared experience through story and song. Little did they know that in the process, they would uncover and understand a migrant story far closer to home. Amrein and de Quadros draw on the personal experiences they revealed to one another under cover of darkness in Tijuana, weaving lyric poetry into a poignant narrative about exile, transit and arrival. With radical vulnerability and love, they reflect on finding home in the context of a friendship that defies age and distance, a friendship that grew to be a source of healing and joy for both.

NOTES

1. The classic reference to this body of scholarship is Murray Melbin's 'Night as frontier' (1978). Within the emergent literature of 'night studies', Robert Shaw in his text on the 'nocturnal city' articulates this strand of Marxist thought as an undergirding principle of research into 'night economies': 'The prolongation of the working day beyond the limits of the natural day, into the night, only acts as a palliative. It quenches only in a slight degree the vampire thirst for the living blood of labour. To appropriate labour during all the 24 hours of the day is, therefore, the inherent tendency of capitalist production' (Marx 1887 cited in Shaw 2018: 32). See Shaw (2018).

In contemporary debates from related fields, scholars (see, e.g., the Special Issue in *Journal of Urban Technology* dedicated to 'Smart Cities and Innovative Technologies' published in 2018) have discussed 'smart cities' and the colonization of the night as indicative of the Anthropocene in that it reveals how humans intervene into planetary systems of life and general sustainability.

2. Nick Dunn and Tim Edensor's edited volume *Rethinking Darkness: Cultures, Histories, Practices* (2021) is particularly helpful in contextualizing the multi-sensorial and multi-species dimensions of darkness.
3. Tom Western frames much of his research as 'a call to critically connect border experiences with border representations by thinking migration through both politics and aesthetics' (2020: 295 cited in Brambilla et al. 2015: 2).
4. One could cite dozens of important scholarly publications as well as works of fictions regarding the intersectionality of migrancy. One fundamental text in my thinking has been Carolyn Boyce Davies's *Black Women, Writing and Identity* (1994).
5. The phrase 'sensorial citizenship' is a reformulation of the overall argument of Trnka et al. (2013). See also Duyvendak et al. (2016). The Special Issue of *Migrações* journal (Côrte-Real [ed.] 2010) is also significant in the literature of sensorial citizenship.
6. See, in particular, a long passage in which Hurston describes going out to a jazz club with a White man and her momentary transformations, i.e., when her 'color comes', and then back again into 'civilization'.

> The great blobs of purple and red emotion have not touched him. He has only heard what I felt. He is far away and I see him but dimly across the ocean and the continent that have fallen between us. He is so pale with his whiteness then and I am so colored.
>
> (Hurston [1928] n.d.: n.pag.)

7. For example, the work Jean-Jacques Nattiez has been influential, in particular his book Music and Discourse (1990).

REFERENCES

Bae, Suah (2016), *A Greater Music*, Rochester: Open Letter Books.

Bhabha, K. Homi (1994), *The Location of Culture*, New York: Routledge.

Bottà, Giacomo and Stahl, Geoff (eds) (2019), 'Introduction: Because the night…', in G. Bottà and G. Stahl (eds), *Nocturnes: Popular Music and the Night*, New York: Palgrave MacMillan, pp. 1–18.

Brambilla, Chiara, Laine, Jussi, Scott, James and Bocchi, Gianluca (2015), 'Introduction: Thinking, mapping, acting and living borders under contemporary globalization', in C. Brambilla, J. Laine, J. Scott and G. Bocchi (eds), *Borderscaping: Imaginations and Practices of Border Making*, London: Routledge, pp. 1–9.

Cohen, Sara (1991), *Rock Culture in Liverpool: Popular Music in the Making*, Oxford: Oxford University Press.

Connor, Steven (1996), 'The modern auditory', in R. Porter (ed.), *Rewriting the Self: Histories from the Renaissance to the Present*, London: Routledge, pp. 202–23.

Côrte-Real, Maria de São José (ed.) (2010), Special Issue: 'Music and Migration', *Migrações*, 7 (October).

Davies, Carolyn Boyce (1994), *Black Women, Writing and Identity*, Abingdon: Routledge.

Deleuze, Gilles and Guattari, Félix (1987), *A Thousand Plateaus* (trans. Brian Massumi), Minneapolis: University of Minnesota Press.

Dunn, Nick (2016), *Dark Matters: A Manifesto for the Nocturnal City*, Winchester: Zero Books.

Dunn, Nick and Edensor, Tim (eds) (2021), *Rethinking Darkness: Cultures, Histories, Practices*, London: Routledge.

Duyvendak, J. W., Geschiere, P. and Tonkens, E. (eds) (2016), *The Culturalization of Citizenship: Belonging and Polarization in a Globalizing World*, London: Palgrave Macmillan UK.

Farrer, James and Field, Andrew David (2015), *Shanghai Nightscapes: A Nocturnal Biography of a Global City*, Chicago: University of Chicago Press.

Hurston, Zora Neale ([1928] n.d.), 'How it feels to be colored', *World Tomorrow*, https://www.wheelersburg.net/Downloads/Hurston.pdf. Accessed 1 November 2020.

Jhumpa, Lahiri (1999), *Interpreter of Maladies*, London: Flaming Books.

Kasinitz, Philip and Martiniello, Marco (2019), 'Music, migration and the city', *Ethnic and Racial Studies*, 42:6, pp. 857–64.

Khosravi, Shahram (ed.) (2021), *Waiting – A Project in Conversation*, Bielefeld: Transcript.

Kun, Josh (2016), 'The aesthetics of all: Listening like a Sonidero', in R. Radano and T. Olaniyan (eds), *Audible Empire: Music, Global Politics, Critique*, Durham: Duke University Press, pp. 95–115.

Larkins, Erika Robb and Angelion, Joe (2020), 'Policing and incarceration: Dispatch from a Brazilian prison', *City and Society*, https://doi.org/10.1111/ciso.12359. Accessed 1 December 2020.

Lashua, Brett, Spracklen, Karl and Wagg, Stephene (eds) (2014), *Sounds and the City: Popular Music, Place and Globalization*, London: Palgrave Macmillan.

Melbin, Murray (1978), 'Night as frontier', *American Sociological Review*, 43:1, pp. 3–22.

Nattiez, Jean-Jacques (1990), *Music and Discourse*, Princeton: Princeton University Press.

Sánchez, Martha I. Chew and Henderson, David (eds) (2021), 'Introduction', in M. I. C. Sánchez and D. Henderson, *Scattered Musics*, Jackson: University of Mississippi Press.

Sardo, Susana (2019), 'Presentacíon: O deconforto de escrever sobre música' ('The discomfort in writing about music'), *En Pedazos*, Antonio Gutíerrez: ACCI, pp. 9–17.

Seeger, Charles (1958), 'Prescriptive and descriptive music-writing', *Musical Quarterly*, 44:2, pp. 184–95.

Shaw, Robert (2018), *The Nocturnal City*, Abingdon and New York: Routledge.

Stokes, Martin (2020), 'Migration and music', *Music Research Annual*, 1, pp. 1–29.

Toynbee, Jason and Dueck, Byron (eds) (2011), *Migrating Music*, London: Routledge.

Trnka, Susanna, Dureau, Christine and Park, Julie (eds) (2013), *Senses and Citizenships: Embodying Political Life*, London: Routledge.

Weinstein, Deena (2014), 'Birmingham's postindustrial metal', in B. Lashua, K. Spracklen and S. Wagg (eds), *Sounds and the City: Popular Music, Place and Globalization*, London: Routledge, pp. 38–53.

Western, Tom (2020), 'Listening with displacement sound, citizenship, and disruptive representations of migration', *Migration and Society: Advances in Research*, 3, pp. 294–309.

PART 1

COLLABORATION

2

Music, Memory and Migration at Night: Relational Ways of Knowing Through Arts-Based Collaborations

Katie Young and Ailbhe Kenny

Introduction

This chapter explores nocturnal music memories for migrants, the African diaspora and Black-Irish musicians based in Cork and Galway, Ireland. We do so through an analysis of the online web project titled, 'Music, Memory and the Night'. As part of the project, four musicians (with diverse musical styles ranging from a multi-genre singer-songwriter to a DJ collective) were asked to select one memory of the night in Galway or Cork and to narrate this nocturnal memory through an audio recording. Musicians were able to select any memory of their choice and memories were recorded without researchers present. Once their memories were recorded, the four musicians were then paired with four visual artists, whose work ranges in style from painting to digital design. Similar to musicians involved in the project, each visual artist has familial or community ties to, or has personal experiences of, migration in Ireland. On the website, visual artists identify in varying ways, including as Irish, biracial and migrant activists, with some visual artists sharing regional ties and connections on the website, including Morocco, Nigeria and Zimbabwe. After each visual artist listened to a musician's memory, the artist-musician pairing connected through a recorded phone conversation without researchers present, where they could delve into the recorded nocturnal musical moment in more depth, encouraging a dialogic process of forming memories. The visual arts participants drew inspiration from these sonic memories and conversations for a commissioned artwork. The audio memories, digital artworks and the recorded musical work of project participants were brought together on an online platform that readers can explore in more depth here: http://www.musicmemorynight.com (accessed 3 August 2022).

The inter-arts nature of the four collaborations discussed in this chapter affords sensual perspectives and relational ways of knowing music in Irish cities at night. The project focuses on Cork and Galway, two secondary Irish cities that are home to diverse communities of migrant, diasporic, second-generation and Black-Irish musicians. Cork and Galway are often overlooked in scholarship on Irish migratory experiences, with a greater focus on Dublin as the nation's capital. Through the project, we show how nocturnal memories of the night in Cork and Galway can be remembered in more ways than one through dialogue across the arts, as each embodied and emplaced nocturnal memory addresses issues of migration, including identity, belonging, place and gender. For example, in the first collaboration discussed below, singer-songwriter Tolü Makay and visual artist Somto Amadi-Obi reveal the value of wandering and meandering through night spaces in Galway, exploring what the night offers in the realm of musical experimentation and growth for the youth of migratory families moving to new cities as young adults. In another collaboration, Ubuntu DJ Collective member Kimbly presents a spoken-word piece detailing the significance of togetherness at night through her embodied experiences in Galway's Halo nightclub; Kimbly's experience is re-imagined through digital artist Fay-Orion Antar's layering of dancing bodies, emphasizing movement and connection in the night through design. Visual artist and cultural activist Elton Sibanda's poster-style artwork on canvas depicts one of musician Wally Nkikita's night-time community projects in Galway, where Wally asserts belonging through musical activism at an Irish traditional music venue. In the final collaboration, DJ Safarii and visual artist Grace Enemaku visualize feelings of musical flow felt between DJ and diverse dancing communities in Cork city at night.

Commonalities and shared experiences of the musician and visual artist pairings became both audible and visual through their dialogic encounters. The unique experiences shared between each pairing underscores the potential for knowing migratory musical moments in new ways through relational, arts-based collaboration. As a dialogic project, 'Music, Memory and the Night' encourages musicians and artists to think through nocturnal musical and migratory moments in layered, collaborative and sonic ways, affording dynamic insights into how music is experienced in Irish cities at night.

Nocturnal musical moments

bell hooks (2009: 5) writes, 'We are born and have our being in a place of memory […]. We know ourselves through the art and act of remembering.' We view this web project as encapsulating both the art and act of remembering. This pursuit is both an individual but also a collective endeavour – rooted in particular urban spaces, streets, sounds, venues and experiences, while at the same time invoking memories of our own drawn from different cities and sounds. Thus, in both the 'art' and 'act' of remembering, the project goes beyond the direct participants, to include the reader, listener, viewer and researcher. Pardue (2019: n.pag.) claims there is a 'creative incomplete-ness of memory' which invites 'collaborative meaning-making'. Resonating with this, the visitors to the project website are invited (both implicitly and explicitly) to conjure up their own memories, contribute and perhaps make meaning (see https://www.musicmemorynight.com/your-memories [accessed 3 August 2022]).

Henri Lefebvre's concept of 'moments' is also useful to consider in this exploration of musical memories at night. He defines a 'moment' as a 'higher form of repetition, renewal and reappearance and of the recognition of certain determinable relations with otherness (or the other) and with the self' (Lefebvre 2002: 344). Thus, the 'moment' becomes transformed through space and time but also 'in relation' – again highlighting the above point about the individual and collective nature of nocturnal musical memories in this project. Lefebvre continually argues that space is always produced 'trialectically'; it is *lived, perceived* and *conceived*. Therefore, the materiality of space, its conception and also its lived experiences rely on the production of knowledge. Through the dialogues, memories and artworks explored in this chapter, we contend that these 'moments' represent relational ways of knowing and so to extend Lefebvre's concepts, a co-production of knowledge.

The obvious ability of 'moments' to repeat, renew and reappear through a digital space further pushes us to consider Lefebvre's concept in relation to the audiovisual memories captured. 'Moments' emerge from everyday experiences (or arguably *everynight* experiences) yet, for Lefebvre, are not part of everydayness. He contends: 'Once profundity and beauty are lived (and not simply gazed at or seen as a spectacle) they become moments, combinations which marvellously overturn structures established in the everyday, replacing them by other structures, unforeseen ones, and fully authentic' (Lefebvre 2002: 66). The 'moments' depicted by the musicians and artists similarly challenge and 'overturn' structures to reveal new experiences of night spaces in Irish cities by all who experience them.

The four arts-based collaborations discussed in this chapter centre around nocturnal experience, engaging with the distinctiveness of the night as a time for a musical encounter. As Dunn (2016: 10) suggests, the night 'appears somehow more porous [...] and perhaps of greater significance, it fosters a different way of thinking'. The sonic and artistic weaving together of disparate nocturnal moments in this web project encourages participants and site visitors alike to think through the night as a time of spatial, sensual and personal exploration and experimentation.

Below, each collaborative exploration of the night calibrates nocturnal experiences for migrant, diasporic and Black-Irish musicians in particular: in one musical 'moment', a starry night sky shines through onto an open roof waffle bar; the scent of crepes permeates a small Reggae music venue in Cork, to reveal a Black-Irish female DJ exploring her musical style during one of her first DJ gigs. In another musical 'moment', the specific emancipatory powers of the night are explored through colour, as a bright, multi-coloured poster-style artwork relays the practices of a former asylum seeker, who pastes posters in a Direct Provision[1] Centre, encouraging asylum seekers to 'shake off worries of the daily grind' in the night through music and dance (Dunn 2016: 12; Kenny and Young 2021). Each 'moment' discussed below reveals a dismantling, questioning or probing of racial, gendered and societal boundaries and structures during the night. These moments situate the nocturnal city as a 'place and time within which escape from the calibrations and shackles of the daytime [...] a state of *being*' (Dunn 2016: 7).

Making nocturnal musical moments

This chapter and the data analyzed within it reflect relational understandings of the memories explored in http://www.musicmemorynight.com (accessed 3 August 2022). The conversational and artistic intersections throughout the chapter are purposefully presented in a dialogic manner with the conversations between artists and musicians interwoven with the artworks and our perspectives as researchers. The recorded conversations between artists and musicians, musicians' audio memories and visual artworks combine in our analysis to provide insights from arts-based and digital methods. Thus, as Western explains, 'sounds are always moving, and can help us rethink society itself [...] plugging sonic perspectives into practices of representation allows for an unsettling of storytelling [...] and circulation, encounter, and friction are placed front and center in the mix' (2020: 296). The discussion below follows the four musician-artist pairings just as the website does and so we journey through the spaces, cities and collaborations in text, image, sound and digital forms together. In doing so, we also aim for 'an unsettling of storytelling' from remembered migrant and diasporic moments and experiences of music at night in Irish cities.

Tolü Makay and Somto Amadi-Obi

In their collaboration, musician Tolü Makay and visual artist Somto Amadi-Obi explore Tolü's musical memory at night in Galway (see http:// www.musicmemorynight.com/tolu-makay [accessed 3 August 2022]). Both artist and musician are

FIGURE 2.1: Artwork by Somto Amadi-Obi, 'Music, Memory and the Night' commission, 2021.

currently based in Tullamore, County Offaly. As well as living in the same large town currently, they also hold personal connections to Nigeria. In their conversation, Somto and Tolü explore experiences of music at night through wandering and meandering:

> TOLÜ: I went to Galway [for university] ... it felt like another village. Another village, but like a bigger village in comparison to Tullamore. So it was quite familiar, homey. But it was mostly students, which was different as well. And then that's actually when I saw more Black people ... so Galway was different. Seeing different people from different backgrounds and all quite similar ages, it was all new. And I was coming from a Christian family and singing in my local choir.
>
> My number one duty my mom wanted me to do was to make sure I found a church ... and then when I did, people started recruiting you. 'Do you want to be an usher? Do you want me to be in choir? What do you want to do? You have to give your service to God.' So naturally, the choir was where I was placed, and I was leading praise and worship ...
>
> It wasn't until my third year [that I started trying to see] how other musicians perform. I was out with a friend of mine, and he had a band set up ... And yeah, it was like a bar, but it's known to be one of the most famous places in Galway for music ... I [sang an] acapella piece for an

open mic night [there] ... but when I saw [my friend] perform, I think that's when I was like, 'Oh. I'd really love to just do this ... but with my own songs' ... before then, it was just like, 'I want to be a Gospel singer.' That's what I thought I'd be. You know?

... Going out in uni ... there are students everywhere. There's [*sic*] nightclubs on both sides. Girls wearing really short dresses, and you know they're cold. Even I, myself, we are all cold, but because it's the time to go out, it's fine. It's okay. We go into the club, the music is pumping ... after nightclubs, the location to go to is Supermac's. And every single night, there was always a fight ...

Galway was really the place that I started ... having my own mind. It really made me more inquisitive about life ... It made me want *to lead my own life how I see fit.* Yeah. It made me question a lot of human behaviour ...

SOMTO: You're away from your parents.

TOLÜ: Yeah, exactly. When you have to start making decisions by yourself, thinking by yourself. But as much as I had people around me, I always felt quite lonely, if that makes sense. Because I felt like my upbringing was very different. Even though I was amongst other Black people, I felt quite distanced ... that's the story of my life in Galway ...

SOMTO: ... I'm new to Ireland. And I don't really know much about Galway. I couldn't name any [Irish] counties if you put a gun to my head ... but I like Ireland because while I'm with family here, music ... there's always music playing ... *I don't have like a straight genre* that I listen to. Like, it *meanders.* Like, my dad listened to Reggae. I like Reggae. My mom listened to Enya, church music, all sorts of things. My dad liked Turkish music ... On my way to school, we bumped into some Arabic tunes ... With me and drawing, well ... *I always have to set up my own playlist ...*

Both in her nocturnal musical memory and in the above conversation, Tolü Makay describes her musical experiences of the night in Galway over time, wandering between seemingly disparate nocturnal musical moments across her four years living in the city as a student. She draws connections between nights out in the cold wandering between rows of nightclubs, attending a friend's rock band performance in a famous traditional music venue, and leading Gospel choir worship in a church that her mother encouraged her to attend. Tolü's musical journey is reflected in her movement through diverse night-time spaces: a church, Supermac's,[2] a nightclub and a traditional music venue. As Dunn (2016: 9–10) suggests, 'the uncanny character of the night-time city squeezes and stretches places', inspiring a 'jumbling of ideas and problems, the half-lives of previous projects and memories all stirred deeply within'. Tolü's time spent exploring the night through music with other young adults led to moments of collaborative exploration and experimentation, bending musical expectations in multiple directions.

In her memory, Tolü recalls her friend's rock band gig, noticing differences between her own experience singing in a Gospel church and that of her friends performing at a night-time rock gig:

> One thing I noticed is that with rock bands, they never have a keyboardist. It's always a guitarist, a bassist, a singer and a drummer. And I found that so fascinating because in the church you always need a keys player. That was so fundamental. So, it was so different seeing that kind of dynamic and seeing music could be played that way. There was just some something so electrifying about it.

By entering into a range of night-time venues in the city, Tolü explored, encountered and experimented with the boundaries of her own musical output. As she reiterates in her conversation with Somto, her time spent attending her friend's rock gig encouraged her to chart new musical paths in her work, moving in more musical directions than what she initially anticipated when moving to Galway. Just as Tolü's meanderings in the nocturnal musical city reveal moments of exploration, her pathways also reflect vivid encounters with racism. In her recorded memory, Tolü recalls a time at a Galwegian nightclub where her Black male friends were denied entry on a night out: 'they told the guys, not tonight. And it was just like we were all kind of taken aback. I think that was the first time I witnessed like something racial face-to-face'. Tolü's memory reflects an ongoing process of systemic racism in Galway's night-time club scene, one that continues to shape Black-Irish youth's experiences of the night in the city (Young 2022).

After listening to Tolü's memory and her story in Galway, Somto discussed his own experiences of listening to music while making artwork and throughout his daily life in Offaly. He explained that while making art in his home but also through his experiences walking, he engages with a range of musical genres from different regions: listening to Turkish music or Reggae inspired by his father or Enya from his mother while drawing, and Arabic language music from when he walked to school. He explores his musical listening practices as 'not a straight genre' but rather a practice that meanders. His practice of listening parallels the meandering explorations that Tolü took through Galway's night scene as she explored the diversity of musical performance and listenership at various venues, clubs, churches and late-night communal spaces.

Tolü's memory encompassed a series of moments in different spaces throughout the nocturnal city. As Somto listened to Tolü's memory, he creatively engaged with meanderings between nocturnal moments and spaces. During their conversation, Somto explained that he did not know much about Galway and furthermore was not familiar with the counties of Ireland generally. However, in his final artwork, Somto etched out the towns and cities within county Galway in detail, filling each settlement with curved, bending lines that move in unexpected ways. In listening to their conversation and Tolü's memory, we as researchers were afforded the chance to engage creatively *with* Somto's artwork through sonic means. For example, through our practice of listening, we heard the lines in Somto's artwork reverberating Tolü's musical journey in Galway's night spaces, including her time spent in the choir and the open mic night with her friend. As we listened, we experienced the lines – or 'meanderings' – of Tolü's memories woven together through conversation, art and Somto's artistic (and cartographic) explorations of Irish space. While Somto may not have experienced Galway's night-time musical spaces and moments through his own lived experience, he comes to know the nocturnal city by listening to and being in dialogue with Tolü's memory. Similarly, site visitors come to know about Tolü's nocturnal musical experiences by engaging with the sounded voice, dialogue and visuals. Memories of the night can thus be experienced and understood in new ways through the practice of collaborative meaning-making (Pardue 2019). In her memory, Tolü presents a collage of nocturnal moments, and in his artwork, Somto listens carefully to this sonic constellation, weaving together musical moments across a map of Galway city. Through the memory, dialogue and artwork, participants, researchers and site visitors are encouraged to 'know' the musical city at night in new ways, by thinking across and between sound and visual art.

Ubuntu DJ Collective and Fay-Orion Antar

FAY-ORION: I was really interested in the part where you guys are performing and you're in the middle of performing and I just wanted to expand a bit on like the visuals ... are you like aware of your surroundings or are you more aware of the lights or like what kind of visuals are the most intense for you when you're like in the middle of performing essentially?

KEITH: The lights, the lights go on ... everyone is like shining lights.

FAY-ORION: Yeah.

KEITH: Red lights, green lights, going all over, strobing kind of thing.

FAY-ORION: Cool.

KEITH: You can see outfits, people's outfits depending on what light is on.

BONGANI: Yeah, for me it would be the same. The lights are probably one of the most captivating things in the club. It's like they actually can make and break a set sometimes. So depending on what sort of atmosphere is there – let's say, if it's in the middle of the night and the vibe is great and you're playing upbeat music and the lights are just like a strobing sequence everywhere. And like, now everyone is going crazy ... the lights match to the BPM or the songs as well.

FAY-ORION: That sounds amazing actually ...

KIMBLY: I just focus on the dancers, who is dancing. If you're not dancing, I'm not looking at you.

FIGURE 2.2: Artwork by Fay-Orion Antar, 'Music, Memory and the Night' Commission, 2021.

In the above conversation, the Galway-based DJ collective Ubuntu DJs reflect on their recorded memory of DJing in Galway at night, in conversation with digital animator Fay-Orion Antar. As revealed from this conversation excerpt, the lights on a given night are all important to creating atmosphere and often pulse to the beat of their music set. Not only this but the lights are also remembered as a means of illumination, allowing the DJs to observe outfits, dancing and 'everyone [is] going crazy'. The memories explored in this conversation weave light, colour, sound and movement together, an approach paralleling Ubuntu collective's nocturnal memory on the 'Music, Memory and the Night' website (http://www.musicmemorynight.com/ubuntu-collective [accessed 3 August 2022]). During the phone conversation between Fay-Orion and the collective, participants make connections between sensory elements of the night, revealing additional layers and 'moments' (Lefebvre 2002) to their memories. For example, when Fay-Orion asked the collective what colours they saw when they remembered the night, DJ Bongani described 'violet and crimson'; Bongani explained that these colours were most often used by lighting technicians when he played slow music in the club, an aspect that transitioned the atmosphere of the night. Fay-Orion's questions around colour conjure up the significance of coloured lights as they relate to temporality in the nightclub for Ubuntu DJs. Violet and crimson are subsequently central to Fay-Orion's design, with her colour choices symbolizing Bongani's experience of sound and time in the artwork. The artist and artwork thus point to the co-production of knowledge of that space, both through the recollection of this 'moment' by DJ collective members who experienced it first-hand, but also through the repetition and re-interpretation of that 'moment' in dialogue and in Fay-Orion's resulting artwork design (Lefebvre 2002).

Exploring Ubuntu DJs' memory on the website, we hear an individual embodied experience of a night DJing at Halo nightclub in Galway, related through spoken word written by collective member Kimbly. As a member of the collective, Kimbly highlights an experience of both sound and movement in her composition. Again, dancing is all important to the recollection as referenced earlier, but there is also a focus on the journey to the club – punctuated by specific geographical landmarks (passing Eyre Square, a neon sign), entering and then moving within the nightclub space itself. Here, Kimbly relates a physical negotiation of space, for instance, setting up equipment ('untangling wires at rocket speed, running around an almost empty club like headless chickens, just to be ready for opening time'), moving across the dancefloor ('I felt trapped moving through the masses that seemed determined to keep me locked in the dance floor') and jostling for a gap at the bar to order drinks ('behind a hoard of thirsty strangers, waiting patiently for a merciful bartender'). She further juxtaposes her time in the smoking area where the air is still with the music from the club 'sound[ing] like thuds hitting against glass doors underwater'.

This nocturnal memory is therefore very embodied, linking space with sensory experience and thus the artwork itself pushes the viewer to consider these aspects further through visuals. As Dunn (2016: 11) reminds us, 'The city is not simply out there – a built construction separate from ourselves – but in the here of our bodies: its particles inhaled and exhaled; its materiality and textures.'

As a collective, the support of a circle of DJs is particularly distinctive in the materials gathered for this web project. For instance, within the phone conversation between musicians and artists, the DJs spoke of friendship, support and a sense of community often:

> BONGANI: You do need to put in time and kind of like develop your craft for you to be able to feel like you're in your element. And for me at the times when I feel like I'm in my element the most, almost every time is when I'm DJing with my mates. When I'm DJing alone, sometimes you just don't have it in you; do I really have to do this? ... for things I really enjoy, I like bringing my friends there ... you know, that gives you the freedom to put more time in your craft and become even better at it. So you can pull a bigger crowd and all that.
>
> FAY-ORION: So it's definitely more fun with friends. I mean, I feel like that goes with everything, but would you all agree that, like, when you're, when you're with each other on stage ...
>
> KIMBLY: ... even if I know I'm DJing by myself, I always bring someone with me. I would call one of the guys or any of the other members to come with me, just to help me in case I get stuck or whatever.

Extending the spirit of the DJ collective itself as alluded to here, their memory also encompasses the power of 'the group'; for Kimbly, the co-presence of Ubuntu DJ members in the nightclub aids in moments of stasis, working to collectively move music throughout the night. This sense of community went beyond the DJs and included the night revellers too. From the spoken word memory, this temporal night-time community is very much 'placed' within the nightclub itself, encapsulating an energy that builds through dance, alcohol and strobe lighting as the music itself builds up to the last tune of the night:

> I remember when we finished our set, everyone was chanting, 'One more tune,' their voices growing louder by the second, until the bouncer gave in, giving us the

> go ahead. And as 'Sicko Mode' began to play, the bouncer couldn't help but start dancing too. Suddenly everyone in the collective had abandoned the decks, dancing with him; that night in retrospect is the reason why I do this.
>
> (Music Memory Night n.d.: n.pag.)

From this excerpt, a sense of togetherness and liberation is related that is experienced within the nightclub space – that even includes the bouncer, a role normally associated with control and surveillance over the space. As well as this, Kimbly asserts her motivation as to why she DJs, just as the other DJs explained in their phone conversation discussed earlier (for more on Kimbly's DJ experiences see Kenny 2022). It is about relationships, collective endeavour and shared interest that connects the musical to the social. This exploration of togetherness through movement and sound is re-imagined in Fay-Orion's digital design, depicted in the multiple waves of colour as well as layered moving bodies.

Wally Nkikita and Elton Sibanda

WALLY: I'm originally from the Democratic Republic of Congo ... when I came to Ireland in 2010, I thought that I have to do something to promote my culture. So, that's how I started the Afro music night.

ELTON: ... So do you only recruit people from Direct Provision? Or is it for everyone who is interested? Or is it for only Africans?

WALLY: Yeah. As an Afro music night event, we invite African artists from Galway City and those in Direct Provision to come ... so we can see the talent, and promote the native African countries' culture. So it's, really involves everyone, let's say, who lives in Galway and belongs in the community.

ELTON: That's cool Wally. I'm glad to hear that. Yeah, so can you please tell me, what did you expect when you were planning the event? Did you expect a small event, or did you expect a large event?

WALLY: Yeah. We started small ... since 2017, our Afro music night. Then it was not really known. But as long as we go along, people knew

> that each and every month there's an Afro night event, so they have come and taken part. Everyone African or Irish and everyone in the city ... We feel so happy because we always have a good crowd now, which makes us to feel the sense of belonging and be part of the Galway community.

FIGURE 2.3: Artwork by Elton Sibanda, 'Music, Memory and the Night' commission, 2021.

The previous conversation between Galway-based musician, Wally Nikkita and Cork-based artist, Elton Sibanda, very much centres around both cultural maintenance of a 'homeland' identity while simultaneously aiming to integrate into the country and city Wally has lived within for over a decade. This signifies a distinct shift of focus from the other artist-musician pairings described in this chapter. During their conversation, Elton and Wally spoke Ndebele[3] and English, switching between languages often. Despite Elton being approximately 30 years Wally's junior, there was a clear commonality found between the two in dialogue and shared experiences. While not made explicit, this was evident in a shared language, their community activist approaches, desire for creative expression and connection to 'homeland'.

It is most interesting to consider this shift of focus in light of the fact that both Wally and Elton came to Ireland seeking asylum. Wally spent the first six years of his time in Ireland living in the Direct Provision (DP) system, while Elton still resides within a DP centre in Cork. Despite the barriers these two have encountered (and continue to encounter) as a result of this, they both actively seek opportunities to create and be part of their surrounding communities. As Western has found, 'sonic, street-level assertions of belonging remake and rearticulate the polis' (2020: 295). For instance, Wally performs in several live bands in Galway, is a DJ and leads a community choir. He often works in partnership with community organisations and events in the city (for more on Wally and African diasporic experiences in Galway, see Kenny and Young 2021). Elton is a self-taught artist who also actively engages within Cork organisations such as The Glucksman Gallery, Cork Migrant Centre and Cork Printmakers. Thus, connecting with others through their art forms is important to both of them but more than this, as Wally claims, there is a desire to feel a 'sense of belonging'.

Wally's memory related to the project website, akin to the others explored earlier, is place-based. He homes in on Afro music night at the venue Áras na nGael in Galway city which he organizes and performs at (see http://www.musicmemorynight.com/wally-nkikita [accessed 3 August 2022]). As well as providing a space for cultural and social connection through music, Wally is explicit in the activist nature of the event in his recollection:

> [W]e can let people know that there are Africans living in Galway city too. As a performer myself, as a DJ, I feel like doing what I do is really uplifting me and telling me that I have to go and go and do more as I live here. That means I belong here. So everything I do has to be for here and for the people of Galway city.

We hear again the importance of belonging to an urban space that recognizes the diversity of its inhabitants. This resonates with the work of Berg and Sigona (2013: 352) who write of how 'specific locations have histories (and memories) of migration'. While Wally wishes to integrate, he does not wish to assimilate – rather he strives for recognition of a distinct African diasporic identity in the city amongst multiple other identities. Elton in his artwork, therefore, produces a poster-style painting that encompasses a dancing, faceless crowd in shadow who he claims 'show their support and appreciation' for the two male musician figures holding guitars – one who is Wally. In the background, Elton depicts what he sees as 'popular African colours and patterns' that Wally emphasizes in his memory are needed to 'make the pub have the feels and smells of Africa'. Elton further highlights the emplaced nature of the memory in displaying the venue, musicians on the billing, and even a start time. Furthermore, he repeats the motto that Wally is so keen to emphasize in his memory and recorded conversation, 'together we can do more'. Elton recognizes the importance of this sentiment for Wally and in a similar activist spirit, includes it in the artwork.

FIGURE 2.4: Artwork by Grace Enemaku, 'Music, Memory and the Night' commission, 2021.

DJ Safarii and Grace Enemaku

DJ SAFARII: ... The setting, it was very dark in there ... the place was quite dark ... I was really nervous... you know when you can't even look at the crowd nervous? I was that nervous. But eventually, when I saw the way the crowd reacted to the songs I was playing, that gave me the confidence I needed. And then after that, then it's just ... *you get into the flow of things*, and yeah. I felt good afterwards.

GRACE: ... So what kind of songs were you playing? I know you said you had Reggae and Afrobeats. Would you have a couple of songs that you'd recommend that I go and listen to? Because I like to work with music in the background sometimes as well, to get me in *the vibe*.

DJ Safarii: I definitely played Vybz Kartel anyways ... because I was so paranoid about playing Afrobeat as well because I felt like it was just a pure Reggae type of crowd. The name of the event is literally called 'Reggae Reggae with Gwada Mike'. So I was thinking, oh crap, I need to play Dance Hall and Reggae. No, like when I played Afrobeat and even played a bit R&B as well, and they all loved it ...

In their conversation, DJ Safarii and digital artist Grace Enemaku explore the first time DJ Safarii performed at the Sextant in Cork. Throughout their conversation, DJ Safarii and Grace tease out moments of encounter with diverse dancers and attendees in this night-time venue, but also with different music technologies and new night-time spaces. Together, they explore how feelings of uncertainty and anticipation over what is expected of night-time musical performances can give way to experiences of ecstasy in the dark. In the fuzziness of a small, dark venue, DJ Safarii falls into sync with the crowd through their audible and physical reactions – through which DJ and dancers connect in 'flow' and 'vibe'. The lack of light imbalances the senses, obscuring DJ Safarii's vision; the darkness allows for a 'heaviness' – such as DJ Safarii's moments of uncertainty and anticipation in the unseen – while also inspiring a kind of 'weightlessness' – afforded through the optics of anonymity, encouraging DJ Safarii to take musical chances (Dunn 2016: 15). DJ Safarii's recollection reveals alternate ways of experiencing darkness and light in comparison to Ubuntu DJs' memory above. For DJ Safarii, the absence of light reflects another kind of temporality in relation to 'flow'.

In the first portion of their conversation, DJ Safarii draws on her selection of music as a point of departure to reflect on feelings of nervousness when DJing for the first time. As she recalls in her memory (see http://www.musicmemorynight.com/dj-safarii [accessed 3 August 2022]), the venue was attended by an eclectic group of dancers and attendees, including 'your Rastafarians, your frickin hippies, your French crowd, all just vibing to the music'. In the previous excerpt, DJ Safarii remembers the feeling of uncertainty on how a diverse crowd might react as she introduced musical genres – such as R&B and Afrobeats – outside the regular expectations of a 'Reggae Reggae' night might sound like. In a dimly lit space, DJ Safarii transitions from not looking at the crowd out of fear, to feeling the 'vibe' of the room, basing the crowd's affirmations on the continued movement of bodies on the dance floor.

Grace asks DJ Safarii to recall songs from her playlist that night, in order to listen to the music while creating the artwork. Just as DJ Safarii was unable to see the crowd as she experimented with playing Afrobeat and R&B music at a 'Reggae Reggae' night, Grace is unable to see the event itself through videos or images, instead drawing on the music DJ Safarii played that night in order to (re)create 'the vibes' of openness while creating her artwork. In doing so, Grace engages with music as a way of entering into DJ Safarii's nocturnal moment, in order to re-imagine this experience in new ways through digital design.

Grace not only relates to this nocturnal moment through sonic means but through visual aspects, such as colour. When Grace asks DJ Safarii the kinds of colours that might reflect DJ Safarii's feeling that night, DJ Safarii replied:

DJ SAFARII: My feeling as a colour, it would be maybe ... Purple ... I felt ecstatic, so, I don't know what colour would link in to ecstatic. But, yeah, we'll say purple.

GRACE: Okay, fab, I'll use purple as a good base. It's a good kind of night colour as well ...

As DJ Safarii links the colour purple to the energy of the night – a feeling of nervousness followed by the confidence garnered through reactions of a new crowd interacting with her music – Grace relates the colour purple as a 'night colour'. Grace places the energy of ecstasy onto the night sky.

The artwork itself layers a series of individuals onto this night sky, representing the significance of the crowd in DJ Safarii's memory:

DJ SAFARII: The only thing I would say that stood out was, you had just different kind of people, like the way they dressed, do you get me? So to me, what really stood out was like the pure hippy crowd ... I'm used to Afrobeats and everyone getting done up and shit, but they just came through with their dreads, they had ... do you know the huge pants? The loose pants? Just wavy, they were just wavy ... I feel like just the different crowds was what really stood out to me. The fact that everyone just came together, and ... they were lit.

GRACE: Everyone came together and vibed to the music ... So you said that you felt it went from being kind of nervous and apprehensive, and then just having the feeling of ecstasy.

DJ SAFARII: Exactly, that's the word – ecstasy.

GRACE: And getting lost in the moment.

DJ SAFARII: Yeah. That's it, that's it.

In Grace's art, the crowd is woven into DJ Safarii's specific sensual memories of the night. For example, in her memory, DJ Safarii detailed the significance of a waffle bar near where she played, recalling: 'there was this little section, open roof section by the bar. And there was this chef and he would make freshly made waffles and crêpes for the evening'. In Grace's work, dancers 'vibe' on top of whipped cream, shaped to reflect clouds floating through the night sky. Senses further blur together, as the waffle-making station becomes part of a vinyl deck, reflecting DJ Safarii's first experiences of DJing with vinyl that night:

> GRACE: Can you think of any other objects that were present on the night that were interesting? Is there anything else that kind of jumps out at you? That'd be an interesting object, that would have stood out from the night?
>
> DJ SAFARII: To me, the only thing really that stood out like that to me was ... Obviously I came through with my decks, the SB2. And then there was this other DJ ... he came through with vinyl ... and I just found that interesting, because I had never seen that in real life before.

DJ Safarii's encounters with vinyl are not only significant to her experience of night but reflect highly gendered processes of learning to DJ in Ireland's night spaces (for more on DJ Safarii's experiences learning to DJ, see Kenny 2022). Through her art, Grace works to 'know' the memory in more ways, bringing varied aspects of DJ Safarii's night into dialogue with one another (Lefebvre 2002: 344). The crowd floats into the ecstatic purple night sky, moving between the whipped-cream clouds and waffle-shaped vinyl records. The crowd are literally spinning on the deck, as DJ Safarii moves the crowd in new ways.

Conclusion

In this chapter, we present four art-based collaborations between Black-Irish, African diasporic and migrant musicians and visual artists, as part of the web project 'Music, Memory and the Night'. Nocturnal musical memories are encountered and explored through a range of means, including digital and canvas-based artworks, recorded memories ranging from free-form recollections to spoken word and conversations that reconfigure these nocturnal musical moments in relational ways. The collaborative nature of this project underscores the 'trialecticality' of the musical moments discussed (Lefebvre 2002). Artworks emerge through conversations with musicians who *lived* these moments, but also through engagements with artists who *perceive* these moments through the lens of shared experience. In each musician-artist collaboration, musical 'moments' are *conceived* in new ways, as memories conjure up shared experiences of music at night for each pairing, subsequently reflected through visual art.

The kaleidoscopic nature of the memories presented in this project makes clear the value of sonic engagements with audible memories, that encourage an 'unsettling of storytelling' placing 'encounter and friction [...] front and center in the mix' (Western 2020: 296). Just as artists and musicians in this project have journeyed through Galway and Cork's nocturnal spaces through an engagement with the audible voice, musical sound and artistic forms, others are invited to engage in these 'moments' as they visit the site. In this way, the 'moment' continues to extend, as new visitors participate in this 'unsettling of storytelling' by listening and perhaps connecting to moments and experiences of music at night alongside the project's musicians and visual artists.

NOTES

1. Direct Provision was set up in Ireland in the year 2000 as a state system of housing those seeking international protection while in the asylum-seeking process. Residents receive a weekly allowance in addition to food and board.
2. Supermac's is an Irish fast food restaurant chain, with restaurants located in major cities and towns throughout the Republic of Ireland and in Northern Ireland. These restaurants are usually open late at night and as such, they are often spaces where people gather for food at the end of nights out.
3. Ndebele is related to the Zulu language, spoken mainly in Zimbabwe and parts of South Africa.

REFERENCES

Berg, Mette Louise and Sigona, Nando (2013), 'Ethnography, diversity and urban space', *Identities: Global Studies in Culture and Power*, 20:4, pp. 347–60.

Dunn, Nick (2016), *Dark Matters – A Manifesto for the Nocturnal City*, Winchester: Zero Books.

hooks, bell (2009), *Belonging: A Culture of Place*, New York: Routledge.

Kenny, Ailbhe (2022), 'Becoming and being a DJ: Black female experiences in Ireland', *Journal of Popular Music Education*, 6:2, pp. 235–46, https://doi.org/10.1386/jpme_00087_1. Accessed 25 November 2022.

Kenny, Ailbhe and Young, Katie (2022), '"The House of the Irish": African migrant musicians and the creation of diasporic space at night', *Ethnomusicology Forum*, 31:3, https://doi.org/10.1080/17411912.2021.1938623. Accessed 25 November 2022.

Lefebvre, Henri (2002), *Critique of Everyday Life: Volume Two*, London: Verso Books.

Music Memory Night (n.d.), 'Ubuntu DJs: Artwork by Fay-Orion Antar', http://www.musicmemorynight.com/ubuntu-collective. Accessed 3 August 2022.

Pardue, Derek (2019), '"Connotative Memories": Writing with light', Cultural Anthropology website, http://www.culanth.org/fieldsights/connotative-memories. Accessed 1 April 2021.

Western, Tom (2020), 'Listening with displacement: Sound, citizenship and disruptive representations of migration', *Migration and Society* 3:1, pp. 294–309.

Young, Katie (2022), '"Watering my roots": From Lagos hometown meetings to Galway's "G Afro Vibez"', *Crossings: Journal of Migration & Culture* 13:1, pp. 11–26.

3

Resonating Restrictions: Dreaming with EDM 'In-between' Casablanca and Montreal

Jillian Fulton-Melanson

Taqsīm, barzakh, hope

This chapter is a reflexive account of the migration of electronic dance music (EDM) producers between Casablanca and Montreal. Through this in-motion spatialization of sound, sentiment and people, I move with my collaborators – musicians, artists, DJs and dancers – who frequent overlapping, underground EDM scenes of various subgenres within house and techno, and who use music as both a means for migration as well as a place of refuge where they can dream.[1] Although my interlocutors dream of 'immigration', which suggests movement from the centre (point of origin) to the periphery (diaspora), in this chapter I also account for their oscillation between these two points and the restrictions they have faced along the way.

Throughout this chapter, I 'sound' the improvisatory techniques used in methods of migration. Compartmentalizing migration into departure, arrival and return, I analyze the different barriers that four Moroccan musicians – Khalil, Younasse, Oussama and Fouad – have come up against during their trans-Atlantic crossings to Montreal over the course of their migratory lives. EDM production and nightlife events offer each of them sonic and physical spaces to hope and dream as they improvise and navigate such barriers. As will unfold in this chapter, each of these musicians has a unique experience with the process of migration and does not necessarily cross over from one category to the next; neither departure, arrival, nor return are guaranteed events. I employ these categories with the intention to focus on the improvisatory navigation that occurs in-between them using the Arabic musical concept, *taqsīm* (*taqāsīm*, pl.), which is both an improvisatory genre of music as well as a reference to the act of musical improvisation. I apply the concept of *taqsīm* to the creative improvisation that restrictions generate during migration. *Taqsīm* is a form of musical storytelling that employs a regulatory structure. I argue that individual and collective histories of migration co-produce the *taqāsīm* that are written into the sounds that bounce off city walls and echo throughout the night.

Taqsīm has been written about extensively by ethnomusicologists such as Racy (2000a, 2000b, 2003, 2009), Shannon (2003) and Marcus (2007). *Taqsīm* incorporates relativity, individuality, inspiration and tradition. It is located in an intangible space between individual and collective pasts, presents and futures, and it creatively re-defines musical direction. Musically, *taqsīm* is also considered to be a genre, for it incorporates its own structure, rules and placement within a performance. According to Racy, 'the special significance of improvisation centres around the musical substance, the individual artist, the community, and life in general' (2000b: 303). Ethnomusicologists such as Ellen Waterman support this statement through the study of improvisation more generally, developing it *as* a social theory in the context of intercultural encounters (2019: 161). Waterman argues that the complex behaviours practised during improvisation make it 'good to think with', and that it 'provides novel ways to theorize the aesthetic and the social as co-constitutive and dynamical' (2019: 163). In response, although *taqsīm* is a musical term – a term that musicians playing traditional Arabic music would employ for the improvisational sections of a piece – my use signifies a deeper connection to the individual, community and life.

While *taqsīm* can simply be defined as improvisation, the improvisatory nature of *taqsīm* is also culturally associated with narrativity in the Arab world. According to Marcus, the improvisatory genres – *taqsīm* (instrumental), *layali* and *mawwal* (both vocal) – are 'understood to be from a distant past within Arab culture (pieces and genres in this category are dubbed "*min it-turāth*," literally, "from the heritage")' (2007: 104). This explains why *taqāsīm* is said to tell a story. The genre tells the story not only of collective memories from the past but also of musical patterns learned, personal memories, schools of playing and the lineage that any given musician might associate with these patterns. Arabic musical terms embody Arab cultural metaphors, which is why they fit so well in a discussion about the experience of social improvisation.

Creative *taqāsīm*, which I will exemplify throughout this chapter, can be thought of as the sound of intertwining movements and restrictions that can be heard in underground EDM events not only on both ends of the Casablanca–Montreal spectrum of migration but also during the processes happening in-between these cities. I think of restrictions as showing at once the simultaneity of movement and stasis, similar to the in-between state of Deleuzian 'becoming', which he describes as an identity crisis that occurs when a sense of self is 'flipped upside down' or 'folds onto itself' (1990 [1969]). However, using Western (2020) as part of my foundation, I aim to destabilize the idea of crisis and frame this state of being as an obstacle that generates *taqsīm* in the form of a hopeful pause. Making this argument culturally specific, I employ the term *barzakh*, a Sufi word that Ibn 'Arabi developed and centralized in Andalusian modes of being.[2] *Barzakh* is defined as an isthmus and can be translated as limbo in esoteric Arab thought. It was developed as such by Ibn 'Arabi as a state between the corporeal and the spirit worlds. *Barzakh* also refers to the imagination: a place located between the conscious and subconscious. Vincent Crapanzano translates this in-between through the words of a Moroccan interlocutor as 'the silence between words and dreams' (Crapanzano 2004: 57). Scholars such as Matthew Sharpe (2005) have used *barzakh* to describe the liminality of migration for the Maghrebi people. I combine *barzakh* and *taqsīm* in order to frame an in-motion temporality showing at once the simultaneity of movement and stasis as well as a form of improvisatory dreaming that is particular to the creative navigation of Moroccan migrants through migratory restrictions.

One might feel as though their mundane life is in stasis while they are literally, energetically dancing at an EDM event. Fieni (2016) and Kaufman (2012) both make similar claims regarding the mutually informative component found within movement and stasis. Nocturnal EDM events in the city are where my interlocutors go to seek refuge at night when their minds are under siege from various legalities and bureaucracies. The music they perform and produce crosses nations, class barriers and cultural barriers and accompanies people dancing in various city dwellings. In such dwellings, when participants have completely surrendered to the music, they often close their eyes and enter a state of trance between words and dreams.[3] Although this moment is not 'silent' as Crapanzano's research on *barzakh* suggests, the soundscape of EDM drowns out virtually all other forms of sound and becomes a location for dreaming. *Barzakh*, in this sense, can be thought of as the social space in-between the self and the society where one is physically moving, a space that is in-between various worlds.

Engaging with the city at night, I employ Dunn (2016) and Minh-Ha (2016) to dance with my interlocutors through the EDM spaces of Casablanca and Montreal. Mirroring *taqsīm*'s storytelling ability, I recount the words of Khalil, Younasse, Oussama and Fouad, along with our collaborative moments. Adopting *taqsīm* as a research methodology allows me to improvise with my interlocutors between Montreal and Morocco, flowing through nightclubs, cafés, pubs, living rooms, beaches, streets and alleyways. These improvisatory movements, which would intensify as the sun would set and the day turned to night, inform how I have written their stories and encounters of music and migration into performance ethnography. Our musical encounters took place from 2018 to 2019, but many interviews and casual conversations continued into 2021. My interlocutors from Morocco express that they have migrated to or are planning to migrate to Canada because they are in search of what they hope will be a better life with more stability. However, they are faced with varying challenges as they progress through the necessary steps towards migration. Through the memories recounted in this chapter, *taqsīm* and *barzakh* are felt in the emotional processes such as the loneliness of displacement, the excitement for departure and the anxieties of returning.

Casablanca, Morocco

Morocco is said to exist 'on the edge' (Berque 1955). This edge exists in relation to the 'grid' (Lefebvre 1992; Gupta and Ferguson 1992), which can provide a problematic structure for understanding intersectional identities, as a grid is a rigid visual aid for accurately processing the flux and flow of identity and performance. A grid, however, is the 'macro-social contextual issue' (Brettell 2003: 7; Vertovec 2007: 969) and can also be visualized as the borders of a nation-state, or the walls of a nightclub, within which people explore intersections of their identities with liminality, uncertainty and indeterminacy. Individuals who are connected to many different nodes or located on the edge of a node must incorporate more complicated *taqāsīm* into their social navigation. Existing on the edge, for Moroccans, might seem limiting, but the experience also eloquently gestures towards the proximity in which Moroccans live to so many objects and places that are just out of reach. Using edges and grids to think about social boundaries and border crossings highlights the restrictions that Moroccan people face on a daily basis.

Moroccans live on the edge of the grid, but they are still located in a particular square on the grid. Living on the edge means being in close proximity to more than one thing, but not being in the centre of any one thing. Living on the edge of multiple geographic places – the Mediterranean Sea, the Atlantic Ocean, the Sahara Desert, the continent of Africa and the Strait of Gibraltar – has put Moroccans in a unique position regarding the signature sound of their music. Morocco's position on the grid creates room for improvisation and simultaneously boxes musicians into Arab and African sounds.

The general sentiment among Moroccan alternative musicians is that music in Morocco that does not feature obviously Arab or African elements does not earn an artist much popularity there. Oussama is an industrial techno producer born and raised in Rabat who moved to Casablanca in 2018. Oussama's industrial techno and noise productions embody 'Moroccanness' in a way that fits into the genre of industrial music rather than with typically Moroccan or Arabic-sounding EDM. Industrial genres resonate with Oussama because he feels he can express his Moroccanness with subtlety and obscurity; using industrial sounds to produce traditional rhythmic modes allows him to blur the lines between European and Arabic musical categories. As such, his productions have gained traction in European techno hubs since 2018, and he has had the opportunity to travel to France and Germany for DJ performances. In Morocco, however, the industrial scene is small, and he frequently expresses distaste for Moroccan society because of the lack of success he receives at home. Music that is considered to be transgressive generates more barriers in Morocco, and his events have been shut down by authorities in turn.

Oussama's productions are more popular outside of the grid of his home and are positioned on the edge of Moroccan EDM because they do not contain typical Moroccan or Arab archetypes. As stated by Joseph Klett and Alison Gerber, 'Noise musicians seek to expand the language of music while creating a space of direct engagement with sound, and each other' (2014: 287). This expansion and engagement is evinced by Oussama's productions and the tight-knit community his performances bring, a community that makes him hungry to continue to musically overcome the interference posed by Moroccan authorities. Oussama's dissatisfaction with home, however, made him want to escape to Europe by any means possible. His complicated feelings about the hurdles his music faced at home, coupled with a low-paying salary at an internship he was completing for his master's degree, made him feel stuck in stasis. The difficulties Oussama frequently experiences with authorities have made him question the importance his events hold, even though they carve space for his community to feel at ease while expressing their alternative Moroccanness into the night.

During the first couple of years of our friendship, immigration to Canada seemed out of the question for Oussama due to the great distance between Canada and Morocco. As much as he wanted to leave, he also wanted the opportunity to return frequently and visit his home. He wanted a European passport and the mobility that accompanies it. As time passed and he began to hear about the many young, skilled workers who had successfully completed direct-entry, permanent-residency applications, he began to open up to the idea of immigrating to Canada; both Oussama and his techno productions were situated on the edge of Morocco, ready to make the leap across the Atlantic.

The centre of the grid of EDM in Morocco is Afro-house. The Moroccan influence on the genre fuses African instruments, rhythms, vocals and subgenres (such as Afrobeat) with the EDM techniques of house performance. The Moroccan fusion of African, Mediterranean and Arabic music, however, gives the Afro-house from Morocco a unique sonic signature that differs from the sub-Saharan

Afro-house. Moroccan producers frequently incorporate samples that are unique to that region, such as samples from popular, local bands, traditional music performed at weddings or other rituals and regional cinema. Each of these sounds would in essence highlight the linguistic and cultural differences between the various regions to whom Morocco exists on the edge.

Moroccan Afro-house has 'departed' from Morocco and 'arrived' in Montreal along with those who carry it. Nightclubs in Montreal favour this sound as DJs incorporate it into their sets frequently. Migratory patterns align with the music, and although I will not focus on my fieldwork conducted in Toronto here, I can say that Moroccan Afro-house is neither incorporated into African-themed events in Toronto nor is it considered to be part of the canon of African-produced EDM by the culture of that city. Due to immigration policies in Canada differing from province to province, Moroccan people have a long history of migrating to the province of Quebec than to Ontario. Their ties to the French language and culture also influence this pattern. The lack of Moroccan music in Toronto is a reflection of the small population of North African migrants who have settled in Anglophone Canada, and this migratory divide in turn constitutes the music played in each city's respective nightclubs.

Moroccan Afro-house evinces presence, movement, limitations and the boundaries of music and people. In Morocco, these boundaries obstruct Moroccan nationals differently than they do in Quebec, largely because of the invisible borders between the economic and social classes. According to my interlocutors, the Moroccan state creates solutions for the public's problems but keeps those solutions just out of reach. The appearance of solutions to problems makes people believe that they can change their socio-economic class, filling them with dreams of a brighter future possessed of both mobility and stability. Like Nikolas Rose suggests, citizens are trying to shape their lives, but the government acts upon the choices they make in order to do so (1989: 10). Because Moroccans sit on the edge, there is a boundary between them and the solution, and the government works to keep such a solution out of reach without reason. This results in an indeterminate state for my interlocutors, who then find themselves sitting and/or dancing in nightclubs in a state of *barzakh* while contemplating their futures as artists and members of society, uncertain how to effectively proceed. Although my interlocutors in the EDM scene are of Morocco's middle to upper class – a status that changes as they migrate – they still bear witness to social inequalities on a daily basis and experience them as the social boundaries of their lives. These invisible borders are akin to the grid.

The grid, as previously mentioned, is a social structure that individuals live within. The grid also provides ethical guidelines to follow alongside its other array of identifiers and rules. In many societies – Canadian and Moroccan alike, although for different reasons – EDM does not fit in the grid of good citizenship. In Canada, EDM is considered to be loud, noisy and disruptive to heteronormative living. In Morocco, it is anti-Islamic due to its club and counter-cultural elements. The grid influences the relationship that any given individual can have with EDM.

EDM is still present in Morocco, however. Rather, the grid influences whose presence is deemed to be appropriate in EDM spaces, but even in regards to that evaluation, a final position differs between each event and venue:

> I arrived at La Banquette, a nightclub in Rabat. Dex Le Maffo, a local DJ, was on the decks, opening the night with a DJ set that floated between Moroccan funk and techno. He waved, gesturing me to come toward him into the DJ booth, after he had transitioned into the next track. We had a long embrace, for I had just arrived in Morocco earlier that day, right on time to see Acid Arab, a duo from France who would be playing later that evening. Dex was playing brilliantly, and the club filled with excitement in response. I turned around to see my friend, Younasse, arrive dressed in a fashionable tracksuit jacket, paired with jeans and stylish sneakers. His long dreadlocks were tied back, draping down his neck, falling below his shoulders, the occasional bundle of locks falling onto his chest. He was immediately escorted out of the club by security. Because it wasn't the first time that I had witnessed my contacts being denied entry at La Banquette, I approached the owner to ask what had happened. Younasse simply 'wasn't dressed' for entry, the owner told me. The owner's pale face and smooth blonde hair spoke to a social issue that cut deeper than his response was willing to admit.

Younasse had been denied at the first border crossing of the evening, except this 'border' was an attempt to 'cross' into the nightclub.

Morocco's geographic grid is infiltrated by the social grids of those inhabiting the space. The social grid of Morocco acts as borders between social classes. Within each square of the grid, one must understand the social etiquette at play. At the border of certain spaces such as La Banquette, the question of who is welcome cannot be answered simply with money, but rather requires a certain vocabulary that is dispersed across language, appearance and movement – a certain style of *taqsīm*. The divide between the upper and lower classes in Morocco is nuanced in ways that I, an outsider, could not understand, at least at first. Friends of mine who I thought would have no issue being granted entry to an event were obviously not welcome according to the mores of certain owners and guards. Like racist encounters in North America and much of Europe, although Younasse was stylishly dressed, his 'urban' look was not appropriate for such a venue. Younasse's socio-economic status is unknown to me, but the boundaries limiting Younasse's movement had clarified themselves.

Departure

Departure and arrival carry with them more weight than a simple exit and entry. They are largely based on socio-economic situations. Few of my interlocutors have prepared for a tangible departure to Canada by obtaining a travel visa and booking their flights. The majority of my interlocutors, however, anticipate a departure in a manner similar to hopeful dreaming. Regardless of whether or not their dreams will come to fruition, each of them anticipates their departure and plans for it in different ways, depending on their unique situations. The preparation for departure is often based on what can be described in terms of the social imaginary of one's destination (Pessar and Mahler 2003; Coletto and Fullin 2019).

Sitting in nightclubs, taking a pause from dancing, I would watch my friends gaze up at the ceiling in a state of *barzakh* as they would ask me questions about life in Canada. Although I would try to be honest about less commonly discussed variables, such as the isolation often experienced in winter and the high cost of living, their dreamy eyes showed that they were not absorbing my anecdotes – life in Canada, as they imagined it, would be smooth and easy.

Whether or not my interlocutors are preparing for or dreaming about immigration to Montreal, the common thread between them is the music they produce and perform, which becomes an outlet for improvising with their excitement, frustration, anxiety, fear and dreams while living in the in-between. Khalil, a musician and photographer from Rabat, immigrated to Canada on a student visa shortly after we first met. His sister had already settled in Montreal for a couple of years, so he did not have to arrange any accommodations for his arrival. They planned to live together. The excitement and anticipation Khalil felt at the idea of leaving Morocco was immense. He had experienced moments of excruciating frustration when dealing with the bureaucracy regarding his visa documents. To counter this frustration, he booked a handful of DJ performances before his departure. Improvising with his emotional process, he imagined a grand exit, believing that he would reify it with his best performances and a celebration held among his closest friends before the upcoming journey.

Instead of a grand exit, each of his performances suffered complications. During the first, where he played fast-tempoed techno featuring samples from jazz standards – music that resonates with his style as a DJ and producer, but that did not fit the deep house and Afro-house enthusiasts present at the event – he did not receive any pay from the promoter. At the following gig, technical issues with the hardware led to the promoter kicking him off the decks and inviting the next DJ to play early. The grand send-off that he had imagined was turning into an escape punctuated by resentment. Khalil's anticipated departure illustrates the emotional turmoil one often feels when leaving behind their home.

Montreal, Quebec

The Moroccan origins of many immigrants in Montreal can be seen through storefronts and restaurants; it can be tasted, smelled and heard through language and music that seeps through nightclub walls onto the streets. This builds a home away from home for those in Montreal's Moroccan diaspora. The sonic environment of Montreal is not the same as the soundscape of Casablanca, but the sound of Moroccan music and the Moroccan dialect of Arabic still evoke a sense of comfort and familiarity according to many of my interlocutors who call Morocco 'home'. Montreal embodies Morocco similarly to the way Moroccan people embody home when they are abroad.

The embodiment of home lies within my interlocutors in diaspora, albeit differently from person to person. Home, for my interlocutors, is an accumulation of different places, cultures and worldviews. This can be heard through the unique samples that each artist uses in their DJ sets to sound their Moroccanness into the night. Considering the city as a social actor and not just a map upon which humans live makes the encounter with a cosmopolitan city similar to that between individuals and institutions. Such encounters result in intersecting stories, non-linear meetings and missed connections between social actor and city (Kenny and Young 2021). Reducing cosmopolitan and alternative identities to a form of crisis would be assuming that home, its culture and embedded morals, ethics and rules in the Arab world, always exist in direct opposition to a newly emplaced home in the western world. This framing maintains the binary of Orient and Occident and does not allow for a cosmopolitan living (Chakrabarty 2000; Chibber 2013). My interlocutors each embody home differently, and this interior connection is in turn performed differently in each of their musical and social *taqāsīm*.

Arrival

Migrants often feel a sense of disappointment or loneliness, depending on their situation upon arrival, especially immediately after landing. As previously mentioned, Khalil landed in Montreal in January 2019 after going through many frustrating experiences with both bureaucracy and performance. Although he had travelled to Northern European countries for music festivals before, and thus had experienced a Northern climate, he described moving to Montreal as landing on 'another planet'. Immigration, for Khalil, could be best described in one word: vertigo.[4]

Khalil began describing this vertigo to me by explaining that the sun appears visually different in Montreal. It feels different on the face and body, and its light illuminates the architectural cut of the city differently as well. As such, this 'new sun' affects the way he photographs the world around him. Paired with the sun's lack of presence on short winter days, Khalil's bodily interface with his world felt altered, and his interior subjectivity was being altered in turn. His new relationship with the Montreal sun made the city at night feel more comforting.

I have a distinct memory of the time during which he felt uncomfortable in his body. Although my reflective conversation with Khalil did not take place until he had been settled in Canada for over two years, his behaviour still left a distinct impression. A few months after his arrival, I travelled to Montreal and invited him to join me for a night out at Stereo, the world-renowned afterhours club. Khalil was quiet and sombre. He did not participate in the experience of clubbing as he once had with me in Morocco. His excuse, at the time, was that he was focusing on improving his body through strength training and weight loss, and he could not afford to indulge as such. After gently asking him probative questions about why he was acting out of character throughout the night, he eventually opened up about the college programme he had enrolled in and how it was not living up to his expectations. There were only a limited number of programmes that he would be able to switch to in order to keep his student visa status. Although he did not mention the feeling of vertigo at that time, his body language had changed due to the unexpected disappointments of his migratory journey. His frustrating exit was matched by a frustrating arrival. Although Khalil was not dancing at the afterhours club as I had seen him previously, he still sought refuge there by quietly sitting and absorbing the frequencies of the night.

Moving to Montreal was harder than he thought it would be, so much so that he even considered giving up and going back to Morocco. He did not, however, want to look like a failure in the eyes of his social network there. Financially, he felt overwhelmed by the cost of living. Improvising with his situation, he saved money by eating cans of tuna and chickpeas so that he could afford to enjoy himself by attending nightlife events. He had become noticeably thinner, his muscles more lean and visually defined, to the point that he was pushing the limits of his bodily alignment. Although he was achieving his goals of self-actualization, he continued to feel depressed. He began to spend the late-night hours in quiet solitude producing ambient electronic music with the theme of 'aether'; musical tracks that would eventually be released on Oussama's record label in Morocco. In July 2019, he travelled back to Morocco for a month-long visit. Pushing mental and physical boundaries, feeling vertigo, surrounded by aether, his financial and social stress combined with homesickness came to require a remedy that he felt could only be synthesized by being immersed in the nightlife culture of Morocco.

Casablanca, Morocco

One often feels as though their sense of self has changed when they return home after being away for many years and that it can be difficult to reconnect with their loved ones (NDiaye 2004). This interior change can affect interactions and the dynamics of relationships. As I will expand upon below, some of my interlocutors have returned home for visits and vacations, and others have returned home because of family issues. The reason for return has a great impact on the experience the individual has once they arrive.

Return

Fouad, a musician from Casablanca, left his life in Montreal after ten years of establishing himself there. He had a high-paying job as an accountant, purchased his own condo in the city centre and lived a balanced life by obtaining multiple DJ residencies at nightclubs where he played deep house and Afro-house that resonates with his identity as a 'modern Arab from Africa'. He told me that he lived a very fulfilling life in Montreal, but that he had to return to Morocco to be with his family. His parents were both approaching their mid 70s, so when his mother had been seriously ill, his father was not strong enough to offer her the care she required; furthermore, his younger brother was struggling with his own issues, which indirectly pressured Fouad with the familial obligation to return.

In June 2018, when we first met, he had been in Casablanca for approximately one year and was experiencing mixed feelings about his situation:

> During Ramadan, Fouad and I whipped across Casablanca on his Vespa. Casablanca was empty; everyone was fasting. We went to Hassan II, a mosque located right beside the ocean, and walked around its courtyards quietly. We both felt an inexplicable sense of calm and tranquillity. After our stroll, Fouad told me stories about his family. They were beginning to accept him as a musician, but they hadn't taken him seriously until he started playing at large festivals. Even still, they were having a hard time understanding why he wouldn't live a 'normal' life. He described them as 'typically Arab' and 'traditional in their thinking' even though they are educated and well-travelled. The conversation unravelled into our mutual silence as we looked up at the minaret of the mosque and heard the waves crash onto the rocks: a moment in the middle the most spiritual month of the year filled with the type of despair that only 'prayer' on a dancefloor can fix.

Because of the mindset held by Fouad's family, he believed that he needed to achieve a certain level of fame in his music career to appease them.

This unravelled into feelings of frustration with the deep house scene in Casablanca because of his belief that people in Casablanca are more interested in their own individual success than they are in creating a scene. He stated in an interview, 'A scene requires people to be collaborating, to be creating something together.

Everyone kind of has his role, and together, we create something bigger. It has to be a bit more selfless.' Fouad believes that the strength of a scene can create individual success in turn. He also felt that there was a stronger sense of community in Montreal, a locale that was in Fouad's diasporic home. Fouad's return to Casablanca shattered his dreams of participating in a cohesive scene like the one he had experienced in Montreal.

It is important to note that, although Fouad is well connected in Morocco because of his social and financial capital, he might not have been fully initiated into Morocco's house music collective at the time of our conversation about scenes and selflessness. Although he had an insider's perspective regarding EDM and music production in Montreal, he might not have felt that he fit the Moroccan EDM 'vibe' before speaking to me. Fouad could have been in a state of transition that left him in the trance of his comforting memories from Montreal's scene. If that is the case, his observations about Morocco's EDM scene could have been unfairly coloured by that 'trance'.

Khalil's return was largely different from Fouad's. Khalil had been away for only six months, but Fouad had lived in Montreal for ten years. Although the deep house scene that Fouad was trying to 'get in' with is still considered underground, events are usually located in more expensive bars, and thus cater to an upper-class community that is concerned with status and image. Although Fouad fits this image, the scene is less open to newcomers. Oussama's alternative techno scene situates itself within a more casual, 'come as you are' context, and as such his community – of which Khalil is part – is more welcoming and cohesive. To further this point, Khalil expressed to me that Oussama's alternative techno scene was the driving inspiration for the music he had produced while living in Montreal. Fouad's drive was the inverse. Khalil missed being a part of the scene in Morocco. He spent his month in Morocco travelling to different cities and playing successful gigs for long hours into the night. He mentioned, during our reflective interview in 2021, that perhaps because there were no external stressors about coming and going between the two countries (his visa was obtained and landing was successful), he was able to fully embrace his time there. Although he did not get his grand exit, he received a grand return.

My next field excursion to Morocco occurred just as Khalil's grand return had come to a close, almost as if we had passed each other in mid-air in-between Montreal and Casablanca. During this trip, I met with Fouad, who told me that, although he was still unhappy and frustrated in Casablanca, his music career was finally starting to blossom. He was about to fly to Montreal to sell his condo – a bittersweet visit to his beloved Canadian city. Going back home to Casablanca was not a positive experience for him, but he felt that he had no other choice but to stay and make it work. He believed that he had to do what was right for his family in their time of need. He needed to improvise with the situation that he had been challenged with.

Although he had not yet obtained the respect in the scene that he was hoping for, improvising with the way he worked with the various individuals running the scene was creating movement in his life. At the same time, as Fouad was improvising with his living situations between Montreal and Casablanca, he was collaborating with traditional musicians from sub-Saharan Africa and improvising with them by playing EDM fusions on various stages across the country. This improvisation often brought him to tears. Both *taqsīm* and EDM are thus intimate in their improvisatory experience.

Fouad says that his fusion of traditional genres with EDM is directly tied to his experiences of home in Casablanca:

> When you bring these two worlds of trance together, it's like a third dimension – something new and something ancient as well. A resurgence – an evolution of the music. We try to bring in the aspect of the ancient and the new. 'Bringing the desert into the urban jungle' – a saying in French. The live rooftop [performance] we did is certainly in a white jungle of Casablanca; it certainly is a jungle. But [in the background] there's also the ocean and the mosque. It's a melting pot of new and old.

Although Fouad felt frustrated by his return, it is clear that there are certain aspects of Casablanca that he appreciates, such as the lack of cultural barriers and access to collaborating with African musicians. Fouad is using *taqsīm* to reconnect with people in Morocco, play music and make the most of his situation.

Conclusion

Sometimes peace is found in the in-between. In 2021, after completing his master's degree and working a stable job for over a year, Oussama told me he had changed his mind about his plans for migration again. He told me that he purchased a motorcycle and that the freedom he felt driving along the coast was like no other. Having access to money in Morocco, he explained, could bring one much happiness and freedom. The mobility he felt while riding the motorcycle broke the social boundaries he felt on the grid, he explained. At that moment in our conversation, he felt that he had found the key to living at home while simultaneously being granted the ability to explore. This freedom has given him the drive to continue building his studio, purchasing traditional instruments to sample uniquely in his noise productions and curating alternative EDM events regardless of the opinion of Moroccan authorities. Although I cannot say whether Oussama's opinion will stay the same or change, he now has high hopes for a comfortable future in Morocco. Oussama crossed the border into financial comfort and has regained the energy required to fight for his alternative techno community.

EDM's position in the nocturnal city creates hope and comfort for those experiencing movement and stasis, vertigo, bodily discomfort, frustration, excitement and peace. Bouncing to the beat at an EDM event at night, entering a state of *barzakh*, my interlocutors dream of their wants, needs and desires that have been conjured up from memories of the past, and they project them into the future. In this way, *barzakh* can be thought of as a bridge across all temporalities. *Barzakh* is the bridge between tangible desires and imagined futures; it is the isthmus upon which *taqsīm* takes place. Through dreaming on the bridge of *barzakh*, migrants can reflect upon the borders they have crossed and how they should improvise towards the next.

EDM is known to create a world for people to enter in order to discover new art, let loose and forget about life's anxieties for an isolated moment in time. This chapter argues that EDM carves space for dreaming and improvisation in all stages of the migratory process. This chapter has the intention of illuminating hopes for future migration, plans to navigate through it and feelings about mobility and restriction. Although Khalil, Younasse, Oussama and Fouad each have different experiences with music, migration and the city at night, nightlife has impacted their migratory lifestyles and aided their experiences in both Montreal and Casablanca. Their respective experiences of nightlife mirror their experiences with movement, access and migration. In Casablanca, my interlocutors are forced to navigate through nocturnal lifestyles that are restricted by the state's authorities, who move about the city at night as a form of control. In Montreal, they deal with social isolation, financial stress and noise complaints resulting in fines. The music my interlocutors produce, perform and seek out reflects their emotional responses to these different experiences of movement and restriction. The concepts *taqsīm* and *barzakh* are employed to outline the improvisational movement unique to the Moroccan experience of migration that takes my interlocutors on journeys, thus helping them through frustrating bureaucratic situations, but also 'sounding' what they are hoping for as they dream and make music in their cosmopolitan lives.

NOTES

1. In Morocco, underground EDM scenes overlap due to the small size of the greater EDM collective. Although my interlocutors perform and produce different subgenres of house and techno, they are still often present at each other's events.
2. Ibn 'Arabi (1165–1240) was an Andalusian Sufi mystic, poet and philosopher who was influential in Islamic thought.

3. One of the ways that bodies perform spaces is by 'trancing'. In *Deep Listeners: Music, Emotion, and Trancing*, Becker (2004) analyzes the trancing process by demonstrating that trancing is co-productive. Trancing requires someone to be 'musicking', defined as the action of playing music. In order to activate the interlocking, dynamic process of trancing and musicking, participants must engage in 'deep listening' – listening for meaning – in order to produce the emotional state of trance. As trancing and musicking progress, the body responds through movement or dancing. The terms 'trancing', 'musicking', 'listening' and 'dancing' are each presented in their present participle form, suggesting that they are active in the present and continuously dynamic; a trance is the product of deep listening, but in order to maintain the trance, the music must also continue. Participants in EDM perform *taqāsīm* through a dynamic, interlocking combination of listening, trancing, musicking and dancing.
4. Valorie D. Thomas theorizes vertigo in diaspora, 'vertigo is an element [...] that reveals a habitable space organized by diasporic cosmologies, in which autopoesis, self-creation, can be realized [...] Vertigo captures the relationship of the internal experience of the colonized to the colonized environment' (2003: 82).

REFERENCES

Becker, Judith (2004), *Deep Listeners: Music, Emotion, and Trancing*, Bloomington: Indiana University Press.

Berque, Jacques (1955), *Structures sociales du haut-Atlas*, Paris: Presses Universitaires de France.

Brettell, Caroline (2003), *Anthropology and Migration: Essays on Transnationalism, Ethnicity and Identity*, Walnut Creek: Altamira Press.

Chakrabarty, Dipesh (2000), *Provincializing Europe: Postcolonial Thought and Historical Difference*, Princeton: Princeton University Press.

Chibber, Vivek (2013), 'Capitalism, class and universalism: Escaping the cul-de-sac of postcolonial theory', in L. Panitch, G. Albo and V. Chibber (eds), *Registering Class*, Pontypool: Merlin Press, pp. 63–79.

Coletto, Diego and Fullin, Giovanna (2019), 'Before landing: How do new European emigrants prepare their departure and imagine their destinations?', *Social Inclusion*, 7:4, pp. 39–48.

Crapanzano, Vincent (2004), *Imaginative Horizons: An Essay in Literary-Philosophical Anthropology*, Chicago: University of Chicago Press.

Deleuze, Gilles ([1969] 1990), *The Logic of Sense*, New York: Columbia University Press.

Dunn, Nick (2016), *Dark Matters: A Manifesto for the Nocturnal City*, Alresford and Hants: Zero Books.

Fieni, David (2016), 'Tagging the spectral mobility of the stateless body: Deleuze, stasis, and graffiti', *Journal for Cultural Research*, 20:4, pp. 350–65.

Gupta, Akhil and Ferguson, James (1992), 'Beyond "culture": Space, identity, and the politics of difference', *Cultural Anthropology*, 7:1, pp. 6–23.

Kaufman, Eleanor (2012), *Deleuze, the Dark Precursor: Dialectic, Structure, Being*, Baltimore: John Hopkins University Press.

Kenny, Ailbhe and Young, Katie (2021), '"The House of the Irish": African migrant musicians and the creation of diasporic space at night', *Ethnomusicology Forum*, 2 July, pp. 1–21, https://doi.org/10.1080/17411912.2021.1938623. Accessed 3 August 2022.

Klett, Joseph and Gerber, Alison (2014), 'The meaning of indeterminacy: Noise music as performance', *Cultural Sociology*, 8:3, pp. 275–90.

Lefebvre, Henri (1992), *The Production of Space* (trans. Donald Nicholson-Smith), Oxford: Blackwell Publishing.

Marcus, Scott (2007), *Music in Egypt: Experiencing Music, Expressing Culture*, New York: Oxford University Press.

Minh-Ha, Trinh T. (2016), *Lovecidal: Walking with the Disappeared*, New York: Fordham University Press.

NDiaye, Marie (2004), *Tous mes amis*, Paris: Minuit.

Pessar, Patricia R. and Mahler, Sarah J. (2003), 'Transnational migration: Bringing gender in', *The International Migration Review*, 37:3, pp. 812–46.

Racy, Ali Jihad (2000a), 'The Arab *taqasim* as a musical symbol', *Ethnomusicology*, 44:2, pp. 302–20.

Racy, Ali Jihad (2000b), 'The many faces of improvisation: The Arab *taqasim* as a musical symbol', *Ethnomusicology*, 44:2, pp. 302–20.

Racy, Ali Jihad (2003), *Making Music in the Arab World: The Culture and Artistry of Tarab*, Cambridge: Cambridge University Press.

Racy, Ali Jihad (2009), 'Why do they improvise? Reflections on meaning and experience', in Gabriel Solis and Bruno Nettl (eds), *Musical Improvisation, Art, Education, and Society*, Chicago: University of Illinois Press, pp. 313–22.

Rose, Nikolas (1989), *Governing the Soul: The Shaping of the Private Life*, New York: Routledge.

Shannon, Jonathan Holt (2003), 'Emotion, performance, and temporality in Arab music: Reflections of tarab', *Cultural Anthropology*, 18:1, pp. 72–98.

Thomas, Valorie D. (2003), '"1 + 1 = 3" and other dilemmas: Reading vertigo in "Invisible Man", "My Life in the Bush of Ghosts", and "Song of Solomon"', *African American Review*, 37:1, pp. 81–94.

Vertovec, Steven (2007), 'New directions in the anthropology of migration and multiculturalism', *Ethnic and Racial Studies*, 30:6, pp. 961–78.

Waterman, Ellen (2019), 'Performance studies and critical improvisation studies in ethnomusicology: Understanding music and culture through situated practice', in H. M. Berger and R. M. Stone (eds), *Theory for Ethnomusicology: Histories, Conversations, Insights*, 2nd ed, New York: Routledge, pp. 141–75.

Western, Tom (2020), 'Listening with displacement: Sound, citizenship, and disruptive representations of migration', *Migration and Society: Advances in Research*, 3, pp. 294–309.

Interlude 1

'How "Free" is the Free Africa Festival?'

Willians Santos and Derek Pardue

> *The transcultural African roots are palpable within Brazilian daily life, music and religion being some of the richest among them. These are privileged fields wherein an African 'mother-earth', at the same time close and far, superficial and deeply mystical, is an object of evocation and sometimes devotion. While the candomblé from Bahia highlights an ancestral Yoruba substrate in a highly syncretized form, the axé pop music provides a sense of belonging to a romanticized afro-diasporic world. The almost infinite Brazilian musical universe is the result of old processes, as well as others still ongoing, of cultural hybridization where Africa, or rather the African roots of Brazil, constitute a referential axis in popular music genres such as maracatu, coco, frevo, samba, chorinho, afoxé, bossa nova, samba-reggae, samba-rock, samba-rap, funk and others.*
>
> (Arenas 2019: 126)

> *[...] the black population, who have black Africans ancestors, my fellows from the continent, are the ones with less space in the job market, the ones that have the least basic living structure (because nobody is on this earth to only survive, this is the thing of the oppressor and of dogmatic religions), the ones who always have art relegated to only specific categories just because they're black, and not because of their natural talents, and are the ones who receive less recognition for genius, talent and abilities. I feel deeply provoked and therefore am in favor of more black presence ... thus strengthening this RACE (if it is about racism that we are talking about, then let us call it out) which has a lot, and I mean a lot, more stories to tell [...] So, yes we will be having a black bassist in the band!!!*
>
> (Bahule 2018: n.pag.)

This interlude[1] is an exercise in intertextuality; a conversation in São Paulo among African migrant musicians, Afro-Brazilians, White urban hipsters, a White gringo Brazilianist and a Black Brazilian intellectual, artist and researcher. The above

FIGURE I1.1: Lenna Bahule and her band at Casa de Francisca, 2018.

citations help contextualize the drama. On the one hand, Brazilian culture, including music, has been influenced in multiple ways by African migration. Arenas (2019) describes this process as both historical and ongoing in the production of multiple artistic genres. On the other hand, the lived reality of the majority of Black Brazilians, and more recently Black and African migrants, is one of disenfranchisement and social invisibility. Carlos Hasenbalg, a Brazilian sociologist writing on Black populations in Brazil, put it succinctly, '[t]he symbolic integration of the black, via culture, can walk pari passu with their subordination and social exclusion' (1996: 242). Have the new sounds from African migrant musicians, located in new venues managed by migrant entrepreneurs, changed this story? What sorts of belonging are performed through music? How might artists and public make claims on the city? What sorts of Africanities and Blackness does music-making afford?

In some respects, over the past decade, São Paulo has become increasingly African as tens of thousands of migrants and refugees have made their way to the city from Senegal, Angola, the Democratic Republic of Congo, Togo, Mozambique and Mali along with the large presence of recent migrants from Haiti after the earthquake of January 2010. Brazilian critics and sympathizers often reduce these diverse communities to *Africano*, simply African, including the Haitians.

Among these nationalities, only Angola and, to a much lesser extent, Mozambique have any substantial history of migration to Brazil, due to their shared linguistic and colonial past. While numerically the influx is small compared to the overall population of São Paulo, which approximates 20 million, Black migrant presence is politically, discursively and culturally hyper visible and Brazilians, as well as the migrants themselves, are currently trying to make sense out of the new Black presence. This is occurring inside a country that has a deeply complicated relationship with race (anti-)racism, Black pride, universally heralded Black culture and state violence (Alves 2018; Brandellero, Pardue and Wink 2020; Fernandes 2008; Morais 2020; Sansone 1996). It's a lot to process and even among those, who are generally supportive of immigration, Black politics and culture, there are tensions around fundamental concepts of Blackness and Africanity.

This interlude focuses on music and so it is important to state that migration is a sonic process as much as a spatial one (Kun 2016; Western 2020). Music performance serves to mediate socio-political tensions and augment racial solidarity, thereby creating a more robust Black presence in the city. At times, however, mediation breaks down and expectations are left unfulfilled. The night, understood as a particular time–space, yields to, and even invites musicians to, occupy certain parts of the city and tell their stories as multi-sensorial experiences. This interlude[2] uses fieldwork experiences from the Festival África Livre ('Festival for a Free Africa') and a concurrent art/academic forum, both held in 2018, to reflect on the complexities of Black/African sonic imprints on the city.

What sort of Africanity are we talking about though? The answer is not so straightforward. In the Second Forum Fontié Ki Waze – Fronteiras Cruzadas,[3] during the panel discussion on 'Migrant workers and cultural projects', Hortense Mbuy, a Congolese human rights lawyer, intervened:

> I, as an African, have been seeing a thing, and I wanted to ask you, who are from the art world, to give your point of view. I noticed that there are some Afro-Brazilians who want to identify themselves as African, who want the preservation of African culture. I think that's good. But, what I just noticed is that Brazil is a country which has gone through a lot of influences and these influences ended up changing a lot of things within the culture because Brazil is a country composed of immigrants from various nationalities. Then I see Afro-descendants identifying or wanting to identify themselves with the African Culture, or wanting to preserve African culture, maybe they're wrong in their presentation because they think they are Africans, but they are not. And I also had noticed that Africanity is more represented in what they call religious, right? Like an Umbanda person, I as an African am not [a practitioner of] Umbanda. All these religions linked to Africa, when I look at all these people [...] some practices I do identify myself with, yes, but in general I think they do not present

VIDEO 1[4]: Access at https://intellectdiscover.com/content/books/9781789386967.

> anything African, but they say the dance, the dress are African, there are those who wants to wear a turban ... also in music. Maybe I look at the African dance workshop, I look and I don't recognize myself, and I say what is this? I don't know. Then, what is your take, artists, what is your view, right? And what is the advice you can give in the case of that what I am thinking is wrong?
>
> (Mbuy 2018: n.pag.)

Hortense's narrative embarrassed Afro-Brazilians, who reacted with disapproving glances; meanwhile, white Brazilians reacted by clapping and laughing. Above all, Hortense's criticisms are not a claim of censorship, but the result of encounters and tensions between Africans born on the continent and Brazilians searching for belonging and fighting for citizenship. Lenna Bahule, quoted previously, who also attended the panel, presented another perspective:

> About what Hortense said [...] I have the same doubts you [Hortense] have, because it's very complicated, this question, right? There are several elements here. I think the first element you brought up is what Africa is this Brazil? This artistic Brazil. This Brazil that is speaking. Which Africa is Brazil expressing? Why inside the arts scene the only Africa I see, the one predominating, is the Africa of Guinea-Conakry, and at most Senegal, at most a very specific Africa, so specific that Mozambique has no idea about what happens in Guinea-Conakry, it absolutely doesn't. It's as strange

for you as it is for us Mozambican people to see a Senegalese or someone from Guinea-Conakry [...] regardless of the reasons, this is the Africa that Brazil uses as reference for artistic matters. This is the first point, I also understand that this is a consequence of the fact that as long as Brazil doesn't admit to being multicultural, as long as Brazil continues to erase its history, there will be desperate people, there will be Afro-descendent people desperate to take any reference connected to this minimal ancestry, appropriating it because 'I need to identify myself with something because this Brazil being shown on Globo [a popular Brazilian television network] isn't sufficient, and this is closer, so I'll get near it and appropriate it', I think it is something like that. I don't think it is people's fault, but I think it's more the fault of the dynamic of the Brazilian institutional policies of not admitting to being Afro-descendent, of not admitting to being multicultural. I think the immigrants from Europe too don't know their history, their European ancestry. This huge appropriation the Afro-Brazilians [...] have about their African ancestry is because the history of Black presence in Brazil comes from a history of oppression, comes from a history of silencing [...] It's more connected to this silencing of the pain than due to lack of information. Of course, there is lack of information precisely because of this silencing. One thing is certain, I think these people of the black artistic movement and the arts activists, anyway, of the Afro-descendant music, should do some research. I brought Mozambican artists to give workshops, to give performances [...] but I didn't see the people who engage in the afro dance classes, I didn't see them, they didn't look for me, they

VIDEO 2[5]: Access at https://intellectdiscover.com/content/books/9781789386967.

> knew, but they didn't go. Why? Is it because they didn't want to know this other Africa? Is it because they intend to continue with the same Africanity? [...] There is also this side of not wanting to know this other Africa being a place of comfort [...] I think it's important to have these two movements, I think your provocation is very pertinent.
>
> (2018: n.pag.)

Both Lenna Bahule and Hortense Mbuy point to a paradigm of thought around Africanity.[6] The current flow of African artists from diverse cultural backgrounds has disrupted the smooth line of identification among Black Brazilians, who are 'desperate' to find some constellation of belonging given the representational exclusion they experience every day and *every night*. While some recent *Africano* communities have settled in the urban outskirts, most Black migrants live near the city centre in the vicinity of the few social services dedicated to immigrant issues. Certain neighbourhoods at night have become increasingly occupied by a range of Black presences. From nocturnal religious services to informal get-togethers to the handful of West African pot-pourri restaurants, the São Paulo downtown turns significantly Black at night.

The bar and cultural centre Al Janiah, the site of the Festival África Livre ('Festival for a Free Africa'), has become one such landmark of immigrant presence, in general, and an occasional platform for African music. The festival was conceived by Aboucabar Ngazy Sidibé, who is an actor, composer and percussionist, Sidibé founded the Centro de Estudos da Cultura da Guiné ('Guinean Culture Studies Centre'), where dance and percussion classes, lectures, film screenings and music concerts are held, as well as orientation workshops for immigrants. Al Janiah was founded in 2015 by a group of Palestinian immigrants who first located their humble bar in a dilapidated storefront beneath a downtown overpass. By 2018, they had moved to a more conventional zone of 'nightlife' in Bixiga, a neighbourhood with rich histories of post-abolition Black migration as well as early twentieth-century Italian immigration. In contrast to the Forum, the festival seemed to demonstrate that intra-Black/African and multi-cultural collaborations *are* possible. The festival included a screening of a Brazilian film *Liberdade* ('Freedom') and poetry readings by artists from Venezuela, Angola, Palestine, Haiti and the Democratic Republic of Congo. There were also two musical performances featuring Jéssica Areias (Angola) and the band Les Etoiles de Liberdade (various nationalities).

Jéssica Areias is from Luanda, graduated in Music Education from the Faculdade Paulista de Arte de São Paulo ('College of Arts of São Paulo'), and is a choral singing teacher, composer and singer. Her repertoire ranges from popular Angolan music, popular Brazilian music, fado and Cuban music. At the festival, Jéssica performed at the back of the stage amid the sounds of glasses, plates

FIGURE I1.2: Poster for the Festival África Livre, 2018. © Centro de estudos da cultura da Guiné.

and conversations coming from the open external area, the drinks counter, the kitchen in the centre of the bar close to the exit, and in front of her from the tables and chairs where the audience was distributed. The lights dimmed, the audience shushed and Jéssica confided

> about being an immigrant and being far from home for 9 years I made a song that portrays precisely this sorrow, this longing, this lack of something that we only find at home. So I give you 'Lamento de Pó' ('Sorrow of dust'):

Só Lamento de pó	Sorrow of dust
No peito um nó	In my chest a lump
Que saudade, uó	What a longing, oh

A pé	On foot
Vou levando minha fé	I carry my faith
Pros meus guias peço axé	I ask my spiritual guides for strength
Cada um nasce pro que é	Each one is born to what they are
Deixei meu berço	I left my cradle
Ah, quanto tempo!	Oh, for how long!
Do outro lado da margem	Across the bank
Da coragem faço meu alento	From courage I take my breath
Fingindo esquecer meus medos,	Pretending to forget my fears
escrevo esta canção.	I write this song.

(Areias 2018)

Her performance featured Gustavo Marques on the acoustic guitar and Jefferson Silva on percussion with an instrument similar to the calabash. Another special feature in her last song was by Edoh Amassize on djembe. Jéssica called to Edoh, 'since we are here, the majority of us being African, let us get together to play one last song' (Areias 2018). The composition of low lighting, emotional lyrics and lilting rhythm created a mood of reveal, of vulnerability that genuinely moved audience members. It was a song that any migrant could understand and sympathize with.

Edoh is an artist born in Togo and living in São Paulo. His art navigates through dance and percussive music from sub-Saharan Africa. He was one of

FIGURE I1.3: Jéssica Areias and Edoh Amassize on stage during the Festival, 2018. Access the video[7] of this performance at https://intellectdiscover.com/content/books/9781789386967.

FIGURE I1.4: Les Étoiles da Liberdade at the bar Al Janiah, 2018.

the founders of the group Maobé, which appeared in the middle of 2018, using djembe, dumdum and other instruments, and performing the Tibó, Sakpatá and Idjombi dances in various institutional and worldbeat commercial spaces in São Paulo. The last attraction of the night was the band Les Étoiles de Liberdade:

Formed by six members, among them Edoh on percussion with the djembe, the band contained a drum set, electric guitar, recorder and a kind of *caxixi* or shaker. The last performance of the night made the whole audience dance throughout the show featuring timbres that mixed the improvisation of the djembe, the groove of the electric guitar and percussion, and the melody of the recorder along with the lively voice of Abou. While Jéssica Areias had created a mood of intimacy and confession, for Les Étoiles the night was about charisma, dancing and the festival.

Ongoing thoughts

Artists are in the profession of expression and encourage audiences to imagine as they appreciate. African migrants in Brazil have come with a wide range of aesthetic tastes and politics, and have arrived in a milieu within a society that has historically embraced Blackness as flare and style but has consistently undervalued Black labour and, in general, Black lives. Local organizations focused on migrant issues and Afro-Brazilian cultural politics have built bridges and created venues for information exchange. Indeed, professional collaborative networks have emerged, ranging from a shared interest to procure project funding, to song composition or band formation as well as to event organization and film production. The Festival África Livre was one such moment of artistic encounter.

However, as we reflect on the two events, the festival and the forum, what is clear is that discourses of Blackness and Africanity, including sonic imprints of music, are challenged by those of multi-culturalism in Brazil. The Fontié Ki Waze Forum made clear that categories, such as 'African music' or 'culture', are problematic because they tend to reduce heterogeneity into general stereotypes. Moreover, this dynamic takes on additional layers of complexity when African artists from across the continent migrate to an enormous country, founded on Black African labour and conceptualized as a nation, in great part, through Afro-Brazilian traditions, including music. The Free Africa Festival worked in great part because the goal was not to make a Black Presence but rather speak to a more universal migrant experience and use a variety of African musical genres to that end. The festival was 'free' in that it was inclusive; artists and audience members, Brazilians and immigrants, all had an enjoyable time and felt a sense of community. And, yet, it was obviously ephemeral, a night out on the town. Will these communal feelings and promises of the collaboration last without seriously addressing the myopic views of Africanity that most Brazilians hold, as demonstrated in the forum debates?

NOTES

1. This chapter was partially translated by Filipe Pinheiro. Other sections were written originally in English by Derek Pardue.
2. This research was funded by CNPq (National Council for Scientific and Technological Development), conducted under the Institute of Philosophy and Humanities at the University of Campinas and supervised by Liliana Rolfsen Petrilli Segnini.
3.

> The International Forum Fontié Ki Kwaze – Fronteiras Cruzadas is an academic, social and artistic interdisciplinary initiative seeking to stimulate critical thinking within the field of contemporary transnational migrations, contributing with projects and policies together with people committed to social causes.
>
> (Fontié Ki Kwaze – Fronteiras Cruzadas n.d: n.pag)

4. In this video, we see Ndudzo Siba in a song intervention during the Forum event. Bystanders chant while she sings.

5. In this video clip, we see a performance snippet featuring Bahule, who turns and interacts with the Brazilian Afro-pop star Chico César playing the guitar.
6. See Juan Diego Diaz's recent book (2021) that demonstrates how local Black musicians in Bahia, considered the most 'African' state in Brazil, position themselves critically to the constellation of common sense notions Brazilians and foreigners have about 'African music'.
7. In this clip, we see Areias singing and then ceding to the percussion solo of Edoh, all under the Palestinian flag in honour of the immigrant owners of Al Janiah.

REFERENCES

Arenas, Fernando (2019), *África Lusófona: Além da Independência* (trans. C. Mazzei), São Paulo: University of São Paulo Press.

Brandellero, Sara, Pardue, Derek and Wink, Georg (eds) (2020), *Living (Il)legalities in Brazil: Practices, Narratives and Institutions in a Country on the Edge*, London: Routledge.

Centro de Estudos de Cultura da Guiné (n.d.), 'Centro de Estudos de Cultura da Guiné – About', https://www.facebook.com/pg/centrodeestudosdeculturaguine/about/. Accessed 3 August 2022.

Diaz, Juan Diego (2021), *Africanness in Action: Essentialism and Musical Imaginations of Africa in Brazil*, Oxford: Oxford University Press.

Fernandes, Florestan (2008), *A Integração do Negro na Sociedade de Classes*, vol. 1, Rio: Globo2.

Fontié Ki Kwaze – Fronteiras Cruzadas (n.d.), *Conheça o Fórum Fontié ki Kwaze – Fronteiras Cruzadas*, https://www.fontieforum.org/sobre/. Accessed 10 May 2020.

Hasenbalg, Carlos (1996), 'Entre o Mito e os Fatos: Racismo e relações raciais no Brasil', in M. C. Maio and R. V. Santos (eds), *Raça, ciência e sociedade*, Rio de Janeiro: Fiocruz-CCBB, pp. 235–49.

Morais, Bruno Vinicius Leite de (2020), 'Os primórdios da black music brasileira e da linguagem política do orgulho negro nos anos 1960', *Mosaico*, 12:1, pp. 79–101.

Porta Curtas (n.d.), *Liberdade*, https://portacurtas.org.br/filme/?name=liberdade. Accessed 5 May 2020.

Sansone, Lívio (1996), 'Nem Somente Preto ou Negro: o sistema de classificação racial no Brasil que muda', *Afro-Ásia*, 18, pp. 165–87.

Western, Tom (2020), 'Listening with displacement: Sound, citizenship, and disruptive representations of migration', *Migration and Society*, 3:1, pp. 194–309.

PART 2

STREET SOUNDS

4

Nocturnal Polyphony: Mobile Music-Making as Urban Composition

Nick Dunn

Introduction

The music of Manchester, United Kingdom, is infamous. Successive waves of artists and bands from the city and its region have had their sounds travel around to many different parts of the world. These sonic exports have reflected the changing dynamics within the city itself (Haslam 1999). From the latter days of its industrialized boom to its post-war contribution of 1960s groups, then its angular and motoric post-punk influence through its ecstasy-fuelled 'Madchester' era, perhaps the peak of its provincial power, and into the diverse musical kaleidoscope of the present day. Like many cities around the globe, the grand narratives that emanate from Manchester have proved important in shaping how the city is perceived and, by extension, heard. Yet a city is much more than the officially recorded sounds it emits. The everyday soundtrack of buses, trams, pigeons, people going about the ebb and flow of urban life provides a typical backdrop against which the staccato rhythm of construction work or the shrill vignettes of emergency vehicles add their fleeting flourishes to the sonic palimpsest of the city. Beyond this urban music-making as a form of identity for the city are the diverse influences that have emerged and become interwoven across Manchester's cultural fabric. This tonal shift is perhaps most evident in the inner-city area of Cheetham Hill.

Home to a multi-ethnic community, the identity of the district has evolved through several waves of immigration to Britain (VCH 2011). In the mid nineteenth century, it drew Irish people fleeing the Great Famine, with Jews settling in the area in the late-nineteenth and early twentieth centuries as they fled persecution in continental Europe. During the 1950s and 1960s, migrants from the Indian subcontinent and Caribbean established new communities in Cheetham Hill. More recently, it has become home to people from Africa, Eastern Europe and the Far East. It is immigration policy as an urban landscape (Mason 1977; Bielewska 2011) and its music is vibrant, discordant and ever-mutating.

The area became heavily urbanized following the Industrial Revolution, with its southern edge bordering Angel Meadow, a place described as 'hell on earth' by Engels (1892). It is bisected by Cheetham Hill Road, which is lined with churches, mosques, synagogues and temples, alongside terraced houses that date back from its history as a textile processing district. Thrown into this lively mix of architectural form and function is HMP Manchester, formerly known as Strangeways. This austere, inward-facing brick colossus dominates its patch and despite the adjacency of surveillance and security services, red-light activity is evident in the shadowlands of the prison, the allure of which has been immortalized in the song 'Cheetham Hill' by the post-punk band The Fall (1996). This seedier side to the area, however, belies the rich cultural heritage of the wider district and the corporeal experiences it offers. Specialist supermarkets along the road trade in wares and foodstuffs from all over the world. As olfactory and gustatory encounters go, there is the potential to experience an astonishing variety of smells and tastes here. Yet, as Harries et al. (2019) have discussed, specifically in relation to Cheetham Hill, it is vital to be cognizant of how a label such as 'diverse' can obscure the lived experience and inequalities of ethnic difference and urban living. But what of the night? As Williams (2008: 514) reminds us, '[n]ight spaces are neither uniform nor homogenous. Rather they are constituted by social struggles about what should and should not happen in certain places during the dark of night'. How might we better understand the contribution that sound makes towards the shaping of an identity and experience of place? In the next section, I consider how the practice of nightwalking can support a form of mobile music-making through its capacity to both perform within and relate to the nocturnal city via the entanglements that occur between the body and urban landscape, sound and migration, presence and identity.

Nightwalking as mobile music-making

The role of the sonic arts and their capacity to powerfully inform our experiences is well documented (Crook 2011), including a recent inquiry into how sound can shape the way we perceive darkness in films (Masson 2021). However, the lived experience of being in a city is a far less controlled environment when it comes to our relationship with sound. Urban walking, meanwhile, can often feel like a cinematic experience due to the multi-sensory engagement, the body moving through space in city encounters. I suggest that the affective dimension of this 'audio-viewing' (Chion 2009) is even more pronounced after dark when our ability to rely on visual information is typically reduced due to the lower levels of light available. In addition, long-held associations with darkness tend to recast places, even those that are very familiar to us during the daytime, as having an uncanny and unknown quality to them at night (Dunn 2016). There is also a history of those who are out and about at night as being problematic or somehow not to be acceptable in the way the daytime frames activity (Palmer 2000), so this can produce a complex interaction between bodies when they encounter one another in the nocturnal city, especially in its quieter, emptier and peripheral spaces. This is particularly relevant in relation to migration, where presences may be apparent in ways that are distinctive, or even more pronounced than, during the daytime. Since the movement of the body through space both virtually and affectively shapes place (Atkinson and Duffy 2019), then the act of nightwalking has both a performative and a relational function in being able to simultaneously contribute towards while also comprehending the soundscape after dark.

The sonic environment as Dyson (2014) has shown is essential to both sense and sensibility. I, therefore, propose that nightwalking enacts a type of mobile music that, as a form of sonority, enables the situated, relational and practised of urban environments after dark. In this manner, it seeks to better understand the phenomenal and experiential premises of night and how they might be different from those of the daytime (Handelman 2005) through direct encounters. Nightwalking here is positioned as a mobile method that can reveal empirical sensitivities and new avenues for critique (Büscher and Urry 2009) pertaining to the nocturnal city: how and why it is constituted and, crucially, by whom. By taking this approach, I am deliberately trying to include and make sense of ordinary, banal sonic worlds of the urban night alongside more unusual and specifically musical sounds as part of this process since the former can often be discredited by the normative approach of soundscape (Schafer 1993). This is because the latter aims to preserve certain sounds categorized by an expert figure which for this study is problematic for two primary reasons. First, it implies that the mundane sonic worlds that co-constitute the experience of the city are not important whereas I contend they are vital to sense- and meaning-making in urban places. Second, given this inquiry seeks to identify the various domestic sonic worlds of a multi-ethnic district within which there is considerable diversity and overlap of sound, it's these, often subtle, interactions and dissonances which are integral to the identity of place rather than distinct, pure sounds. In the wider sense, it is my intention that this approach helps represent a degree of the multiple, incommensurate perspectives that are co-present in such multi-cultural and intercultural urban places (Gidley 2013).

In this chapter, I provide an account of my experiences of nightwalking through Cheetham Hill during the third national lockdown in the United Kingdom due to the coronavirus pandemic. It is important to note that the encounters and exchanges that took place are representative of an inner-city suburb within which there was noticeably far less activity than there usually is when not under the restrictions of lockdown measures. Although reasonably familiar with this part of the city pre-pandemic, I conducted a series of 24 nightwalks in the area between 4 January and 29 March 2021. I made audio recordings and autoethnographic notes during each of these nightwalks. At the end of each nightwalk, I first wrote down from memory my experiences, then listened to the recordings to understand any resonances or dissonances between my encounters as recollections and as sonic documentations. This cumulative experience helped me to comprehend the nuances of this district at night and better understand the different rhythms and ambiences it presents, albeit ones that may sometimes be dynamic and fleeting. Building on some of my previous work which sought to capture how various interrelationships between artificial light and darkness were altering and even temporarily disappearing due to the replacement of lamps in the city's streetlighting (Dunn 2019), I have been struck by this new endeavour, by returning to a number of the same places at different times and on different nights, how some of the sounds I have heard have persisted, while others have changed or become absent. This in turn has informed my understanding of the migrations that have occurred and are ongoing in this urban district. In order to convey the embodied and embedded nature of this work and describe how the different tones and rhythms of the urban landscape appear and change by my moving through a place, I provide a detailed, reflexive account of one of these nightwalks in the following section. This particular nightwalk took place on 18 March 2021, starting from Angel Meadow at 8:30 p.m., about two hours after sunset, and lasted approximately five hours. The reason I chose this nightwalk is because it was representative of the series and in this way provides an authentic account of the district with its focus on the 'everynight' of a migrant, multi-ethnic urban landscape.

A nocturnal urban composition

Walking along from the city centre and up Cheetham Hill Road, the eerie quiet and lack of urban buzz due to the national lockdown is palpable. Cars and bike couriers move people and food around the city's circulation system. By Manchester Oratory St. Chad's, the illuminated stained-glass window melds with the late evening sky, capturing its bruised hues in its crystalline fragments. Crossing over and moving down Chatley Street, the roads here all seem to be held together by the background drone of the city beyond. The width of the streets and the style of architecture whispers more of small-town Middle America than the urban centre of North West England. In some ways it is the frontier, still holding off the forces of gentrification and regeneration. Thanks to the bulwark of the prison, the sound here is like nowhere else in the city, huge swathes of brick and stone flank down the roads, reflecting noises in peculiar ways, the low thrum of idling cars trying to blend into the asphalt and not raise suspicion, the fast tick-tock engine of a taxi as it takes its exasperated pant uphill, the unanswered phone at the other end of the guy shouting into it. These are the soliloquies of the urban night. They tell us of its life, its times, through their utterances as they move through the air, and reflect off the city's surfaces. Human activity around this part of the city is all the more conspicuous for its general absence. This is the muffled soundtrack of furtive and illicit movements and transactions, the slow crunches under the rubber of the kerb-crawling car and the buzzes of vibrating mobile phones in hands setting up the next deal. The district around the prison is a micro-climate where many edges of urban activity overlap and co-exist. It is a composition characterized by the sustained spaces and washes of background sounds between its major notes which, when they appear, are often the sharp skronk of the brakes of heavy goods vehicles (HGVs) and careening cars hurtling through the night. There is little here tonight to speak of the city in its third lockdown, so I continue along Empire Street then Sherborne Street, edging along the railings of Cheetham Park to the main road.

An improvised performance of bass drum via a waste bin being repeatedly kicked due to a missed bus and then the scissor snip of a lighter setting a spliff aglow. Distorted percussion crackles out of a mobile phone. Washing lines flutter their wares beyond railings, dancing ghosts swaying to the sporadic traffic hum. Out here the sounds of the night wash through the streets. There is an eerie absence of people and activity in general. As a result, the soundtrack of the night slips out of open windows and doors held ajar. Music and voices intermingle, wafting out of these apertures towards the sky, their rhythms and accents dispersing in the dark. Swatches of reggae, hip hop and soukous uncoil themselves from domestic interiors and weave their way into the street beyond. Tinny ribbons of music escape into the wider world, distorted and shrill from their source, punctuating the night air with their Morse code to unknown recipients. Occasionally they overlap, forming interstitial sonic zones for the nightwalker. The babble of a family couched in the splurge of a television game show adds jingle bursts and audience appreciation to an already heated discussion. Here within the inner suburban fabric of the city, the soundscape is convivial and an open score awaiting your voice to add to its community compared with the urban melee usually found in the city centre. The low-rise housing schemes in this district offer a slower tempo to the feet, this is a landscape at a human scale, and for the body to enter the gentle surround sound of lives behind brick and mortar. Snippets of dialogue join the found sounds of the urban landscape as brakes squeak in the next street, a wheelie bin lid clasps shut and a dog barks its warning over several garden fences. As the pattern-cut architecture gives way to a major thoroughfare, the swooshing of distant vehicles and blinking of a pedestrian crossing bring forth the memory of when this road is busy with its crawling wheels of congested traffic which need to be paused for the scramble of schoolchildren to laugh and shout their way across. Not tonight though. There are very few people around. Where figures can be seen they are usually stood alone and motionless, frozen in time by the blueish-white glaze that emits from their phone, a temporary death mask isolating them from the wider dance of the city.

Onward and upward along Waterloo Road and the low thrum of urban life seems to build. Fried chicken and other takeaway food smells drift towards me, tasty poltergeists drawing the body to their origins. At the top of the road where it is swallowed by Cheetham Hill Road, the plunge and sizzle of deep fat fryers within the brightly lit glass boxes of fast food outlets. Delivery drivers wait with their insulated cubes ready to transport these crispy wonderments across the hungry neighbourhoods. Bright colours of illuminated signage join the visual fray, a private psychedelic showreel for the nightwalker. Above one of these, a leg hangs out into the night air from a window amidst the sweet plumes of a vaping machine providing intermittent succour to the suckling owner of the limb. Urgent Arabic flourishes pinch their way into the night air from the lowered window of a private hire vehicle stopping at the traffic lights. Engine idling, its thrum adding syncopated beats to the treble waves of the music that is playing inside the car. The sounds build as the car accelerates away, streaking its mash-up melody down the road to quick fade out of sight and ear.

Down from the brow of the hill along a curve of townhouses and back into a suburb, this time Crumpsall. Many of the homes along this stretch are semi-detached, conjoined architecture keeping two families apart by a membrane of wallpaper, plaster and brick. Lives are largely muffled, noise kept firmly within domestic spaces save for the occasional one-sided chatter from a passing mobile phone user or the sporadic speech that slips through the night's cracks and crevices. Sound and place become weirdly dissonant. The general quiet envelops the area akin to a vast blanket, yet because of the cold air and the absence of sound when a noise does appear its presence somehow strikes a pertinent chord by contrast. This soundscape is one of deteriorating loops, the circadian rhythms of families' lives slowly and steadily disintegrating in pitch and timbre as the darkness grows in the night. From navy blue sky and ochre clouds to a more solidified bruise of purple-blacks. Feeling uncanny and out of sync with this muted orchestra, I stop. Breathe in. Breathe out. Breathe in. Breathe out. Breathe in. Breathe out.

I walk into Crumpsall Park, dark velvet lawns flank each step, with the spongey shadow forms of trees that stood in attendance to line paths and perimeter. There is no one else here tonight as the obelisk, empty play area and tennis courts can attest. Gathering momentum, I stride back out of the park and into the streets again. I am an instrument. My boots pad out along the pavement in dull clomps suddenly replaced by the scritch scratch of gravel beneath my feet then back to the subdued percussion again. I re-tune, watching the trams glide away on their curvatures into the infinity of night. Two figures snap me out of my reverie, their fast patois stretching out before them as they talk excitedly in an ethnic dialect I was unable to decipher as their sound bubble passes me by and then floats down the street with them.

Moving on and upward towards Cheetham Hill Road again, the rhythmic pairings of homes abruptly stop as the landscape shifts from dwelling to commerce. Now the architecture is one of the brick boxes and car parks, the noise from the nearby main road swirling around these barren places as it reflects from blank surfaces. Too late for shopping tonight. Back onto the artery road and the hubbub of takeaway restaurants sizzle and fizz with fryers and brief chatter between cooks, couriers and customers. Grease, warmth and strongly spiced aromas jab the air, wafting from doorways and opened polystyrene takeaway boxes. Chicken and chips, kebabs, curry and rice, and hot treats provide sustenance for those who share the night. The shuttered, blank expressions of some shopfronts provide unintentional minimalist artworks of aluminium and steel, white and grey planes with the accoutrements of a sticker or a grimy edge. In contrast, those retail and other spaces that bare their glass to the street show a mirror world, my twin through the looking glass and semi-submerged amongst the things actually residing in the interior beyond. The quick staccato call and the response of a Polish couple in minor disagreement before recommencing their walk together enter my sensory field before exiting stage left down a side street. The whump and bump of heavy bass pounds its way down the road at breakneck speed, drumming its route along the asphalt – an under-lit mobile disco for one. Leaving behind the area of synagogues and threading through one with mosques, the latter bookended by Trinity Union Church and the mostly derelict St. Luke's Church.

From here the road tumbles down to the city centre again. Large retail parks bulk into view, their patchwork sheds offering discounted dreams and convenient parking. A budget bit of consumerist Americana grafted onto the skin of the city. Behind these is North Street and a long history of light industrial units stakes its way across the urban landscape. This is a micro-utopia of demand and supply: wholesale clothes retailers, garages, electronics, textiles, materials and foodstuffs. It provides the city and the region with portals to the world through its procurement and logistics of goods and services. The *musique concrète* that can be experienced during the daytime around here is tangibly absent at night. Electric light skims along the bottom of a steel door or illuminates the odd window but whatever clandestine operations are going on inside are not disclosed beyond its walls. The ghosts of intense and poorly paid labour hang heavy around here. A formerly white plastic seat, since speckled with the patina of grit and grime, waits to receive a tired body and provide a brief respite from work. Little gatherings of cigarette butts close to façade apertures rest quietly following a flick and then the arc of their flight from fingers. They are tiny reminders of the soundscape from the day before, spectres of routine and all-too-temporary recuperation. The sleeping hulk of an HGV lies hard against the kerb, its smell of rubber and dust telling tales of highways and byways near and far. Its wide eyes and festive cabin lights sit forlorn and discharged from power. The confetti of foams packing material twitch in the light breeze but the long ribbons of sponge nearby are unwilling to join the dance tonight. The jabber of the unseen city beckons, its babble ebbing and flowing around corners and along streets in relation to my navigation across the warp and weft of the urban fabric. Arcing back again towards the main thoroughfare of Cheetham Hill Road, along which cars and trucks shift to and from the urban centre, their bright white headlights growing and blood-red rear lights dissipating into the long avenue. Hydraulics squeak, stereos pump beats, while further away some light rail transport adds metallic streaks of noise.

Turning back into the city centre, it is striking how different the soundtrack experienced in this area is compared to some of the other districts and neighbourhoods at night. These compositions, often fleeting and accidental, provide aural hints of a complex identity that despite some of its familiarity also remains obscure and can never be fully known as it rewrites and remixes itself with its people, the weather and the dynamics of urban life. Hidden in plain sight, Cheetham Hill is both a promise and a premise. It offers countless opportunities for reinvention in its environs and the ability to have encounter and exchange with a diverse and mobile set of cultures and identities. Its steadfast refusal to acquiesce to the planned power of the city and the latter's ongoing quest for an urban renaissance of renewal has led to its character as much as the forces of late capitalism have shaped its offer of cheap and counterfeit goods, shady operations, and both legitimate and illicit provisions to the wider population. With the return of LED-illuminated hues in the sky, and the very radiance of the city centre, it is time to leave the early hours of the urban landscape behind for another night. Standing and contemplating the music on-the-move and incidences of sublime composition that have been experienced tonight in the city, almost knowingly, lowers its volume and my body is briefly held still, embalmed even, in its soundscape. The veer and thrust of a Salford Van Hire van swerving around the corner then full throttle its way down the road completely shattering the ambience.

Nocturnal polyphony as shifting identities of place

To hear the city at night is to become aware of its utterances and migrations. To listen to the nocturnal polyphony of the city is to experience its mutating tones of knowledge that enable us to begin to understand the character of a place, its multitude of voices and the corporeality, temporality and movements that constitute them. Sound, as with other characteristics of a place, is integral to the formation of an urban environment's identity through its pitch, duration, intensity and timbre. It also is a form of representation in the city at night, one that gives expression to temporary, including fleeting, occupancies of place. Experienced at night, even familiar sounds are received quite differently due to the immersive, multi-sensory way in which the relationship between body and landscape oscillates. Considered in relation to the sonic attributes of urban places after dark, I contend that nightwalking is able to offer what Edensor (2017: 125) describes more broadly as, 'previously unanticipated ways of apprehension, soliciting perceptions that expand the capacities for imagining and sensing place otherwise, such approaches extend the compendium of ways of seeing'. In terms of methodology, nightwalking thus contributes to the ways we might rethink how to conduct sensory ethnography (Pink 2015). It also supports the notion of mobile music-making as a form of urban composition in cities at night, bringing together the situated, diverse and relational qualities of sound to produce an arrangement that is subject to incidental nightly variations but underpinned by the score of lived experience. Music-making here is conceived in a wider sense to account for the practice of nightwalking, where the body becomes an instrument through which the different sounds of the urban landscape are attuned at particular times and places. In this sense, the relationship with sound is both embodied and embedded. It is the shifting dynamics as the body moves in relation to the nocturnal city that enables the music-making to happen.

While this study is primarily focused on the sonic world of the 'everynight', it is important to emphasize the multi-sensory qualities of being in places after dark. In particular, the forms of synaesthesia which evolve through nightwalking as other senses such as smell, sound, taste and touch become more vivid at night, point towards new knowledge and understandings of place that are temporal, material and spatial. Crucially, such an approach puts less significance on sight in the way we comprehend places and I suggest this is valuable in those situations where and when we want or need to establish rich descriptions that may not easily share their identity if considered in visual terms alone. This is especially relevant in those contexts where migrant individuals or groups may not be in view but their presence is detectable in other ways, including sound.

Although this work afforded the opportunity to explore some of the overlapping soundtracks that occur at the in-between of multi-cultural residential spaces at night during winter and the first week of spring, I believe further inquiry especially out of lockdown and also at different times of the year would be insightful. This would enable the different forms of domestic night (Shaw 2018) to be articulated, including migrant and immigrant lived experiences, along with how their contribution to the wider sonic world of the area changes in relation to routines, specific events, weather conditions, etc. It is also important to recognize that different groups make use of the urban night in different ways (Wilkinson and Wilkinson 2018), so another avenue of inquiry would be to engage with various groups in Cheetham Hill to understand how their mobilities shape their identity within the city and vice versa, including the music and sound that forms part of this process. A number of the people I encountered during my research were waiting, for a variety of reasons, and further research would be useful to better understand the micro-geographies and ethnographies (Janeja and Bandak 2018) of their respective versions of the nocturnal city since this lay beyond the scope of my nightwalks. The timeframe of darkness is not consistent and, of course, changes throughout the year depending on context. Through the detailed description of a nightwalk, I have sought to illustrate how being in places after dark provides rich situations for the interplay of moods, creativity and imagination (Löfgren and Ehn 2007). By paying specific attention to a district of a city that by the conventional definition may appear far from spectacular, I have also tried to show how the 'everynight' can be just as revealing and profound as accounts of the more dramatic events occurring in cities at night (Sandhu 2007). Yet, this has been done during a national lockdown when the ability to engage with other people was severely limited apart from very short interactions. A further path of inquiry would be to have substantial time with those who contribute to the collective sound of the city, in particular by listening to those who may be underrepresented or marginalized to understand their issues and how these are articulated (Farinati and Firth 2016).

This chapter has presented nightwalking as a method through which the soundtrack of the urban landscape can be experienced, even remixed, as the body moves through the place. It has provided an account of the ongoing entanglement that occurs at the boundaries of body and urban landscape, sound and time, identity and place. It has also sought to illustrate how relationships between night and migration are encountered through a range of multi-sensory presences, especially with regard to sound. Through this description, I have aimed to convey the phenomenon of mobile music-making at night as an act of urban production. This is of critical importance if we are to develop a wider and deeper knowledge of the situated, relational and practised nature of the city after dark, and be able to rethink and reclaim it as a time and place that gives expression to the many different forms of music-making, mobile or otherwise, it produces.

REFERENCES

Atkinson, Paul and Duffy, Michelle (2019), 'Seeing movement: Dancing bodies and the sensuality of place', *Emotion, Space and Society*, 30, pp. 20–26.

Bielewska, Agnieszka (2011), 'The settlement patterns of Polish immigrants in Manchester in the context of move from modern to postmodern understanding of place', *Geographica Polonica*, 84:2, pp. 19–32.

Büscher, Monika and Urry, John (2009), 'Mobile methods and the empirical', *European Journal of Social Theory*, 12:1, pp. 99–116.

Chion, Michel (2009), *Film, A Sound Art* (trans. C. Gorbman), New York: Columbia University Press.

Crook, Tim (2011), *The Sound Handbook*, London: Routledge.

Dunn, Nick (2016), *Dark Matters: A Manifesto for the Nocturnal City*, Winchester: Zero Books.

Dunn, Nick (2019), 'Dark futures: The loss of night in the contemporary city?', *Journal of Energy History / Revue d'histoire de l'énergie*, Special Issue: 'Light(s) and darkness(es)' / 'Lumière(s) et obscurité(s)', 1:2, pp. 1–27.

Dyson, Frances (2014), *The Tone of Our Times: Sound, Sense, Economy and Ecology*, Cambridge: The MIT Press.

Edensor, Tim (2017), *From Light to Dark. Daylight, Illumination, and Gloom*, Minneapolis: University of Minnesota Press.

Engels, Friedrich (1892), *The Condition of the Working-Class in England in 1844* (trans. F. K. Wischnewetsky), London: Swan Sonnenschien & Co.

Farinati, Lucia and Firth, Claudia (2016), *The Force of Listening*, Berlin: Errant Bodies Press.

Gidley, Ben (2013), 'Landscapes of belonging, portraits of life: Researching everyday multiculture in an inner city estate', *Identities: Global Studies in Culture and Power*, 20:4, pp. 347–60.

Handelman, Don (2005), 'Epilogue: Dark soundings – towards a phenomenology of night', *Paidemua: Mitteilungen zur Kulturkunde*, 51, pp. 247–61.

Harries, Bethan, Byrne, Bridget, Rhodes, James and Wallace, Stephanie (2019), 'Diversity in place: Narrations of diversity in an ethnically mixed, urban area', *Journal of Ethnic and Migration Studies*, 45:17, pp. 3225–42.

Haslam, Dave (1999), *Manchester, England*, London: Fourth Estate.

Janeja, Manpreet K. and Bandak, Andreas (2018), *Ethnographies of Waiting: Doubt, Hope and Uncertainty*, London: Bloomsbury.

Löfgren, Orvar and Ehn, Billy (2007), 'Daydreaming between dusk and dawn', *Etnofoor*, 20:2, pp. 9–21.

Mason, Tim (1977), 'Residential succession, community facilities and urban renewal in Cheetham Hill, Manchester', *Journal of Ethnic and Migration Studies*, 6:1&2, pp. 78–87.

Masson, Damien (2021), 'How does the dark sound?' in N. Dunn and T. Edensor (eds), *Rethinking Darkness: Cultures, Histories, Practices*, London: Routledge, pp. 150–60.

Palmer, Bryan (2000), *Cultures of Darkness: Night Travels in the Histories of Transgression: From Medieval to Modern*, New York: Monthly Review Press.

Pink, Sarah (2015), *Doing Sensory Ethnography*, London: Sage.

Sandhu, Sukhdev (2007), *Night Haunts: A Journey Through the London Night*, London: Art Angel.

Schafer, R. Murray (1993), *The Soundscape: Our Sonic Environment and the Tuning of the World*, Rochester: Destiny Books.

Shaw, Robert (2018), *The Nocturnal City*, London: Routledge.

The Fall (1996), 'Cheetham Hill', *The Light User Syndrome*, CD, London: Jet Records.

VCH (2011), 'Townships: Cheetham', in W. Farrer and J. Brownbill (eds), *A History of the County of Lancaster: Volume 4*, London: British History Online, pp. 259–62, http://www.britishhistory.ac.uk/vch/lancs/vol4/pp259-262. Accessed 30 March 2021.

Wilkinson, Samantha and Wilkinson, Catherine (2018), 'Night-life and young people's atmospheric mobilities', *Mobile Cultures Studies, The Journal*, 3, pp. 77–96.

Williams, Robert (2008), 'Nightspaces: Darkness, deterritorialisation and social control', *Space and Culture*, 11:4, pp. 514–32.

Interlude 2

'Tokyo After Hours'

Nick Prior

In 2017, I held a Visiting Fellowship at the University of Tokyo of the Arts, Japan. During the Fellowship, I was asked to compose and perform a series of electronic music scores that related to my work on the sociology of Japanese popular culture. One of the pieces was called 'Tokyo After Hours' and the following is a reflection on the score and the ideas behind (and perhaps in front of) it.

There are many layers to Tokyo, but the dominant urban imaginary is still one that reduces the city to its frenetic rhythms. It's the ultra-capitalist, high-tech Tokyo at full tilt, subjecting the bewildered urbanite to the constant and ceaseless stimulation of the neon-lit city. It's Simmel's metropolis at warp speed (Simmel [1901] 1971).

But as that other European sociologist of the city, Lefebvre (2004) insists, cities are polyrhythmic. They are sites for garlands of rhythms: seasons, atoms, corpuscles, traffic, heartbeats, commodities and migrants. How do you navigate and orient to these myriad forms, forces and stimulations? Earlier in the European modern tradition, Baudelaire had the poet's (male) gaze and the poignant glance. Photographers had their frozen moments. Impressionists their wispy flourishes. The Situationists insisted on aimless drifting and the politico-cognitive mapping of psychogeography. As for contemporary researchers, urban ethnographers describe thickly while data scrapers scrape, desperately trying to catch up with the networked intumescence of the datafied city.

Like many, I walked and observed when and what I could, going backwards and forwards from the digital maps on my smartphone to their 'real-world' referents. But I also recorded stuff with my digital audio recorder. The sounds are not of the famous Hachiko crossing or Shinjuku's pleasure-soaked streets, but of everyday domestic life and the traces left by the dreamlike city at dusk, as the light drains and the dark settles in.

As Les Back has said, digital audio recorders have not only enlivened our methodological creativity but have also helped us to tune into the 'rhythm and aesthetics of life' (Back 2010: 19). These devices have opened up possibilities

FIGURE I2.1: Akihabara, Tokyo, 2018. Photo taken by author.

for doing social science differently, for new modes of storytelling, making and doing together. In my case, their use supports a shift from a sociology *of* music to a sociology *with* music, where the latter is a meaningful resource to relay something vital about here and there, time and space, solidarity and inclusion, bodies and cities.

The piece begins with two melodies, the first a field recording and the second played 'live' on a MIDI controller triggering piano samples. The second is a melody that connects The University of Tokyo of the Arts with Scotland, where I currently live. It's a folk tune 'Comin Thro' the Rye' that was translated by Takeo Ito while at Tokyo Music School in the late 1920s. The Scottish version was written by Robert Burns, who also wrote the New Year's tune 'Auld Lang Syne', in 1782. The Japanese version of Burns' melody is called 'Kokyō no Sora' and ended up as a children's tune played at pedestrian crossings in Japan to signal to children and the visually impaired that it's safe to cross.

These little urban melodies act like audio punctums (to evoke Barthes's term), injecting the lightest of sounds into the most mundane of duties. They include the most famous, 'Tōryanse', a lilting, plaintive nursery rhyme and 'Yūyake Koyake', which is the field recording and first melody of the piece. This tune is played over public address systems at 5:00 p.m. on a daily basis in many parts of Japan and helps constitute everyday routines. It is a sonic temporal boundary marker to remind children to return to the safety of their homes before dark.

Tokyo *after* hours? There is no *after* of course, not with a city that as the saying goes 'never sleeps'. The city keeps moving. Shift workers shuffle. Clubbers stumble. Tourists look for ways to combat jet lag, while at 3:00 a.m. you can see the lights of many office blocks still blazing. The salaryman's overtime. And yet things are *different* at night. Not a hiatus as such, but a kind of declension. Even in one of the most populous and accelerated cities on the planet, you can moderate your pace; or is it that the city adjusts you, re-fixes its coordinates and invites you to take a breath?

The audio composition is designed to explore Tokyo's less visible rhythms, those that play out in the backstreets, side-streets and quiet passageways of the city. Internal domestic ambiences, too. Rain is a good signifier of ambience, of course, and there is rain here, the result of times spent field-recording in underpasses and over drains. There are washes and sweeps, glitches and cuts. There are nods to my European cultural capital and the techno-orientalism that constitutes my urban-national imaginaries – *Blade Runner* and *Lost in Translation*, Haruki Murakami and ping pong. Nods too, to the British band that got me fixated on this country in the first place, the aptly named glam-rock outfit, Japan. I still reel from the fact that this band wrote a song, 'Life in Tokyo', on an album called *Assemblages* released in 1981. Forty years later I'm still working with the Deleuzian idea that the Japanese virtual idol, Hatsune Miku, is an assemblage (Prior 2021).

At 10 minutes, 46 seconds into the piece, enter Miku. A glitched out Miku to be precise, from the Vocaloid software that generates her voice. She features a lot in the night-time economies of Tokyo: you can catch her synthesized post-human voice spilling out from the karaoke bars, pachinko parlours and amusement arcades of Shibuya. They add layers of distributed creativity to an already hyper-mediated city. But here, too, things are polyrhythmic and steeped in hybridities. One of Miku's most well-known songs is 'The Disappearance of Hatsune Miku'. Like most of the other 500,000 songs, it's written by one of her fans using the Vocaloid software. It's a piece of high-octane electro-pop which comes in at 240 beats per minute. I've been in Karaoke bars when bar hostesses have tried to perform this song. Flesh-and-blood singers affecting their voices to sound like a digitized version of software originally intended to emulate and replace flesh-and-blood singers. They can barely keep up with the tempo but try admirably. It's their work after all, and the night is their stage.

And then at 11 minutes, 30 seconds into the piece, another layer, another rhythm, another memory. This time the delicate pluckings of my partner's koto, and the over-dubbed sounds of the washing machine in her flat. Of laundry smells and dodgy microphone stands; and then eventually the smell of our newborn's hair. In summer, too, the incessant and strangely electronic sounds of the cicadas: their sonic crescendos far outweighing their visibility. It is here in this flat that I first started writing 'Tokyo After Hours'. And, yes, this piece is also an assemblage. I look for its traces three years later: scraps of paper and field notes, digital folders and archives, and hundreds of samples with names like 'water_5', 'arigatou' and 'urban_ambiance'. Some of the files are no longer accessible, the victim of bit rot. But there is an unmastered recording on YouTube at least.

My partner tells me my face changed when I made this: headphones on, folded into the piece. 'In your zone' she says. But that zone, like the night, is never as pure as it seems – it's always multiple, contingent and hybrid. The tech-induced tinnitus and rounded shoulders, for a start, but also the abundant fissures and apertures as MIDI data is enacted, sliced and diced. Spilled coffee and data drop-outs, (uneven) distributions of household labour and insomnia. The relative quietness of the night only serves to make more apparent the spatial intensities and contradictions of these moments. I'm playing across interfaces, calling down audio from data storage centres across the world, pressing the small silicon pads of my controller at a small wooden table in a living room in a tenement in one of the densest cities in the world – all working at slightly different speeds and with semi-autonomous rhythms, logics and pleasures. This is Tokyo, too.

https://www.youtube.com/watch?v=TMQV8eFnG-U (accessed 3 August 2022).

REFERENCES

Back, Les (2010), 'Broken devices and new opportunities: Re-imagining the tools of qualitative research', *ESRC National Centre for Research Methods*, NCRM Working Paper Series, Goldsmiths: University of London.

Lefebvre, Henri (2004), *Rhythmanalysis: Space, Time and Everyday Life*, London: Continuum.

Prior, Nick (2021), 'STS confronts the vocaloid: Assemblage thinking with Hatsune Miku', in A. Hennion and C. Levaux (eds), *Rethinking Music Through Science and Technology Studies*, London: Routledge.

Simmel, Georg ([1901] 1971), 'The metropolis of modern life', in D. Levine (ed.), *Simmel: On Individuality and Social Forms*, Chicago: Chicago University Press.

PART 3

HISTORICITY

5

Manolo D'Aro Postmortem: The Eternal and the Futurible in the Musical Landscapes of Francoist Experiential Capitalism

Pol Esteve Castelló

The text that follows is a non-authorized biography. It is a fictional autopsy of two dead bodies, a human body and an architectural body. The two bodies cannot be dissected separately from each other. Together, like two organs, they function as a single organism engaged in processes of production and consumption around travel, music and the night. It is precisely their 'difference'[1] that ensures the perfect functioning of a larger libidinal body. The two organs are the town of Platja d'Aro and the singer Manolo Escobar; we will call the body experiential capitalism.

Platja d'Aro

Platja d'Aro is a touristic town in the Costa Brava.[2] In the decade of 1950, what then was a fishing village went through an abrupt transformation due to international tourism. In less than ten years, Platja d'Aro went from being a deprived rural enclave to a pioneering night-life spot on the Mediterranean coast. In the 1960s, Platja d'Aro became a biopolitical laboratory: in its nightclubs were being tested the instruments – music, fashion, drugs, youth – of a new global libidinal economy based on experience consumption.

Platja d'Aro was not the only town to respond to the desires of a growing European leisure middle-class,[3] but a paradigmatic example of a larger transformation of the Mediterranean coast into a 24-hour leisure space; day-time on the beach, night-time on the club. Of all the emergent Spanish tourist town, Platja d'Aro, according to sociologist Mario Gaviria, was the 'true capital of leisure' (1971: 161). In winter, it had around 4000 inhabitants, while in summer, the conurbation reached 200,000. All attracted by the Sun and the *fiesta*.[4]

In Platja d'Aro, the *fiesta*, as an experiential event for tourists' consumption, transitioned from being a folkloric show to a postmodern dance floor. Traditional forms of music and dance, like flamenco, were substituted by the rhythms of an emergent global music industry. In Platja d'Aro, the flows of people, capital, technologies and cultural products fostered by international tourism met the Spanish understanding of the night as a space and time for leisure.[5] Supported by new airports and jets, improved roads and recreational cars, prêt-à-porter fashion and bikinis, a new leisure culture crystallized on the dance floors.

This displacement from traditional to new forms of night leisure was accompanied by the apparition of spaces purposely designed for dancing to recorded music. In 1958, the year that stereo sound was made commercially available, at least one nightclub in Platja d'Aro already had a stereo sound system pointing towards the dance floor.[6] In 1964, in Platja d'Aro, the first modern discotheque of Spain and a pioneering night space in Europe was launched.[7]

The renowned writer and critic Manuel Vázquez Montalbán would describe the Costa Brava and Platja d'Aro as 'a paradise of idleness'. The summer, the night and the transient visitors ignited the *fiesta* as 'the most baroque expression of this idleness'. In Platja d'Aro, the *fiesta* was made up of 'a swing of wine, dancing, light and pantomime which free our spirits'. Vázquez Montalbán would conclude: 'The summer creates freedom. The summer cannot be lived without freedom: freedom to think, to speak, to do or not to do – the four fundamental freedoms of the fiesta' (Vázquez Montalbán et al. 1966: n.pag.).

Platja d'Aro preceded and inspired the night scene of Ibiza.[8] Before the Balearic island became a world renown destination, Platja d'Aro attracted international personalities and a national liberal bourgeoisie looking for fun and freedom into the night. The discotheque, as it had been designed in Platja d'Aro, was then copied and exported throughout the coast of Spain and beyond. Some of the discotheques founded in Platja d'Aro opened branches through Europe and the Middle-East.[9]

At the present, Platja d'Aro is still a popular touristic destination with certain night life, but none of the 1960s nightclubs exist anymore. Other towns in Spain have taken over as first destinations for party-trips, from Salou to Magaluf. However, after the golden years of Ibiza, most of the Mediterranean party resorts have fallen into the logics and mechanics of aggressive neocapitalism. The experimental and emancipatory power of the first clubs has been lost.

Through the decades, the Mediterranean discotheque has become a part of a larger infrastructure for the mass production of low-cost pleasures. As philosopher Yves Michaud would say, the discotheque is a vital part of an industry of 'sensations engineering'.[10] This global and contemporary socio-economical project found some of his first expressions in Platja d'Aro by exploiting the difference between the newness of pop dancing against the 'authenticity' fisherman's coastal landscape.

Manolo Escobar

Escobar was one of the most prominent singers in Spain and Latin America during the second half of the twentieth century. He sang Spanish popular music, recorded more than 80 albums – 24 of them gold – and played in multiple films. His disc, *Y Viva España*, was the best-selling album in the history of Spain from 1973 until 1992 – the year Barcelona celebrated the Olympic Games, and the year scholar Teresa M. Vilarós interpreted as when 'the national psychology closes up the feeling of 'change' and transition of the first twenty years of postfrancoist Spain' ([1998] 2018: 39–40).

Escobar has been a paradigmatic figure, incarnating the values of a traditional and picturesque country. His films – one a year for over twenty years – and songs promoted a highly commercial new style of folkloric music. Rumbas, pasodobles and sevillanas were infused with the new upbeat and electronic sounds of 1960s pop. Wrapped with fresh arrangements, often set on beach resorts and recurrently addressing tourism, his work had a latent conservative message praising a traditional understanding of gender roles and religion. Eventually, he would be known as *la voz de España* ('the voice of Spain'). His chorus reflected a sort of national consciousness.

His song 'Moderno pero Español' ('Modern but Spanish') paradigmatically claimed the possible coexistence between a traditional Spanish – sexist and religious – character and a modern consumerist world. In fact, he himself became the most profitable product of an emerging national pop music industry by adapting anachronic macho values to the new regimes of cultural consumption. His Barcelona-based music label Belter earned large amounts of money on the first wave of Spanish folkloric pop in the 1960s,[11] opening a new paradigm for contemporary cultural industries.

Escobar already incarnated a cultural pastiche when in the 1960s literary and architectural postmodernisms irrupted. His work was imbedded in new media, deconstructing the Spanish character into fragments to be sold through the shiny surfaces of screens, vinyl and merchandising. The medium was new, the message was old. He became a pop celebrity, 'a commercial product and tourist attraction' (Crumbaugh 2010: 77), and, for many, an instrument of propaganda for the dictatorial regime.

The Spanish critic and writer Manuel Vázquez Montalbán said Escobar represented an 'eternal Spain'.[12] Precisely at the moment when the country was more fiercely looking towards the future. The lyrics of his songs were the voice of a conservative society shocked by the arrival of liberal capitalism in commercial jets. The rhythms of his music were peoples' sentimental topographies; a contrasting landscape between the cheerful beach and the quiet inlands. He appealed to identarian feelings and proved that Spanishness was not going to be lost when confronted with global consumerism.

Montalbán saw Escobar as 'a representative artist of an alienated popular imagination that feeds consensus, and that maybe can only be justified for its nervous acceptance of all consensus, for his traumatic acceptance of all consensus' (Vázquez Montalbán [1971] 2003: 176). A consensus for oblivion. His pop mixture of the eternal and the contemporary was enchanting enough to impose a collective amnesia of dictatorial repression and its opposite liberation utopias. Escobar infused consensus to transit from authoritarianism into democracy.

Like in Platja d'Aro, it was the friction between the old and the new that made Escobar's music and figure attractive. But while in Platja d'Aro, the discotheque as a sign of modernity contrasted with the backward coastal landscapes, in Escobar's songs, it was the anachronism of his claims what contrasted against the modern musical arrangements. He was selling 'difference' in the form of pop songs' choruses. 'Spain is different'[13] has been the most popular Spanish tourist slogan.

Manolo Escobar in Platja d'Aro

Manolo Escobar entered the reign of the eternal in Benidorm[14] in 2013, the most radical touristic city of the Spanish coast. When alive, he had been asked on several occasions to write his memoirs. He recurrently answered that the truth about his life would probably hurt someone (Escobar 2013: n.pag.).

This text is an attempt to dissect and reconstruct a portion of his biography, which is also the history of Platja d'Aro. The singer and the town best showed their cultural behaviours on the time they encountered each other. This fictional text is based on historical research.[15] Despite its questionable veracity, it is probably through literary fiction that Platja d'Aro and Manolo Escobar as producers of consumable fictions of difference can be best read.

Platja d'Aro was a place of personal and professional memories for Manolo. There, he probably encountered the beat of a new generation for the first time.[16] In Platja d'Aro, Spaniards and Europeans mingled together. The tourists came from the industrialized European north; the workers in leisure industry were migrants from the Spanish dry south.[17] In Platja d'Aro, European postwar scarcities were buried under the pleasures of long nights and long drinks served by Andalusian waiters.

There was a sensual vibe brought by new musical genres that had travelled across the sea. First, the velvety textures of soul; later, the electric sparkles of beat, rock and psychedelia. When the sun went down, the 'eternal Spain' started dancing towards the future at the rhythm of progressive rock.[18] This occurred after midnight, because earlier in the evening they sat down to listen to the folkloric chorus of Escobar's songs. As Vázquez Montalbán said, the 'feet of a young proletarian Spain [...] are moving with the electrosound [*sic*] of the future, but his language is still attached, for unnumerable causes, to the fake metaphysics of a fake man' ([1971] 2003: 177). The night was a space of transgression, where the body was moving along the electric beats of futurist aesthetic regimes. The day was the reign of Manolo, a time of the immovable eternal Spanish sun printed on all holiday advertisements.

Late 1950s – Migrant sounds

Manolo was in Platja d'Aro for the first time at the end of the decade of 1950 – back then, still a small yet anxiously growing touristic resort. Earlier in the 1950s, newly built functional apartments and hotels started colonizing the seafront. Some bright land owners started constructing little huts near the beach to provide drinks and food to the vacationers.

Initially, this *chiringuitos*[19] opened on Sundays; it was a way for the farmers to make some extra money when not working the land. Soon, the success pushed them to remove some crops, enlarge the huts and start opening seven days a week. Then they upgraded the atmosphere by introducing some colourful lighting and hiring some local musicians to play at sunset. In few years, a new kind of beach architecture for night, music and *fiesta* had been invented. The *chiringuito* was a precursor of the discotheque.

Manolo sang in Platja d'Aro for the first time in 1958. It was as a member of a band along with his brothers: Manolo Escobar y sus Guitarras ('Manolo Escobar and his Guitars'). They were hired to play in Salón Fiesta[20] (Figure 5.1). This night venue opened at the beginning of the 1950s and was run by a local family. Originally, it had been an open-air space for dancing, cinema and other activities. By 1957, it was covered in order to host shows and dancing during the summer. Salón Fiesta was a *sala de fiestas* ('party hall', in its literal translation), which was the term used to denominate a night venue for shows, music and dancing before the emergence of discotheques.

FIGURE 5.1: The owners and two waiters of Salón Fiesta, under a picture of Manolo Escobar, Salón Fiesta, Platja d'Aro, *c.*1960. Joan Bassó personal archive.

Like most of the *salas de fiestas* of the time, Salón Fiesta had live folklore shows. Escobar's troupe was at that time still playing a repertoire of traditional Spanish folk, very much aligned with the cliché of the 'typical Spanish'. The Spanish 'authentic' was performed as if the clock had stopped in Don Quijote's times. The public was elegant, women wearing nightdresses and men with tie. The atmosphere was rather distinguished and broad in ages.

The club reminded of a Spanish *cortijo*.[21] The space, decorated with traditional architectural motives and tenuous lights, went along with the style of the performance. That night they offered classic coplas, pasodobles, rumbas and boleros.[22] Manolo would try to give it a personal touch. Influenced by the arrival of new modern beats from the English-speaking world, he started essaying what would become the unique Escobar sound (Escobar 1985: n.pag.); a sound rooted in traditional Latin musical genres but with a fresh commercial production that would make both older and young groove. His smile and Don Juan attitude did the rest. The first show was a success and he was hired to come back the following summer.

Entering the 1960s – Migrant bodies

It was the turn of the 1960s. Spain was about to become the first tourist destination in the world, in volume of visitors. The number of tourists surpassed one-third of the local population at the beginning of the decade and steadily grew thereafter.[23] Northern girls lay on the beach. Manolo was back for his second show; this time he had an agreement with the maître:[24] he would sit the prettier single girls on the first row. The music, the night and the vibrations of his Spanish 'r' melted the hearts of romantic tourists in search of summer love. During the show, he took off his Cordovan hat and put it on a German girl; the day after they had a date in *Flamingo*[25] (Figure 5.2).

Flamingo was a beautiful open-air dance club inaugurated in 1958. In contrast to Casa Vella, the space had a minimalistic style and brought a feeling of contemporaneity. The vernacular decorations had been substituted for the tropes of modern architecture. It had a stereophonic sound system for playing recorded music and two retro-lit dance floors with flickering lights surrounded by plants. It was like a technified garden next to the sea. When he first tried to kiss her (and got a slap back), 'Lonely Teardrops' by Jackie Wilson was pumping through the speakers – melodic,

FIGURE 5.2: Interior view of the nightclub Flamingo, Platja d'Aro, *c.*1960. As reproduced in the magazine *Quaderns d'Arquitectura*, 58, 1964, p. 32.

soft, sexy. The sound was amazing in intensity and definition;[26] that night, Manolo was enveloped by stereophonic sound for the first time.

Three months later, they got married in Cologne. She was called Anita and would be Manolo's wife until his death. There he fulfilled a generational fantasy: the eternal Spanish Don Juan seducing a northern liberal blonde.[27] Just that his wife was a dyed brunette – the body of capital in disguise – and theirs was not to be the promised summer love, but a long-term Christian union. In the following years, Manolo became widely popular singing rumbas like 'El Porompompero'[28] and 'Buscando un Amor' (Escobar 1966a, 1966b: n.pag.).

Ando buscando una novia
ando buscando un amor
una mujer más hermosa
y más linda que un día de sol.
Tan dulce como una madre,
tan serena como un juez,
que me comprenda y me quiera
como se debe querer.
Altiva con la malicia,
orgullosa de su fe,
cristiana buena y sencilla,
una mujer de una vez.
('I'm looking for a girlfriend,
I'm looking for love,
a woman more beautiful,
and prettier than a sunny day.
As sweet as a mother
as serene as a judge,
that understands and loves me,
like one must be loved.
Arrogant with malice,
proud of her faith,
good and modest Christian
a woman finally.')[29]

Mid 1960s – Migrant capitals

Since the beginning of the 1960s, Platja d'Aro had become internationally popular for its nightlife.[30] In 1966, Manolo was hired to perform again. In this occasion, the invitation came from Stanley Bouana, a French-Algerian dancer that decided to invest in Costa Brava's night-business after seeing the major success of another of Platja d'Aro's clubs, *Gogó*[31] (Figure 5.3).

Gogó had opened in 1962 as a 'boîte' – the term used at the time to refer to a night space for music and dancing, before the term 'discotheque' was popularized – in a camping site. Gogó was the first club of Costa Brava to introduce go-go dancers while the censorship of the regime banned naked bodies in films and media. Rather humble, in comparison to the discotheques that opened later, it had podiums and discreet flickering colour lights. It was right next to the beach and, reportedly, the nights ended in the water. In Gogó, the newly arrived twist dancing met the twists of sea waves.

Impacted by the atmosphere of Gogó, Bouana opened Paladium[32] in June 1966. That same year, it organized a Miss Miniskirt contest that ended up in an official fine for public scandal. Paladium shared artists management with Parisian nightclub Don Camilo.[33] Bouana was an example of an international flow of investment towards the shores of the Mediterranean.[34] On this occasion, Manolo sang in front of a larger audience; northern Europeans that had arrived in charter planes through Perpignan airport and French that had driven down with their new Citroëns.[35]

At that time, Bouana's club was not a dancing club but more of a concert hall. Juliette Gréco and a young Johnny Hallyday performed on the same stage that

FIGURE 5.3: Interior of the discotheque Gogó in Calonge, Platja d'Aro, 1968. Ajuntament de Girona. Collection Narcís Sans Prats (CRDI).

summer, but only Manolo knew how to sing to the 'passions' of Spain. He interpreted 'Flor del Sur' (Escobar 1965b: n.pag.).

> *Flor del sur, alondra de los campos*
> *que creciste como una amapola.*
> *Tan llena de encanto, abre tu corola*
> *y recibe el canto de un hombre que añora*
> *tu flor de pasión.*
> ('Flower from the south, lark of the fields
> you grew like a field poppy
> So full of charm, open your corolla
> and receive the singing of a man that longs for
> your flower of passion.')[36]

Late 1960s – Migrant cultures

A while after the show, a few French girls took Manolo to what they said was 'the best club of the Mediterranean'.[37] It had just opened the year before, in 1965, and was a real shock. Simple decoration, dark interior, mesmerizing lights, loud modern music: Tiffany's.[38] Behind it were two Swiss entrepreneurs, Raito Ganzoni and Werner Straub. Tiffany's would be the model for a contemporary concept of discotheque.

People were crazily dancing perched on podiums (Figure 5.4) – this was a radically new form of social dance. Individuals danced separately – rather different from the romantic couples dancing to Manolo's pasodobles. Under the influence of R&B, soul, rock and psychedelia's tripping melodies and trembling bass, the crowd became a common entity. Manolo entered the dance floor and was invaded by a strange feeling; it was like being submerged in an expanded field of affections; this was not the delicate poppy of 'Flor del Sur' but a plastic flower bouquet.

In Tiffany's, Manolo saw a discotheque DJ for the first time. He was positioned at the level of the dance floor with two turntables installed in a panel wall (Figure 5.5). His name was Jean-Pierre Grätzer, from Switzerland, and was playing 'Somebody to Love' by Jefferson Airplane. He would get the hottest sounds on regular trips to New York, London and Zurich. That night he was linking faster and slower tracks without pause, creating a temporal loop, a sinuous soundscape![39]

Manolo had some drinks – they make them large in Spain – and some amphetamines that a friend got from the local pharmacy.[40] Manolo jumped into the

FIGURE 5.4: Interior of the discotheque Tiffany's in Platja d'Aro, 1969. Ajuntament de Girona. Collection Narcís Sans Prats (CRDI).

FIGURE 5.5: DJ Jean-Pierre Grätzer in the DJ deck in the disoctheque Tifanny's in Platja d'Aro, *c*.1968.

dance floor; above him, hundreds of lighten stalactites twinkling at the rhythm of the fast beat. Then appeared the go-gos: Black, Asian and blonde (Figures 5.6 and 5.7) – they came from all around the world. It was like a Babel tower, foreign

FIGURE 5.6: Go-go dancer in the discotheque Tiffany's in Platja d'Aro, *c.*1973. Ajuntament de Girona. CRDI (Collection Pablo García Cortés, Pablito).

music, exoticized bodies, different languages. On the dance floor, the mythical prude woman that inhabited Manolo's songs dissolved in a libidinal mass of hips, tits and lips learning the body gestures of consumer society.

That night there was a guy with a camera, the filmmaker Jacinto Esteva, shooting some footage. This space was not like the previous boîtes, it was something 'different'. It was a modern discotheque; a new kind of aesthetic experience that Jacinto recorded for his film *Lejos de los árboles*[41] (*Far From the Trees*). The film was a cultural critique to the Spanish regime. It started with a scene in Tifanny's to later engage in a journey through Spain unveiling the contrasting and rooted poorness and cultural backwardness in areas not touched by tourism.

Manolo went back to the hotel with a couple of girls; feeling, like he used to sing 'Bohemio' ('Bohemian') (Escobar 1965a: n.pag.). In this case, though he was not a 'bohemio de Dios' ('bohemian of God') as his lyrics praised, but a bohemian of newly born global culture of dancing and the summer.

FIGURE 5.7: Go-go dancers in the discotheque Tiffany's in Platja d'Aro, *v.*1973. Ajuntament de Girona. CRDI (Collection Pablo García Cortés, Pablito).

Entering the 1970s – Migrant minds

Manolo only came back to Platja d'Aro four years later, again to play in Paladium, which by that time had become an institution. Stanley had built a car park for 600 vehicles. He performed some of his classics, like 'Porompompero', and his new sevillana hit 'La Minifalda'.[42]

No me gusta que a los toros
te pongas la minifalda.
La gente mira pa'rriba
porque quieren ver tu cara
y quieren ver tus rodillas
Los niñatos qué pesados
no dejan de contemplarte

Me rebelo y me rebelo
y tengo que pelearme
y a los toros no los veo
('I don't like that at the bull ring
you wear a miniskirt.
People looks upwards
cause they want to see your face
and want to see your knees.
How annoying the brats
they don't stop staring at you.
I get upset and upset
and I have to fight
and I don't see the bulls.')

Anita, his wife, didn't travel with him. It was Saturday night, and Manolo was by himself. Stanley had put some podiums in Paladium, and, after the show, the DJ started playing a potpourri of rock, pop and ye–ye tunes (Figure 5.8). By the early 1970s, thousands of people were dancing all night long in the different discotheques of Platja d'Aro.

Manolo didn't stay long, though. After a bit of chitchat there, he made a move and went to Maddox, the new in vogue club[43] (Figures 5.9 and 5.10). Maddox was a discotheque inaugurated in 1967. The space was designed by the Italian architect Vincenzo Carmenati and lighting and sound designer Cesare Fiorese. The architect designed an elevated DJ booth overlooking the dance floor, from where to control sound, and an impressive light installation.[44] The figure of the DJ was crowned in Maddox.

In 1968, the club was taken by Oriol Regàs[45] and under his direction became a hotspot of the Costa Brava. It was the meeting point between the chic local bourgeoisie, the Gauche Divine,[46] and carefree European youth. Earlier that night, there had been a gig by Màquina!,[47] the latest sensation of progressive rock that counted between their fans, Salvador Dalí (Figure 5.11). He was around and told Manolo he looked like Carlos IV.[48]

Maddox was like a cave from an outer world. All painted white, the design dissolved any Cartesian references: no up or down, no limits. It was an infinite interior space extending between two planes of techno stalagmites and stalactites. When Manolo arrived, the music was very low, and he didn't understand why in a room with four hundred people not a single soul was dancing … when suddenly:

> […] *pum pum pum* […] and it could be heard a voice saying 'here it comes, here it comes' […] then the room was left in darkness. Pitch dark, also the bar. And a long play came in, a song by Spooky Tooth, *tum tum tum tum pang! pang!* […] and the

FIGURE 5.8: Interior of the nightclub Paladium in Platja d'Aro, 1969. INSPAI, Centre de la Imatge Diputació de Girona (Collection Pablo García Cortés, Pablito).

FIGURE 5.9: Interior of the discotheque Maddox in Platja d'Aro, *c.*1968. Emanuela Carmenati personal archive.

FIGURE 5.10: Interior of the discotheque Maddox, Platja d'Aro, *c.*1968. Unknown author. Emanuela Carmenati personal archive.

FIGURE 5.11: Artist Salvador Dalí posing with progressive rock band Máquina! inside the discotheque Maddox in Platja d'Aro, *c.*1969.

> lighting for all the room turned on, like a bullfighting arena! full in red! such an impact! The dancefloor was full. Boys and girls where cinematically shaking their hair under the flickering flash[49] [Figures 5.12 and 5.13].

A combination of soul, rock and psychedelia brought directly from London was the instrument the DJ used to turn the dancers on (Figure 5.14). The crowd exuded waves of desire (Figure 5.15). Deep Purple, Titanic, Marvin Gaye, Soft Machine ... miniskirts were almost too decent for that. Bodies were shaking as if exorcising National Catholicism.[50] This ritualistic dance opened a portal to a techno-future. The guardians of the door were two tourists with promotional t-shirts of Bocaccio.[51] Manolo looked through the threshold yet decided not to cross it.

Manolo was offered drugs. It probably was acid. He didn't know how to dance to the sounds of counterculture and laid down in a circular sofa fascinated by the multi-coloured shadows his body cascaded under the psychedelic lights. He saw UFOs with American flags flying above his head then woke up to silence; the Francoist secret police had stopped the music. The DJ had played 'Santa Espina'.[52]

FIGURE 5.12: A woman and a man dancing inside the discotheque Maddox, in Platja d'Aro, 1969. Ajuntament de Girona. Collection Narcís Sans Prats (CRDI).

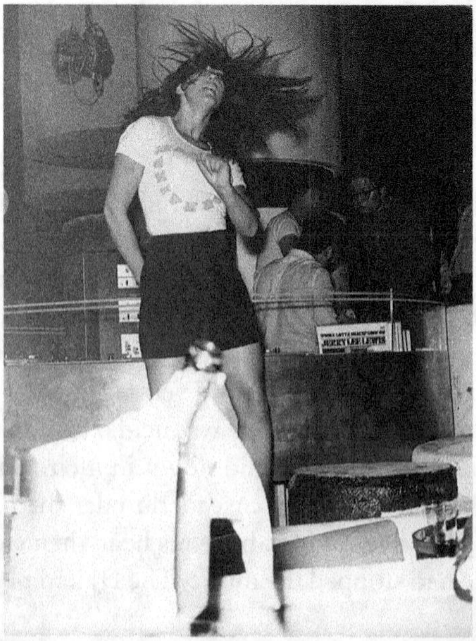

FIGURE 5.13: A woman dancing on a podium in front of the DJ booth in the discotheque Maddox in Platja d'Aro, *c.*1968. Emanuela Carmenati personal archive.

FIGURE 5.14: Interior view, with the DJ booth in the foreground, of the discotheque Maddox in Platja d'Aro, *c.*1969.

FIGURE 5.15: Interior view of people dancing in the discotheque Maddox in Platja d'Aro, 1970. Ajuntament de Girona. Collection Narcís Sans Prats (CRDI).

Still hungover, Manolo left Platja d'Aro two days later. He took a plane from the nearby airport of Girona to Málaga: he was performing the day after in the Festival Internacional de la Canción en la Ciudad Luminosa de la Costa del Sol.[53] Manolo never came back. Maybe he had a bad trip.

He did pay, though, a little homage to the international go–go dancers of Platja d'Aro's discotheques in the video of 'Y Viva España'[54] (Figure 5.16), where he was accompanied by a multiethnic troupe. Probably, his cover of this song was the most sentimental of all the covers in multiple languages that helped to promote the land of summer love:

Qué bonito es el mar Mediterráneo
su Costa Brava y su Costa del Sol.
La sardana y el fandango me emocionan
porque en sus notas hay vida y hay calor.
España siempre ha sido y será
eterno paraíso, sin igual.
('How beautiful is the Mediterranean Sea
its Costa Brava and Costa del Sol.

FIGURE 5.16: Cover of Manolo Escobar's *Y Viva España* single, Belter, Barcelona, 1973.

> The *sardana* and the *fandango* move me
> because in their notes there's life and warmth.
> Spain has always been and will be
> eternal paradise without match.')[55]

Manolo wanted to go back to Platja d'Aro before retiring. He planned a tour through all the towns he had performed in along his career. Yet he died before then and left behind atemporal songs, tunes that at a time created the illusion of the apolitical.[56] His work represented the fantasy of a society beyond history that had its counterpart on summer dance floor's mystifications. Manolo was the eternal, the discotheque the futurible. It was precisely by incorporating the differences between the two into the logics of experiential capitalism that an apolitical and ahistorical postmodernity was born.

NOTES

1. For an insightful account on the cultural production of 'difference' in Francoist Spain in relationship to tourism and consumption see Crumbaugh's *Destination Dictatorship: The Spectacle of Spain's Tourist Boom and the Reinvention of Difference* (2010).
2. The Costa Brava is the name given to the portion of Spanish Mediterranean coast belonging to the area of Girona. It is comprised between the French border and the town of Blanes, having 256 km of rocky coast interrupted by beaches and small bays. The Costa Brava was the first Spanish costal area being renamed with a new toponym for touristic purposes. The journalist Ferran Agulló invented the term Costa Brava in 1908. For an in-depth explanation of the invention of the touristic term Costa Brava, see Vicenç Pagès Jordà's article 'Ferran Agulló, inventor de la Costa Brava' (2014).
3. For a critical approach to the emergence of a new social class in relationship to post-war tourism, see Dean MacCannell's *The Tourist: A New Theory of the Leisure Class* (1976).
4. *Fiesta* is the Spanish word for party. Notably, as found researching in the municipal archive, the word *fiesta* was commonly used in early touristic advertisements of Platja d'Aro to attract tourism.
5. Spanish society has recurrently been seen and presented as cheerful and lively. Tourism presented Spaniards as welcoming and revelling, a society that likes to party and engage in singing and dancing. As an example, a BBC report from the 1950s showed how in traditional parties like the Wine Festival of Jerez people danced late into the morning (Dimbleby 1956).
6. Legal documents kept in the Arxiu Municipal Castell-Platja d'Aro i S'Agaró prove the concession of a permission for playing recorded music for dancing in 1958 to the nightclub Flamingo. A document by the Secretaría General del Gobierno Civil de la Provincia de Gerona dated 10 September 1958 specifies that Flamingo has gained the right 'to host sessions of public dancing with a radio-turntable'. An article devoted to the nightclub Flamingo specifies that the sound system was 'stereophonic' (Viladevall i Marfà 1964: 32).
7. Tiffany's in Platja d'Aro has been considered the first discotheque of Spain including a sound and light electronic installation for dancing. It was built in 1964, opened in 1965 and it was extended in 1966. Historical evidence about Tiffany's has been compiled from Arxiu Municipal Castell-Platja d'Aro i S'Agaró.
8. Ricardo Urgell, founder of Pacha, Ibiza-based night entertainment company owning the first and one of the most popular clubs of the island, has explained in several interviews how he got inspired after visiting the discotheque Tiffany's in a trip to Platja d'Aro, to open the first Pacha in 1966 in Sitges (Bardem 2015). Few years later, in 1973, he opened the first Pacha in Ibiza, setting a corner stone for the development of night leisure and business in the island.
9. As an example, in the late 1960s and the early 1970s, Tiffany's opened branches in Montpellier, Munich, Palma de Mallorca, Perpignan, Tel-Aviv, Toulouse and Torremolinos; the

sound designer of Tiffany's, Quico Riera, would claim to have designed the sound system for more than 100 discotheques around Europe, as it is reported in Xavier Castillón's *Nits d'Aro* (2018).

10. French philosopher Ives Michaud gives an account on leisure industries based on his observation and study of the island of Ibiza in *Ibiza Mon Amour: Enquête Sur l'Industrialisation du Plaisir* (2012).
11. In its heydays, Belter would have a year revenue of 1600 million pesetas, which at the present would be around 1400 million Euros (Editorial 1984: 39).
12.

> There's an eternal Spain that doesn't die, and if it would, there will be a troupe in charge to revive it. In the times of spatial conquest and the infinite scientific possibility, survive the myths of the eternal Spain, they are manifest all over the place and, of course, in the galaxy of showbusiness shine stars of arcane brightness, of carbide brightness, of oily lamp brightness. One of these stars is Manolo Escobar.
>
> (Vázquez Montalbán [1971] 2003: 174)

13. 'Spain is different' was a promotional slogan launched in 1960 by the then Minister of Information and Tourism, Manuel Fraga. The slogan took advantage of the position of exclusion that Spain took within Europe during the beginning of the dictatorship to present the country as an exotic tourist destination. The slogan had a strong impact on Spanish society and is still present on collective imaginaries today.
14. Manolo lived most of his life in Benidorm, a paradigmatic vacation city on the border of the Mediterranean sea. Benidorm, like Manolo Escobar, represents a tourist oriented Spanish product emerging from global neocapitalist fluxes. Benidorm has been a recurrent object of study by Spanish post-Marxist sociologist Mario Gaviria. A comprehensive approach to Benidorm can be found Gaviria's *Benidorm, Ciudad Nueva* (1977).
15. This fictional piece is based on historical research, including archival research in Arxiu Municipal de Calonge, Arxiu Municipal Castell-Platja d'Aro i S'Agaró, Arxiu Municipal de Girona – Centre de Recerca i Difusió de la Imatge and Servei de Gestió Documental, Arxius i Publicacions de l'Ajuntament de Girona; as well as research in private archives (with special thanks to Vincenzo Carmenati's family) and through collection of collective memories as expressed through individual interviews and online platforms.
16. In the words of the architect Vincenzo Carmenati, designer of discotheques in Platja d'Aro and Italy, in Platja d'Aro a 'new youth [was] looking for an international identity', 'the heart of a new city was beating and calling a participative experience, a white page to express the unspeakable' (2003: n.pag.).
17. At the time in Costa Brava, over 60 per cent of the tourist industry workers were not local – 18 per cent from other parts of Catalonia and 42 per cent from other parts of Spain. For more detailed data, see Rogelio Duocastella's *Sociología Pastoral del Turismo* (1969).

18. Accounts of the musical scene of Platja d'Aro can be found in multiple interviews with the DJs and personalities that frequented its nightlife. A collection of these materials has been published in Xavier Castillón's *Nits d'Aro* (2018).
19. *Chiringuito* is a Spanish word referring to a beach bar. Journalist Manuel Costa Pau gives a review of the evolution of *chiringuitos* into leisure architectures for music, dancing and night partying in *Turistas, Sirenas e Indígenas* (1967).
20. Historical data on Salón Fiesta have been compiled from Arxiu Municipal Castell-Platja d'Aro and Xavier Castillón's *Nits d'Aro* (2018), among other secondary sources.
21. A *cortijo* is a typical farm house from southern Spain.
22. Coplas, pasodobles, rumbas and boleros are all music genres rooted in Spanish and Latin-American culture. *Bolero* is from Cuban origin, while the others originated in Spain, although their development was enriched with the cultural exchange with Latin America.
23. As Edward Malefakis has consistently documented in his article 'Spain and its Francoist heritage':

> The number of tourists entering the country equalled one-third of the indigenous population by 1963, exceeded one-half of that population by 1966, and surpassed the entire population by 1972, a level at which it remained for most of the rest of the 1970s.
>
> (Malefakis 1982: 2015–30)

24. This scene is recreated from oral histories recalling how some male singers at that time would ask the person in charge of the venue to sit beautiful women on the first rows of the public.
25. Flamingo was a purposely built dance club designed by the architect J. Claret Ruvira and interior designer M. Majoral Sanfeliu. Historical data on Flamingo has been compiled from Arxiu Municipal Castell-Platja d'Aro i S'Agaró, and the article 'Sala de Fiestas Flamingo' (Viladevall i Marfà 1964).
26. In an article in the architectural magazine *Quaderns* (Viladevall i Marfà 1964: 32), the author explains that the space had a stereophonic sound system and some sections of the venue had to be covered due to the intensity of the sound disturbing neighbours in the surrounding areas.
27. An interesting account on the affective and sexual imaginaries around tourism and specifically about northern liberal women and Spanish macho men can be found in the fourth chapter 'Blondes in bikini and beachside Don Juans: From the comedy of sex tourism to a state perversion' of Justin Crumbaugh's *Destination Dictatorship: The Spectacle of Spain's Tourist Boom and the Reinvention of Difference* (2010).
28. El Porompompero (Escobar 1966b: n.pag.) is one of the most famous songs interpreted by Manolo Escobar. It became a Spanish classic and a generational hit.
29. Translated by the author.

30. In 1967, Platja d'Aro had at least nine discotheques, and 80 per cent of its visitors were foreigners, as Mario Gaviria has documented in *Campo, Urbe y Espacio del Ocio* (1971).
31. Historical data on Gogó has been compiled from Arxiu Municipal de Calonge and Xavier Castillón's *Nits d'Aro* (2018), among other secondary sources.
32. Paladium opened in Platja d'Aro as a *sala de fiestas* and later became a discotheque. It was characterized by an international programme of artists – particularly French due to its business partnership with the club Don Camilo in Paris. Historical data on Paladium have been compiled from Arxiu Municipal Castell-Platja d'Aro i S'Agaró and Xavier Castillón's *Nits d'Aro* (2018), among other secondary sources.
33. Don Camilo is a Parisian cabaret inaugurated in 1954 and still running. Stanley Bouana, who had made a career in Paris as a dancer, had a business relationship with Don Camilo to bring French artists to perform in Paladium in Platja d'Aro.
34. Mario Gaviria defined the 'neo-colonialism of space' as a continental operation of capital investment in the leisure industry on the coast of the Mediterranean Sea that would lead to 'the exploitation and control by foreigners of the production and use of the quality space in Spain' (1974: 13).
35. For Roland Barthes, the Citroën was 'the supreme creation of an era' (1972: 88). The popularization of recreational cars, e.g., the Citroën, allowed millions of tourists to cross the French border into Spain. In 1966, 7,745,928 French people came on holidays to Spain; the majority entering the country by car through the Costa Brava as reported in Rogelio Duocastella's *Sociología y Pastoral del Turismo en la Costa Brava y Maresme* (1969).
36. Translated by the author.
37. English singer George Fame said of Tiffany's: 'This is marvellous, without doubt the best of its class in Europe' (Miñano 1965: 9).
38. Tiffany's was the first recorded dance club in Spain to have a lighting and sound installation that created a psychedelic atmosphere. Historical data on Tiffany's have been compiled from Arxiu Municipal Castell-Platja d'Aro and Xavier Castillón's *Nits d'Aro* (2018), among other secondary sources.
39. Instead of talking between tracks, as it was usual at that time, DJ Jean-Pierre Grätzer in Tiffany's started linking tracks to create a continuous sound atmosphere.
40. Antonio Escohotado explains how during the decade of 1960s in Franco's Spain, amphetamines were legal and could be easily bought without a doctor's prescription. A survey between students showed that more than 60 per cent where consuming amphetamines and that during popular parties and celebrations, the consumption would surge. For a thorough historical account on drug use in Spain and beyond, check Antonio Escohotado's *Historia General de las Drogas* (1998).
41. Jacinto Esteva is one of the most relevant authors linked to the avantgarde Barcelona School of Film. *Lejos de los Árboles* was shot during the 1960s, but it was only released on 1972 by Filmscontacto.

42. 'La Minifalda' ('The Miniskirt') (Escobar 1971) is one of the most famous songs sung by Escobar and one of the Spanish hits of the decade of 1970s. The lyrics, rather sexist, contrast with the spirit of social and sexual revolution that supposedly Spain was undergoing on the verge of the death of the dictator.
43. Historical data on Maddox have been compiled from Carmenati Family's private archive, among other secondary sources.
44. Carmenati's design is the oldest found record of an architectural drawing of a DJ booth.
45. Oriol Regàs was a prominent member of the Gauche Divine – see Endnote 46.
46. In the words of the architect Oriol Bohigas, the Gauche Divine was something like 'the first postwar version (deformed by the particular political circumstances of the country [Spain]) of a certain Catalan persistence: a liberal high bourgeoisie with superficial attachment to the "progressive"' (Moix 2014: 89).
47. Màquina! ('Machine!') was a psychedelic rock band from Barcelona that was managed by Oriol Regàs, director of Maddox. Màquina! represented a new wave of youth counterculture that would spread throughout Spain, preceding the later and commercially endorsed *Movida* cultural movement.
48. Carlos IV was King of Spain between the eighteenth and nineteenth centuries.
49. The description of the DJ show has been extracted from an interview with Maddox's historical DJ Ángel Pérez, in the TV programme *El Cucurutxo* from Palamós Comunicació, on the 9 September 2015.
50. National Catholicism was at the core of the ideological identity of Franco's dictatorship, giving to the Catholic church a dominant position in both public and private life.
51. Bocaccio was a nightclub inaugurated in 1967 in Barcelona that, like Maddox, was run by Oriol Regàs. Bocaccio is well known for being a meeting point of the progressive Gauche Divine (see Endnote 46). Architects, writers, models and other liberal professionals mingled in a festive manner challenging the dominant atmosphere of cultural castration during the dictatorial regime.
52. 'Santa Espina' is a *sardana* (popular Catalan musical genre), which considered a patriotic anthem for Catalan people. Largely, during Francoist regime, it was forbidden to interpret the piece in public. Reportedly, Ángel Pérez, Maddox's historical DJ, was arrested one evening for playing 'Santa Espina' and spent a couple of nights in the police station (Castillón 2018: 110).
53. Festival Internacional de la Canción en la Ciudad Luminosa de la Costa del Sol was one of the many festivals organized during summertime on the Mediterranean coast of Spain and which served to the promotion of a mainstream music market. Other festivals were the Festival Español de la Canción de Benidorm and the Festival de la Canción Mediterránea.
54. 'Y Viva España' (Escobar 1973) is one of the most famous songs sung by Manolo Escobar and an anthem to tourism. Praising the wonders of the country, it was also sang in many other languages by other artists.
55. Translated by the author.

56. Despite the fact that the lyrics sung by Manolo Escobar were strongly aligned with conservative social ideologies and National Catholicism, he would consider himself as 'totally apolitical' (Escobar 1975: n.pag.).

REFERENCES

Bardem, Miguel (2015), *Pacha: El Arquitecto de la Noche*, Spain: Shine Iberia.

Barthes, Roland ([1957] 1972), *Mythologies*, New York: Noonday Press.

Castillón, Xavier (2018), *Nits d'Aro*, Castell-Platja d'Aro: Ajuntament de Castell-Platja d'Arp.

Carmenati, Vincenzo (*c.*2003), *Carmenati*, Platja d'Aro: OTIM.

Crumbaugh, Justin (2010), *Destination Dictatorship: The Spectacle of Spain's Tourist Boom and the Reinvention of Difference*, Albany: SUNY Press.

Dimbleby, Richard (1956), *Jerez Wine Festival*, London: BBC.

Duocastella, Rogelio (1969), *Sociología Pastoral del Turismo*, Madrid: Confederación Española de cajas de Ahorros.

Editorial Office (1984), 'Suspendió pagos Discos Belter, con un pasivo de 1.160 millones', *La Vanguardia*, 7 November, p. 39.

Escobar, Manolo (1965a), 'Bohemio de Dios', *Mi Canción Es para Ti*, Vinyl, Barcelona: Belter.

Escobar, Manolo (1965b), 'Flor del Sur', *Manolo Escobar*, Vinyl, Barcelona: Belter.

Escobar, Manolo (1966a), 'Buscando un Amor', *Manolo Escobar*, Vinyl, Barcelona: Belter.

Escobar, Manolo (1966b), 'El Porompompero', *Manolo Escobar*, Vinyl, Barcelona: Belter.

Escobar, Manolo (1971), 'La Minifalda', *Sevillanas*, Vinyl, Barcelona: Belter.

Escobar, Manolo (1973), 'Y Viva España', *Y Viva España*, Vinyl, Barcelona: Belter.

Escobar, Manolo (1975), interview with P. Ruiz, ¿Lo Conoce Usted?, Televisión Española, 7 January.

Escobar, Manolo (1985), interview with R. M. Sardà, Ahí te quiero ver, Televisión Española, Barcelona, 9 May, https://www.youtube.com/watch?v=NB0V-q9L_ew. Accessed 3 May 2022.

Escobar, Manolo (2013), interview with S. Vives, Els Optimistes, Catalunya Radio, Barcelona, 9 May, https://www.ccma.cat/catradio/alacarta/els-optimistes/manolo-escobar-vaig-coneixer-la-meva-dona-a-platja-daro/audio/726685/. Accessed 3 May 2022.

Escohotado, Antonio (1998), *Historia General de las Drogas*, Barcelona: Espasa Libros.

Gaviria, Mario (1971), *Campo, Urbe y Espacio del Ocio*, Madrid: Siglo XXI de España Editores.

Gaviria, Mario (1974), *España a Go-Go: Turismo Charter y Neocolonialismo del Espacio*, Madrid: Ediciones Turner.

Gaviria, Mario (1977), *Benidorm, Ciudad Nueva*, Madrid: Editorial Nacional.

MacCannell, Dean (1976), *The Tourist:. A New Theory of the Leisure Class*, Berlin: Schocken Books.

Malefakis, Edward (1982), 'Spain and its Francoist Heritage', in J. H. Herz (ed.), *From Dictatorship to Democracy: Coping with the Legacies of Authoritarianism and Totalitarianism*, Westport: Greenwood Press, pp. 215–30.

Michaud, Ives (2012), *Ibiza Mon Amour: Enquête sur l'Industrialisation du Plaisir*, Paris: NiL Éditions.

Miñano, Fulgencio (ed.) (1965), 'Tiffany's', *Los Sitios de Gerona*, 24 June, p. 9.

Moix, Ana Maria ([2001] 2014), *24h con la Gauche Divine*, Barcelona: Lumen.

Pagès Jordà, Vicenç (2014), 'Ferran Agulló, inventor de la Costa Brava', *Revista de Girona*, pp. 66–68.

Pau, Manuel Costa (1967), *Turistas, Sirenas e Indígenas*, Barcelona: Dima Ediciones.

Vázquez Montalbán, Manuel, Miserachs, Xavier and Coughtry, Peter (1966), *Costa Brava Show*, Barcelona: Editorial Kairós.

Vázquez Montalbán, Manuel ([1971] 2003), *Crónica Sentimental de España*, Barcelona: Grupo Editorial Random House Mondadori.

Viladevall i Marfà, Assis (ed.) (1964), 'Sala de Fiestas Flamingo', *Quaderns d'Arquitectura y Urbanisme*, 58, p. 32.

Vilarós, Teresa M. ([1998] 2018), *El Mono del Desencanto: Una Critica Cultural de la Transición Española*, Madrid: Siglo XXI de España Editores.

6

Dancing Down Memory Lane: (Re)experiences of Cape Verdean Nightlife in Rotterdam

Seger Kersbergen

Oh pove bzot ben oiá	Oh people come and see
Êss kriol na porta de Habanera	These creoles at Habanera's door
Frontode num pavio dôde	Crazy with excitement
Na finta dês holandesa.	For conversations with the Dutch ladies.

(Morais 1967)[1]

In this song, we are placed at the entrance of the Latin American nightclub Habanera in the city of Rotterdam. Some men from Cape Verde decide to try their luck and chat with some Dutch ladies, earning bragging rights. Comically, the song urges the listener to wait until four o'clock, when 'the puzzle is solved': as it happens, the ladies actually charged between 70 and 100 guilders for their company. This entertaining scene is a testimony of Rotterdam's lively nightlife, recorded by renowned Cape Verdean singer Bana (1932–2013), who arrived in the city in 1965. Many of his fellow countrymen arrived around the same time, looking for work (in what was then the largest port in the world), as well as escaping poverty and political oppression by the Portuguese colonial regime on the archipelago. Waiting and looking for a ship to board, they were eager to spend some time somewhere in the city's bars, nightclubs and cafés.

Rotterdam was not simply a popular destination for Cape Verdean economic migrants, however. The city became a hotbed of political activism directed towards the anti-colonial struggle of Guinea-Bissau and Cape Verde, led by revolutionary leader Amílcar Cabral. The leader's assignment for João Silva, one of the pioneers in the Dutch diaspora, was to safeguard and disseminate the culture of Cape Verde. He founded Morabeza Records, the first Cape Verdean record label of the world, in Rotterdam. Silva became a representative of the revolutionary party PAIGC and was much involved in political activities, seeking to stimulate a sense of Cape Verdeanness in the diaspora. Albums that were produced by Morabeza, containing not only music but also political speeches and poetry, were sold in the diaspora or secretly smuggled to Cape Verde (Cidra 2008a: 194–95).

Seeking ways to spend their evenings with co-nationals, Cape Verdeans started to engage with a night circuit that encompassed their own community. Cape Verdean musicians and artists found their way to Rotterdam and the first so-called 'Noites Caboverdianas' ('Cape Verdean nights') were organized. These served as important occasions in which the socialization of the rapidly growing community was a central goal. In present-day Rotterdam, these historic nights, as well as the places in which they were celebrated, have become part of the Cape Verdean community's memory of the city. Engaging with Deleuze and Guattari's conceptualization of assemblage, geographer Robert Shaw proposes to approach the night-time city as an 'affective atmosphere' created through assemblage; the city is continuously produced and constructed 'through practices and the movement of materials', bringing together 'people, objects, ideas, affects and discourses' (2014: 87–93). This contributes to an understanding of how space and identity cohere and interfere at night, as bodies collide, music flows, and conversations are struck, creating a flow of impulses that work one's imagination and generate a sense of belonging together with those encountered, where past and present are interwoven.

The city is in constant movement and (re)construction, and many historic venues have been re-purposed or demolished as of today. Cape Verdeans have an active memory of community nightlife and the various locales in which events were hosted. The histories of particular places and memories where Cape Verdeans used to meet and have fun together are re-appropriated not only in songs but also in contemporary nightlife, as organizers draw on collective memories of historical nightlife events. These events are promoted through narratives of the nocturnal city, where both the community's and the city's past are reflected through practices of re-memory (Brah 1996) and re-experience, where an imagination of the nocturnal past is constructed.

Drawing on a variety of materials from several events, places and organizers – including music, newspaper articles, promotional material and interviews – this chapter discusses the memory of Cape Verdean nightlife and the associations with specific locations in the city, thereby demonstrating how current generations of nightlife organizers (and partygoers) imagine the city's different night scenes and consequent implications for diasporic identity and belonging.

The first part of this chapter includes a historic account of early nightlife. Early night venues visited by Cape Verdean migrants became important spaces of encounter, where ties with fellow nationals were forged and important processes of belonging took place. This becomes evident in both interviews and testimonies in music of that time. In the second part, more contemporary nightlife events will be analyzed, discussing how historic nightlife practices are re-imagined and re-appropriated in present nightlife practices.

Rotterdam nights in the 1950s and 1960s

On 14 May 1940, Rotterdam, the second-largest city in the Netherlands, was bombarded by the German Luftwaffe. Dropping almost 1300 bombs in thirteen minutes, the German invaders left little intact of the historic centre of Rotterdam and destroyed a major part of the port area. In fact, Rotterdam was the only major city in the Netherlands that came out of the Second World War destroyed to such an extent. With reconstructions in full swing in post-war Rotterdam, the development of night-time spaces of leisure such as nightclubs had not been a large priority. However, on 28 February 1948, the social-democratic newspaper *Het Vrije Volk* (*The Free People*) announced the re-start of nightlife in Rotterdam:

> Whatever has already been or is being rebuilt in Rotterdam, the world of going out still lacked one facet: nightlife. For a world city that wants to attract foreign nationals (you already know: foreign currencies), insiders say it cannot be missed and that is why the gap has been filled from tonight onwards. Rotterdam started its post-war nightlife with permits given to three establishments. [...] The main thing is that it can no longer be said of Rotterdam that it is so far behind other cities in this term of entertainment [...] in view of visitors from elsewhere, of course.
>
> (Anonymous 1948: 2)

Rotterdam has a rich history of inland shipping as well as maritime shipping. Especially after the construction of the Nieuwe Waterweg (The New Waterway) in 1872, which created a better connection with the sea, the number of ships and therefore sailors in the city increased. Many of them enjoyed the nocturnal city, whether outside, in cafés, bars, restaurants or nightclubs. Several neighbourhoods in the city served as red-light districts or offered other forms of entertainment. In the years that followed the end of the Second World War, the city and port area were in reconstruction. Several new establishments opened, while others were remodelled after having served as 'emergency nightclubs' during the war. Large flows of sailors from all regions of the world, such as the Cape Verdean archipelago, visited the city in their off-time between journeys. In 1958, socialist public broadcaster Vereeniging van Arbeiders Radio Amateurs (VARA)[2] emphasized the variety of cultures represented in Rotterdam's nightclubs of the late 1950s, with 'South Slavonic' sounds in 'Engels' and Italian ones in 'Belmont' (Anonymous 1958: 7). Later in 1966, the local tourist information office De Vereniging voor Vreemdelingenverkeer (VVV)[3] emphasized that Rotterdam was ahead of the capital city Amsterdam in terms of entertainment available, offering a large variation of amusement:

> An establishment where you can hear chansonnettes ('t Winckeltje), places where you can dance and are regularly treated to a floor show (La Bonanza, Bristol, Casino de Paris, Habanera, l'Ambassadeur, El Amra), a place where one can 'twist' for hours (De Wieck, where beat group The Hot Jumpers plays), an establishment where one can drink a glass with piano or accordion on the background (Doofpot and Drie Musketiers).
>
> (Anonymous 1966: 9)

Cape Verdean migrants and sailors started arriving in Rotterdam, especially since the 1960s. They left the islands to escape from drought, famine and poverty. At the same time, many fled the oppression by the Portuguese colonizer, avoiding conscription for the Portuguese armed forces which fought their compatriots on the mainland of Guinea-Bissau. At that time, no Cape Verdean clubs, associations or music spaces existed in Rotterdam. However, the city counted several clubs which were frequented by Cape Verdeans. In the newspaper excerpt above, two places stand out. In 1950, Habanera was opened, a venue we encountered at the beginning of this chapter. It was a dancing bar 'completely furnished in Cuban style' where 'Rotterdammers and non-Rotterdammers can find amusement' (Anonymous 1950: 5). Habanera was a popular club for young Cape Verdean sailors. Bana, one of Cape Verde's most famous artists, regularly played at this venue and attracted a significant Cape Verdean audience. As one sailor recalls:

> I started working for Heineken for some time, but I only earned 90 guilders per week. During the weekends, I went to Habanera, two nights, and it was all gone! So I thought, I'm going to sea, this way at least I will be able to save some money!
>
> (Interviewee A 2020)[4]

Many men who came to Rotterdam were still young and keen to go on nightly adventures in one of Rotterdam's nightclubs, such as Habanera, when off from work. The realization that this was not a very sustainable lifestyle often came later. Three years after Habanera, another dancing venue, La Bonanza, opened that would later become a hotspot for Cape Verdeans in Rotterdam:

> South America is now also represented in the entertainment life of Rotterdam. In six weeks' time, the earlier café De Kroon [...] has been transformed in La Bonanza ('Prosperity'), a tastefully decorated bar. Lou Hidalgo holds sway over it and the Don Alvino Garcia orchestra receives visitors with South-American tunes.
>
> (Anonymous 1953: 3)

La Bonanza was run by the first Surinamese club owner in Rotterdam, Lou Hidalgo. Even though Cape Verdeans attended the nightclub, the space was shared with a predominantly Dutch but also migrant – Antillean, Spanish, Portuguese, Surinamese – audience. Over the years, Hidalgo contracted many migrant and foreign musicians, and it became a place known in particular for its exotic performers, Black Surinamese jazz performers such as Teddy Cotton and Kid Dynamite, a variety of Latin American performers, floorshows and stripteases. La Bonanza was also one of the first nightclubs in Rotterdam to contract the Cape Verdean music group Voz de Cabo Verde, which would soon become a popular icon of Cape Verdean music. The group was managed and created by João Silva, mentioned in the introduction, who was the owner of the first Cape Verdean record label and considered an important actor in the resistance against the Portuguese. As mentioned, many of the recordings included hidden messages, often denouncing abuse by the colonizers and stimulating a sense of Capeverdeanness. A band was formed with the idea of recording these politically tinted albums, 'conceiving the recording of Cape Verdean popular music as a means of documenting the cultural sovereignty of Cape Verdeans and legitimizing the nationalist claims to self-determination' (Cidra 2015: 311). Leaving his life as a sailor behind, former member Morgadinho explains how he became involved in the band:

> Meanwhile, Luís Morais, João da Lomba and Toy d'Bibia met Frank Cavaquim, who already lived in the Netherlands. And when I got there, I was told: 'You are not going to work for any ship. What we're going to do is form a band'. So, instead of leaving on one of the ships, we stayed on land and got a job. And we were encouraged by Cape Verdeans who lived there to form such a group, because they wanted to have a group in that country.
>
> (Anonymous 2004: 2)

The group, first named Os Verdianos and later renamed Voz de Cabo Verde in 1966 to appear more professional, started playing at 'creole parties' almost every weekend, and according to Djunga, Cabral was very content with the group as they 'symbolized and represented Cape Verde' (Silva 2009). The term 'creole' has an important role in the genesis of Cape Verde and the formation of a national identity. Although it insinuates national unity in this context, the term is also in constant debate given the variation of life experiences, cultural traditions and migration trajectories on each island. In the nineteenth century, the Portuguese colonizer even saw creole as an intermediary stage 'on the way to speaking and being Portuguese' (Pardue 2015: 42). In the description above, however, the term creole is rather used as a badge of honour for the Cape Verdeans striving for independence. Voz de Cabo Verde was one of the first international Cape Verdean music groups to be integrated into a diverse landscape of night scenes: as well as performing in Cape Verde, they played in Dutch and Belgian clubs, and also in nightlife venues of the Cape Verdean communities across Europe, in France, Luxembourg and Portugal. Silva landed a contract with Latin American nightclub La Bonanza in 1968, where they became the house band.

In La Bonanza, Voz de Cabo Verde played a repertoire of mainly Latin American music styles, including Cumbia, Merengue and Samba. Cape Verdean music styles were for the most part played for recordings and Cape Verdean parties, even though the stirring rhythms of coladeira would be played in La Bonanza too. The owner of the club wanted them to play mostly Latin-American and Brazilian music, thus performing in line with the 'tropical' Latin label of the club. The group even switched vocalists, replacing Bana with Djosinha (José Vieira Duarte, born 1934), to satisfy Hidalgo's wish. The group's adaptability and versatility are well-reflected in their music production:

> Along with the dance styles in vogue in Europe, the group recorded in their phonograms a substantial repertoire of mornas and coladeiras,[5] vocalized or in instrumental versions [...] which circulated in Portugal, in the then African colonies and in the centres of the Cape Verdean diaspora.
>
> (Cidra 2008b: 114)

The first popular Cape Verdean music group was in a sense entangled in both political and commercial circuits, each of which had a particular place and time. Whereas recordings were integrated into streams of information and images oriented towards Cape Verdeans in the context of political struggle, the group was also integrated into a nightclub scene that offered transnational forms of entertainment. At the same time, these spaces still offered room for generating a sense of belonging in the diaspora.

In this regard, La Bonanza offered a space of transnational encounter (both musical and between communities) and re-encounter with fellow Cape Verdeans. Interactions with strangers were common: sailors from other countries, tourists, locals and visitors of the other sex mixed in this space. The dancefloor functioned as a space of inevitable cultural mixing, and sometimes collision. It also served, however, as a space of re-encounter: of those Cape Verdeans that departed from the same country and were able to socialize with each other 'between ships', or with those that had already settled on the land. The dancefloor was simultaneously a space in which common cultural references could be enjoyed collectively. In a Rotterdam neighbourhood newspaper, a migrated Cape Verdean man remembers his first experiences of La Bonanza as a sixteen or seventeen-year-old young man, while waiting on land to board another ship:

> You saw so many familiar faces […] greeting […]. Kisses […] shaking hands at tables […] a couple of beers to warm up […] We danced the cumbia […] When 'Quem tem ódio' or 'Terezina' were played the dancefloor exploded. Merengues, sambas, coladeiras, yeah yeah […] Djosinha was the king on the podium, he jumped right in the middle of the audience. Luis Morais was the joker – always teasing, always with a drink: "Listen, there is no bad grogue,[6] it's about how you feel – FORMIDABLE!"
>
> (Hart 2012: 12)

In La Bonanza, both artists and the audience appropriated cultural forms, and enjoyment of this blend is emphasized. It was a space of entertainment and leisure where Cape Verdeans danced to both foreign and occasionally to Cape Verdean hits of that time. Early nightclubs were a privileged site to accommodate encounters in an informal, casual setting. As such, these spaces simultaneously functioned to generate a sense of community through shared experiences of enjoyment and encounters with common cultural references through music.

Experiences of nightlife in Rotterdam are well recorded in Cape Verdean music of the 1960s, 1970s and 1980s. Narratives involve and uncover processes of belonging and identity seeking, of 'placing' a community or finding the right place within the context of a diaspora:

Nacionalidade o que bo e? |	What nationality are you?
Mim e fidju di caboverdeano …	I am a child of Cape Verde
U ke k bo tem feito desd que bo txiga ki?	What have you done since you are here?
Nha vida e rodea ta ospia traboi …	Walking in circles looking for a job.
Nos ba, nos ba,	Let's go, let's go,
dança na Martinique	Dance in Martinique
Ka bo preocupa	Don't you worry.
Virgem Maria ta ramedia	Virgen Mary will solve it.

(Gonçalves 1980)

In 'Lucy d'Nho Morgode', a 1980 song by Bana, a conversation takes place between two men from the islands of Cape Verde that meet each other somewhere in Rotterdam, at night. One man inquires what the other man's nationality is and finds a compatriot seeking some distraction in the night-time city. Having a hard time finding work during the day, describing life as mainly consisting of 'walking in circles', the man invites his fellow national to go out to a club in Rotterdam: blowing off some steam, interrupting the cycle of boredom and stress that migrant life brought, meeting fellow Cape Verdeans, and perhaps, a lady. Martinique allegedly was a pseudonym for the Latin-American nightclub La Bonanza.[7] For many, the night was an outlet for the hard work that was done during the day, either in the ports, the factories or alternatively for extended periods at sea. These lives lived collectively stimulate the creation of common places to get together for the purpose of entertainment and relief, a way in which people with similar experiences can collectively detach themselves from their circumstances in the diaspora and connect to common cultural expressions such as music and entertainment from the homeland.

When the first Cape Verdean migrants started arriving in Rotterdam in the 1960s, no Cape Verdean clubs, associations or music spaces existed. Rotterdam counted several clubs in the 1960s which were frequented by Cape Verdeans, such as La Bonanza and Habanera. A night scene directed towards and created by Cape Verdeans started appearing when larger numbers of Cape Verdeans settled in Rotterdam from the mid 1960s onwards and community organizations were founded. In the early 1970s, many events started to be organized by Cape Verdean clubs and associations that were committed to the well-being of the community in Rotterdam. Often, these organizations strove to contribute to the independence of Cape Verde and did so by organizing cultural and social events, including night-time music events. One important organization was the Associação Caboverdiana (The Cape Verdean Association), founded in 1967 to meet the needs of newcomers for housing and mutual contact (Duarte Rodrigues Pires 2006: 10). As sociologist Doris Pires mentions, this organization was founded by pioneers such as João Silva and other members of the Cape Verdean resistance against Portugal, and had an emancipatory goal: to create awareness among the Cape Verdeans of their own culture. Members and sympathizers of the independence movement actively joined to promote their Cape Verdean identity. The Associação would regularly organize dance nights. With the income of the bar and entry fees, they would finance their other activities. These included, for example, literacy lessons, card evenings and the establishment of a Cape Verde football club. In the 1970s, a small childcare centre was also organized for working mothers (Duarte Rodrigues Pires 2006: 104–05). As one prominent member of the association recalls, 'Cape Verdeans organized many dance evenings. But the dances were there to get people involved, to sell their political story' (Interviewee B 2014). As Gonçalves mentions:

> The purpose of those parties was to gather people, give people a good time, make people aware of … hey, remember, our youth? Cabo Verde, Cabo Verdean music, we are not Portuguese, those are elements that always came back at parties. The people who organised it did it consciously, but the people who went there, it was giving those people a good feeling, so that they could have some fun and be a Cabo Verdean for a while. It was something psychological, but it wasn't something handed to you on a pamphlet.
>
> (2021, translation added)

Night spaces were fundamental in bringing a community together and 'out there' in order to create a sense of 'us'.

Night spaces served to relieve pressure of the daily persecution of Cape Verdeans by the colonial regime and became an instrument for generating Cape Verdean consciousness in the diaspora. Simultaneously, they provided a means for integrating into the urban spaces of Rotterdam. Early Cape Verdean nightlife in the 1960s and 1970s was predominantly organized in venues owned by Dutch citizens, where organizers would simply rent a hall. A band would be contracted, either from the Netherlands, elsewhere in the Cape Verdean diaspora or Cape Verde, and an entrance fee would cover the costs for rent and the music group. Even so, a collective memory of space has formed over the years in relation to particular locations in the city. Organizers often built relations with particular venue owners and would host their parties at the same location for extended periods of time. There were also a handful of venues that were owned and run by Cape Verdeans since the 1970s, which became important meeting points and have been captured by several musicians in their lyrics, emphasizing both fun times but also critical views on how to behave properly in another country (to be briefly discussed below, in the second part of the chapter). Audiences in these common locations thus produced connections with particular places that grew to become spaces of community. As Lidskog explains, 'the construction of community requires a place for reproduction and contestation. Musical performances are places where marginalized cultures find public expression and contribute to the construction of a particular community' (2016: 31–32). Even though the lives of immigrants are transnational, they are still involved in creating 'belonging in the receiving society' (Ehrkamp 2005: 361), which is done through processes of place-making in the host society.

In the history of Cape Verdean migration to the Netherlands, each decade had its particular places that were significant for the construction of a community. The next section will focus on the re-appropriation of the memory of several significant night spaces for the Cape Verdean community, and how they are promoted in contemporary nightlife in terms of belonging.

Parties in the 2000s

Cape Verdeans have an active memory of community nightlife and the various locales in which events were hosted. With a sense of nostalgia, particular places and memories thereof are mentioned, where Cape Verdeans used to meet and have fun together. Music is an important binding element, connecting not only recent migrants with each other and with Cape Verde but also with descendants of previous migrants (Duarte Rodrigues Pires 2006: 119). La Bonanza and Habanera became the first places where Cape Verdean music was played and Cape Verdean men came together to enjoy music during nights out, and where both Cape Verdean classics and Latin American music got the crowd going. In the 1970s and 1980s, several Cape Verdean-owned establishments opened in Rotterdam, such as the Butterfly Bar and Scotch Inn. Centrally located in the Weena area (which is now a business district) was Sató, a discotheque established in the 1970s and owned by Luis Fortes.[8] These places are also connected by the fact that various Cape Verdean artists have sung about these places over the years, often through various lenses. Some, for example, criticize the fact that sailors and migrant men would spend all their money on alcohol at night, whilst others express the enjoyment of smoking a joint, drinking a pilsner, and dancing. Others emphasize the need to connect with Cape Verdean forms of nightlife and not be disloyal to cultural expressions of the homeland in another society.

A night-time party scene continued to evolve throughout the 1980s and 1990s, establishing new relations with night-time venues. Several of these places have since been swallowed up by urban development projects during the 1980s, as the city council focused on 'the development of prestige projects' in several areas including the city centre (McCarthy 1999: 306). New places arose that became central to the nightlife of the Cape Verdeans in Rotterdam. In the 1980s, several locations opened on the Schuttevaerweg, located opposite the Spangen neighbourhood, Delfshaven district; locations included Sun Club, Blokhut, Scouting, Real Parbo Football Club and Voorwaarts Football Club. Not only was this close to the district in which the majority of Cape Verdeans have historically lived and still live, but it was also close to the Van Nelle Factory, where many Cape Verdeans that had settled in Rotterdam had been working since the 1960s. The area was popularly renamed 'Vanella' by Cape Verdeans and served as the main location for Cape Verdean parties during the weekends from the 1980s until 2017 when it was demolished. Whereas the parties in Sun Club attracted a somewhat younger audience with more modern sounds of that decade, such as zouk and swingbeat in the 1980s, and caboswing, cabozouk and R&B in the 1990s, the other halls mentioned in the area attracted an older generation that mostly enjoyed the more traditional Cape Verdean coladeiras (Interviewee D 2020). In fact, in a recent song by Nelson Freitas (one of the most famous contemporary Cape Verdean artists who was born in Rotterdam), an encounter at Vanella is narrated:

Mbem paxoná	I fell in love
Pum loira na Vanela … bnitinha	With a blonde at Vanella', pretty.
Dicidi fka má ela	I decided to stay with her,
Nha passaporte kaduká	My passport expired.

(Freitas 2019)

A sacred place: Sun Club

As the above lyrics in Freitas's song demonstrate, the artist engages with memories of nightlife in Rotterdam that are strongly linked to a particular place in the city. This can be explained not only by the fact that these places, in contrast to other temporary locations, have served for an extended period of time as a nightlife venue but also because of the necessity for a diaspora to 'engage in creating places, transforming the urban landscape of contemporary cities' as both 'symbolic and material expressions of local and translocal connections' are created (Ehrkamp 2005: 361). It is on the local level that spaces are created in which 'some sense of being a citizen is made possible', which is often done in 'everyday spaces of the city' (Kalandides and Vaiou 2012: 264). In contemporary nightlife, one way of 'theming' an event is to re-appropriate the memory of one particular nightlife location, seeking ways to re-experience the place:

> Saturday, June 30, we bring you back to the 80s / 90s / 2000s when SunClub was a phenomenon in Rotterdam, for many Cape Verdeans. Remember how fun going out with your friends used to be in the then-popular SunClub venue? Parties such as Tcholda, Dominginhas, Ribeira Alta, Santiago, Maense were super fun! […] The best classics from the 80s / 90s / 2000s in Pakhuis, which will be transformed into SunClub. In addition, the best Coladeira, Funaná, ZoukLove, R&B and house music! We'll make sure you move. The nice people, the atmosphere of the past and the beautiful warehouse location take care of the rest and we'll make SunClub Reunion a unique party.
>
> (DJ Guide Website 2018: n.pag.)

Sun Club, located on the 'Vanella' terrain, was an event hall that had been used for Cape Verdean parties from the 1980s until January 2017, when it was forced to close. The Sun Club reunion was organized in 2018 by two Cape Verdean DJs that used to be regulars at the venue. Several party organizations that were established by immigrants from the same place of origin (Ribeira Alta, Santiago), and football clubs (Maense) used Sun Club and several other neighbouring venues as their main party locations since the start, establishing long-term relationships with the renters over time. Several organizers see these venues, in particular Sun Club, as a home port and part of Cape Verdean history in Rotterdam, or as one organizer mentions, it was seen almost as a 'holy place' (Interviewee C 2020). He argues that 'Cape Verdeans go to parties everywhere, but when it's a Cape Verdean party, it had to be in Sun Club'. Another DJ confirmed that when organizers tried hosting an event at another location, visitors would even 'look around and say "what is this?", this is not Sun Club. It was hard for DJs to get people on the dancefloor because they were ill at ease' (Interviewee D 2020).

Do you remember?

Contemporary nightlife directed towards Cape Verdeans or organized by Cape Verdeans still comes in diverse forms: from traditional morna performances in small-scale venues such as restaurants and bars to large parties, including DJs and international artists, in popular city-centre venues. As seen in the previous example, a common phenomenon in the Cape Verdean night scene is that of contemporary commercial organizers drawing on the history of Cape Verdean nightlife in Rotterdam by organizing events that invoke reflection upon common memories in these places. These are memories that have been collectively shaped in particular places in the city, and are in this sense, memories of place. The following commercial text demonstrates the relation between place, memory and community:

> Lembra in the Thalia Lounge is a household name since the previously sold-out edition. It turned out to be a party that a lot of 25-plus people were waiting for: with many memories of the atmosphere, the people, and mostly the golden years of Cape Verdean music. Lembra brings visitors back to the time of parties in Fountain Paradise, Imperium, Palace, Ocean Paradise, and the golden years for bands like Livity, Rabelados and Gil & the Perfects. Whomever recognizes this, should feel invited to relive these days. The Lembra band accompanies the popular band Cabo Verde Show, the tough boyband Jocel and the Cape Verdean Diva Dina Medina with their greatest hits from the eighties and nineties. DJ Triumph and Sir Edward will spin the best (disco) tracks from those years and an airline ticket to Cape Verde can be won.
>
> (Metro Rotterdam E.O. 2014: 3)[9]

Lembra, a music event directed towards the Cape Verdean community in Rotterdam, makes use of the collective memory of Cape Verdean nightlife spaces. The advertisement connects specific venues – Fountain Paradise, Imperium, Palace, Ocean Paradise – to a particular atmosphere and memories of the so-called 'golden years', glorifying the 1980s and 1990s in which many Cape Verdean artists reached fame and Cape Verdean party nights and shows were still extremely popular within the community. As the organizer explained, in this time period many Cape Verdean artists produced their greatest hits and the Cape Verdean night scene thrived, thanks in part to this reason. The organizer's marketing strategy for this reason focused on 'bringing back the feeling of that time' (Interviewee E 2020). It is not, however, exclusively a feeling of time but also a sense of place which is produced in this advertisement, demonstrating that historical places of community are still actively imagined and appropriated as places of community and belonging while demonstrating their relevance in the present for commercial nightlife organizers. In an interview with Danilo Tavares, the most important contemporary producer of Cape Verdean music in Rotterdam and bassist of Rabelados, a group that also caused the kick-off of musical careers from artists like Suzanna Lubrano and Beto Dias (Nogueira 2016: 447), he confirms the feeling of the time that Lembra refers back to:

> We also played in Rotterdam, that was [...] yeah [...] Especially the band Livity, wow [...] They have done so many beautiful performances. I can also speak of this, because I often went to these shows, it was always a blast. Always a full house, 1500 people, and in those times there was not as much violence as now, it was always a joy, for everyone. We had Fountain Paradise here, Kings Place, we had Imperium, that was one of the most known places.
>
> (Tavares 2020: n.pag.)

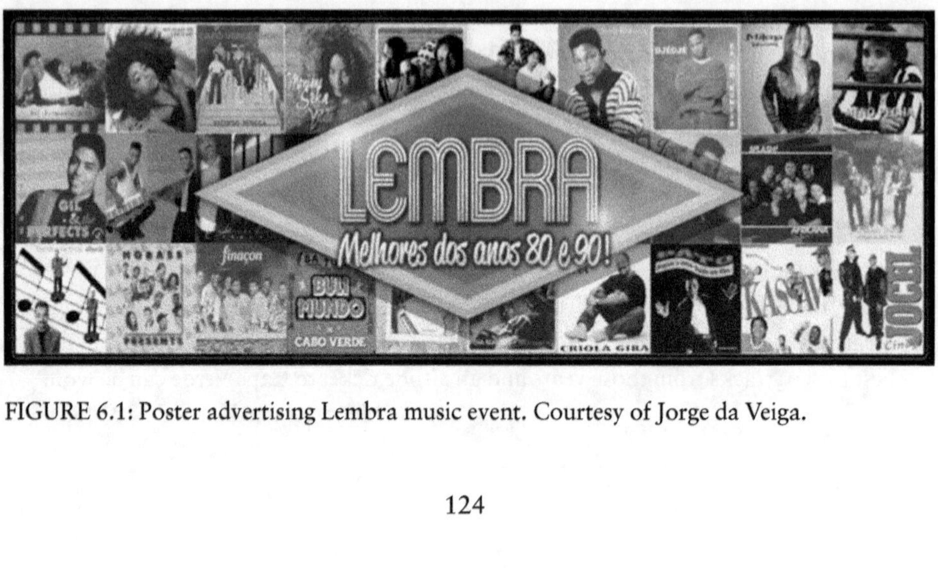

FIGURE 6.1: Poster advertising Lembra music event. Courtesy of Jorge da Veiga.

Drawing on collective memory is a common practice in the party scene, which is also visible in the name of the promotion, translating to 'remember'. But if a reference to a time in history brings memories back to life, it is the place that specifies and situates these memories, charging them with emotion and the particular atmosphere of that place. The ability of a place to be situated in memory comes through its familiarity with a person, being 'a container of experiences'. As such, a place will 'invite certain memories while discouraging others' and conversely, memories 'seek out particular places as their natural habitats' as they are a 'mise en scène for remembered events'; often, the memory of a place is provoked by feelings of nostalgia, in which a 'place's extraordinary memorability is found', making it possible to 're-experience' a place (Casey 2000: 183–201).

There are several elements that create and refer to a symbolic 'us' in the event's logo above. It is worth noting that Lembra, in a classic retro font, is contained within the green, yellow and red colours of the flag that Cape Verde adopted after independence, associated often with socialist and pan-Africanist policies. The flag reflects times of solidarity and mutual assistance within the diaspora and the homeland and thus reverberates particular values and affiliations towards these places. The background includes album covers of artists in their heyday that are most familiar to the party-going generation of the 1980s and 1990s targeted by the event.

The albums included in the background of the Lembra logo feature many familiar faces, including Gil & the Perfects, Beto Dias, Cabo Verde Show and Splash and Bulimundo, each of which have their particular histories and stories in the Netherlands since the 1980s. Some artists came to the Netherlands at an early age or were born there, and others often performed in the Dutch Cape Verdean diaspora or recorded their albums at one of the many recording studios in Rotterdam and surrounding areas. For example, Gil Semedo, from Gil & the Perfects, came to the Netherlands at only 6 years old, in 1980. At 15, he participated in a classic Dutch television talent show called *The Soundmix Show*, as a young imitator of Michael Jackson, finishing second after arguably one of the most successful Dutch singers, Marco Borsato. His later creations, a combination of modern and traditional Cape Verdean sounds, became known as caboswing, which would soon conquer not only the Cape Verdean night and music scene in Rotterdam, but diasporic music circuits worldwide (Nogueira 2016: 208). Groups originating from the Cape Verdean islands, some of which are featured in the event poster, could often be found in Rotterdam, to record and perform for periods of time. Bulimundo, for example, recorded several albums at Black Power Records in Rotterdam, incorporating Dutch-based artists such as Suzanna Lubrano and Milena Tavares as background vocalists.

Lembra adopts a particular narrative by imagining these night-time venues mentioned before as places of mythical proportions while presenting both performance and place simultaneously as the collective memory of nightlife for the community. 'Lembra', either as an imperative or a question ('Remember?') calls the recipient to actively remember specific experiences related to historic music scenes and spaces, during which many Cape Verdeans flooded music halls and other venues to assist performances and shows by these popular groups. What this event builds is indeed a nostalgia of place through common references in music and historical spaces of community.

Conclusion

Night spaces have historically been the spaces where people would be able to meet other Cape Verdeans after a week (or day) of work and find a place to socialize, drink and dance. Music played an integral part in this experience as a highly valued cultural reference and symbol, connecting music, space and memory. The night provides an opportunity for encounters that stimulate a sense of belonging in the diaspora, often provoking feelings of nostalgia towards other times and places through music practices. Bana, the 'King of Morna', captured one of the first experiences of nightlife in Habanera, a club popular with Cape Verdean sailors, during the migration history to the Netherlands. Since then, artists have integrated their realities of Rotterdam nights into their music, creating a web of nocturnal testimonies.

Nightlife and music practices in the Cape Verdean diaspora have also been extensively used to mobilize Cape Verdeans politically for the struggle for independence from colonial Portugal, especially during the 1960s and early 1970s. Cape Verdean music practices and night scenes developed parallel to the (political) institutionalization of the Cape Verdean community. While the diaspora in Rotterdam grew, a night scene directed towards Cape Verdeans started appearing through efforts of community organizations, providing a space for socialization with co-nationals and generating a Cape Verdean consciousness entangled with night-time entertainment.

Nightlife practices evidence the entanglement of politics, culture and commerce in the construction of spaces of belonging. Nightlife was, and still is, a means to generate cultural affiliation and generate a connection to the imagined homeland for younger generations, while simultaneously seeking integration into the Dutch context. Night spaces, in this sense, also play an important role in the construction and positioning of migrant communities towards both the local and the global, host society and homeland. Present nightlife events re-construct and re-imagine past nightlife experiences through commercialized promotional narratives. The importance of particular places that are remembered, re-appropriated and re-imagined, brings to light the intimate connection people have with particular locations in the city as shared community nightlife spaces.

NOTES

1. Own translation. Luis Morais is the composer, yet this song was recorded and performed by Bana. The title of the song is 'Problema'.
2. 'Association of Workers Radio Amateurs'.
3. 'Association for Tourist Traffic'.
4. From an in-person interview with a first-generation Cape Verdean migrant and sailor.
5. Morna is a genre from Cape Verde characterized by its melancolic sentiment. Coladeira, on the other hand, is known for its more uplifting rhythm.
6. Grogue is strong alcoholic beverage from Cape Verde, made from sugarcane.
7. This was explained in conversations with Jorge Manuel Oliveira Lizardo, with whom I translated and analyzed many Cape Verdean songs related to Rotterdam.
8. Luis Fortes is otherwise known as Luís Karaté because of his martial arts background and participation in Dutch Kung Fu movie *Dai Xang Li Dai Nao Ou Zhou* (1974).
9. Not only has the landscape of nightlife venues changed over the years because of which many of the previous venues are not available anymore, but contemporary organizers seek more centrally located, often more upscale venues for their events. Thalia Lounge – now called Club Villa Thalia – where Lembra was hosted for example, is a popular venue in the city center of Rotterdam for a young and ethnically mixed audience:

    > Villa Thalia, located in the former movie theatre Thalia, is the biggest and best-known event venue in the centre of Rotterdam. The history as (movie) theatre can still be seen today, just like then, luxury and style predominate Villa Thalia today. At Villa Thalia you can eat, dance, relax, enjoy a drink and meet new people in a chic ambiance.
    >
    > (Villa Thalia Website n.d.: n.pag.)

REFERENCES

Anonymous (1948), 'Rotterdam Start zijn nachtleven', *Het vrije volk: democratisch-socialistisch dagblad*, 28 February, p. 2, https://resolver.kb.nl/resolve?urn=ddd:010949472:mpeg21:a0068. Accessed 29 April 2020.

Anonymous (1950), '"Habanera" geopend', *Het vrije volk: democratisch-socialistisch dagblad*, 30 September, p. 5, https://resolver.kb.nl/resolve?urn=ddd:010950554:mpeg21:a0154. Accessed 29 April 2020.

Anonymous (1953), 'La Bonanza', *Het vrije volk: democratisch-socialistisch dagblad*, 4 September, p. 3, https://resolver.kb.nl/resolve?urn=ddd:010951594:mpeg21:a0112. Accessed 29 April 2020.

Anonymous (1958), '"Vlieg er eens uit" was aan Rotterdam gewijd: Rijke variatie zomerklanken', *Het vrije volk: democratisch-socialistisch dagblad*, 7 July, p. 7, https://resolver.kb.nl/resolve?urn=ddd:010953195:mpeg21:a0197. Accessed 29 April 2020.

Anonymous (1966), 'Klokje rond met VVV: "Er is geen centrum" Rotterdam geen stad om uit te gaan? ACH KOM!', 18 February, p. 9, https://resolver.kb.nl/resolve?urn=ddd:010955964:mpeg21:a0256. Accessed 29 April 2020.

Anonymous (2004), 'Morgadinho', *A Semana*, Kriolidade, 19 November, pp. 2–3, https://www.asemana.publ.cv/PDF/41a3cb3d77b4c.pdf. Accessed 4 August 2022.

Brah, Avtar (1996), *Cartographies of Diaspora: Contesting Identities*, London: Routledge.

Casey, Edward (2000), *Remembering: A Phenomenological Study*, Bloomington: Indiana University Press.

Cidra, Rui (2008a), 'Cape Verdean migration, music recordings and performance', in L. Batalha and J. Carling, *Transnational Archipelago: Perspectives on Cape Verdean Migration and Diaspora*, Amsterdam: Amsterdam University Press, pp. 189–203.

Cidra, Rui (2008b), 'Produzindo a música de Cabo Verde na diáspora: redes transnacionais, world music e múltiplas formações crioulas', in P. Góis (ed.), *Comunidade(s) Cabo-Verdiana(s): as múltiplas faces da imigração Cabo-Verdiana*, Lisboa: ACIDI, pp. 105–26.

Cidra, Rui (2015), 'Politics of memory, ethics of survival: The songs and narratives of the Cape Verdean diaspora in São Tomé', *Ethnomusicology Forum*, 24:3, pp. 304–28.

DJ Guide Website (2018), 'SunClub Reunion 30 juni!: Remember the good old times!!', https://www.djguide.nl/nieuws.p?id=47014&language=en. Accessed 1 May 2021.

Duarte Rodrigues Pires, Doris (2006), *Nha tambor: onderzoek naar het cultureel erfgoed van Kaapverdianen in Rotterdam / Uma investigação sobre a herança cultural dos caboverdeanos em Roterdão*, Rotterdam: Stichting Avanço in het kader van het Project Cultureel Erfgoed Kaapverdianen.

Ehrkamp, Patricia (2005), 'Placing identities: Transnational practices and local attachments of Turkish immigrants in Germany', *Journal of Ethnic and Migration Studies*, 31:2, pp. 345–64.

Freitas, Nelson (2019), 'Bolo Ku Pudim', *Sempre Verão*, CD, Lisbon: Nelson Freitas Music.

Gonçalves, Adriano (1980), 'Lucy d'Nho Morgode', *Teresa*, Vinyl, Lisbon: Discos Monte Cara.

Hart, André (2012), 'De Kaapverdiaanse Muzikale Revolutie van Djunga & Voz de Cabo Verde', *Buurtkrant Oude Westen*, June, n.pag.

Kalandides, Ares and Vaiou, Dina (2012), '"Ethnic" neighbourhoods? Practices of belonging and claims to the city', *European Urban and Regional Studies*, 19:3, pp. 254–66.

Lidskog, Rolf (2016), 'The role of music in ethnic identity formation in diaspora: A research review', *International Social Science Journal*, 66:219, pp. 23–38.

McCarthy, John (1999), 'The redevelopment of Rotterdam since 1945', *Planning Perspectives*, 14:3, pp. 291–309.

Metro Rotterdam E. O. (2014), 'Kaapverdiaanse nostalgie op Lembra', 27 February, p. 3.

Morais, Luis (1967), 'Problema', *A Paris*, Vinyl, Lisbon: A Voz de Cabo Verde.

Nogueira, Gláucia (2016), *Cabo Verde & a musica: Dictionário de personagens*, Primeira ediçâo: Campo da Communicaçâo.

Pardue, Derek (2015), *Cape Verde, Let's Go: Creole Rappers and Citizenship in Portugal: Interpretations of Culture in the New Millennium*, Urbana: University of Illinois Press.

Shaw, Robert (2014), 'Beyond night-time economy: Affective atmospheres of the urban night', *Geoforum*, 51:1, pp. 87–95.

Silva, João (2009), *De Ribeira Bote a Rotterdam*, Mindelo: Gráfica do Mindelo, Lda.

Villa Thalia Website (n.d.), 'Villa Thalia Events', https://www.villathalia.nl/en/. Accessed 1 May 2021.

Interlude 3

Karingido: Vigilante Tricksters and Feedback-Loop Approaches to a Liberation Struggle

Masimba Hwati and Austin T. Richey

Under the cover of night, Zimbabwean guerrilla fighters in the 1970s took back their land from colonial settlers. The night time allowed the Zimbabwean combatants to control the battle on their own terms, both militarily and ideologically. In this interlude, we discuss the role pirate radio frequencies and late-night liberation choirs played in capturing the hearts, minds and ears of Zimbabwean people. Based on our lived and learned perceptions of Zimbabwean sonic cultures, we play with the politics of listening by remixing wartime choir broadcasts via two homemade cassette instruments. What emerges is a sonic work that simultaneously echoes the multiple pirate frequencies penetrating colonial borders and the many listeners who joined the wartime chorus.

From 1967 to 1980, the Second Chimurenga ('liberation' or 'struggle') was a Zimbabwean independence movement against Ian Smith's White majority Rhodesian regime.[1] The anti-colonial struggle took place on multiple fronts: internally against the apartheid-style rule; externally through guerrilla training camps in neighbouring Mozambique, Zambia and Botswana; and across borders through radio frequencies. These migratory radio broadcasts were a crucial sonic tool for revolution.[2] Guerrilla radio stations such as Voice of the Revolution (VOR), which broadcasted messages from the Zimbabwean African People's Union party, and Voice of Zimbabwe (VOZ), which broadcasted messages from the Zimbabwean African National Union party, served as an auditory foil to the Rhodesia Broadcasting Company's (RBC) colonial propaganda.

The VOR and VOZ distributed their messages through transnational radio channels. The Chimurenga was supported by adjacent African independence movements situated outside of Zimbabwe in Zambia's capital Lusaka (VOR) and Mozambique's capital Maputo (VOZ).[3] These migratory frequencies spurred migratory movement; pro-independence radio broadcasts influenced prospective liberation fighters to uproot from Zimbabwe and move to training facilities just across national borders, thereby creating a feedback loop of armed struggle between the distribution of revolutionary sounds and the re-distribution of people.

Some of the most compelling sonic indices were the broadcasted songs of Chimurenga liberation choruses. These songs emerged from pungwes, all-night political rallies for the revolutionary parties. The night was unmonitored and uncensored by Rhodesian colonial powers and the Selous Scouts, the Rhodesian special forces. Guerrillas took advantage of this open channel and the liberated nocturnal frequency to creatively adapt multiple dissident personalities. The darkness helped blur the identities of the guerrillas and attendees, thereby shielding them from easy recognition so that they could operate without limits.[4] Leaders such as ZAPU's Comrade Chinx and ZANU's Comrade Paul Chigango wrote songs for mass choral performances, which inspired revolutionary participation both in person at pungwes held in transnational camps, as well as distant listeners tuned in to guerrilla radio frequencies at home in Zimbabwe.

The liberation choruses could number in the hundreds, and most recordings took place outside of a radio studio and in the fields of the camps themselves; the liveness of these night-time events is evident in the sounds of crickets and other nocturnal creatures audible in the background of the songs, while the impressive sonic force of many voices responding to the calls of the choral leaders often distorts the microphones recording the sessions.

The lyrical content of the choruses mixed indigenous metaphors with the Marxist–Leninist ideologies stemming from Chairman Mao and Fidel Castro. For example, Comrade Chigango's chorus 'Kune Nzira Dzemasoja' ('The Way of the Guerrilla') dictates proper conduct for Chimurenga soldiers utilizing Mao's teachings.

'Kune Nzira Dzemasoja'	**'The Way of the Guerrilla'**[5]
Kune nzira dzemasoja dzekuzvibata nadzo	There are ways of soldiers to conduct themselves
Tereererai mitemo yese nenzira dzakanaka,	Listen to all instructions and follow the good ways
Tisave tinotora zvinhu zvemass yedu,	We should not take things from the masses
Taurai zvine tsika kuruzhinji	We should speak politely to the public

Rwevanhu kuti mass inzwisise	So that they understand the purpose of the struggle
zvakananga musangano	
Dzorerai zvinhu zvose zvamunotora kumuvengi	Return everything you take from enemies
Tisanetsa vasungwa vatinenge tabata	We should not ill-treat captives
Musaita cheupombwe	We should not take liberties with, and abuse women
Bhadharai zvamunotenga nenzira dzakanaka	We should pay for everything we buy in a good way
Aya ndiwo mashoko akataurwa kare naivo vaMao vachitidzidzisa.	These are the words of Mao when he was teaching us.

Tuning into these pungwe broadcasts was an act of sonic warfare; the Rhodesian government had banned the distribution of revolutionary songs, as well as popular Chimurenga music of artists such as Thomas Mapfumo, whose music presented an electric, guitar-based re-imagining of indigenous Shona spiritual culture such as the syncopated arpeggios of the *mbira dzaVadzimu* ('mbira of the ancestors') and the deep metaphorical lyrics that were woven within the sonic texture.[6,7]

The pungwe war choruses were created by bending and stretching language, in the process creating a new kind of language – a transitional-liminal Shona. This re-interpretation and play with language parallels Deleuze and Guattari's proposal in *A Thousand Plateaus* to, 'make language stammer, or make it 'wait,' stretch tensors through all of language, even written language, and draw from its cries, shouts, pitches, durations, timbres, accents, intensities' (1987: 104). The night vigil becomes a place of linguistic experimentation. When we (Hwati) grew up in the rural areas in Zvimba, a district within Mashonaland West province and the birthplace of my Mother, we used to go out at night with our elder brothers to *chibhandhuru/ngoma/jiti*, which were post-independence recreational night vigils.[8] Songs were being composed and re-composed, while hybridized new words were created and thrown into the liminal ether.

For example, the term *karingido* from the song 'Karingido amai here' roughly translates to 'trickster' or 'juvenile agitator'. The root of the name is a verb, *kuringa* ('to look') and *do* is an onomatopoeia for an object falling. *Ka* is a descriptive that captures the size rank of the noun's object. Nicknames are given in social satirical situations by patching together a verb and a descriptive, often an onomatopoeia.

'Karingido amai here'	**'Young man, really?'[9]**
Mwana wenyu uye amai nhingi	Your son, Mother
Karingido	The one who fells (takes down everything he sees)
Anopedza rofu ne freeziti[10]	He finishes a loaf of bread with a Freezit
Karingido	The one who fells (takes down everything he sees)
Koi we mfana zvaita sei	Hey young man what is wrong with you?
Karingido	The one who fells (takes down everything he sees)
Anopedza rofu ne freeziti.	The one who finishes a loaf of bread with cockerel stew.

It is only in particular social satirical circumstances that names are created by meshing several elements together and stretching language. Sometimes the meaning of the trans-locative word is not important – it's the shape, tone and sonority that is key.

The transnational and migratory nature of these guerrilla broadcasts, as well as variations in linguistic and auditory performance, position Chimurenga choruses and the liminality of pungwe participation as a part of a rhizomatic performance space. In response to this sonic history, we (Hwati and Richey) have created

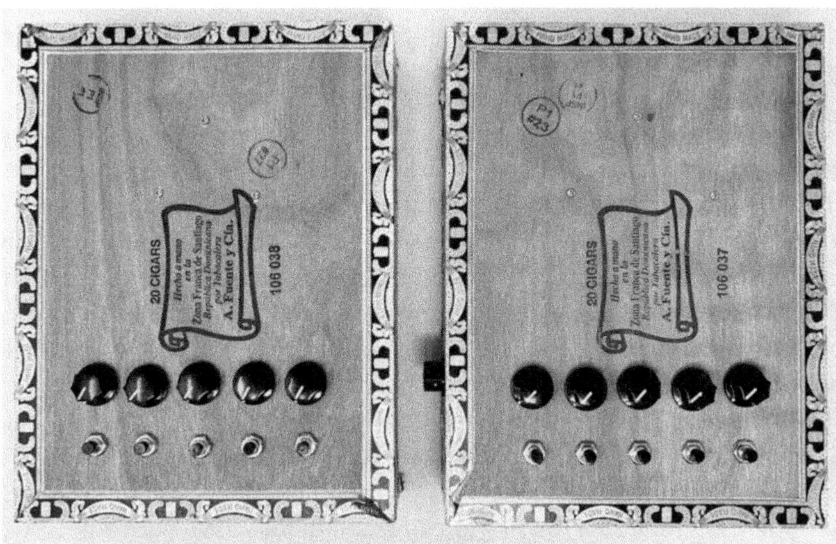

FIGURE 13.1: Karingido, covert cassette instruments.

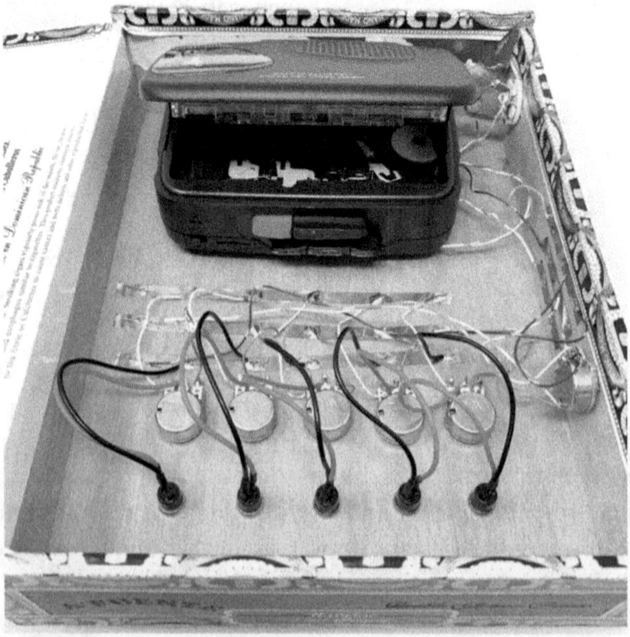

FIGURE I3.2: Interior circuitry of Karingido.

a series of instruments, named Karingido, that tease out further roots of this rhizome; through the re-inscription and re-presentation of cassette recordings of the choruses as well as the re-mix of multiple broadcasts, these instruments act as mechanisms to create ahistorical and sonically diffuse modalities.

The aesthetics of the Karingido instruments reflect the covert nature of pre-independence listening practices: a modified cassette tape player is stashed inside of a Honduran cigar box, with five temporary push buttons and corresponding potentiometers on their face. A single quarter-inch stereo output jack and a single potentiometer are positioned on the left side of the box. Inside the instrument lays a network of telephone wire, salvaged from a scrapyard in Detroit and strips of conductive copper tape. Together, these materials form a circuit which allows the performer to modify the speed of the tape player via the individual knobs.[11]

This is an extension of the printed circuit board within the player; Richey bent the internal circuit by removing the factory-installed speed control and rewiring those regulator points to the external circuit. With this system, the speed of the cassette inside the player can be modified at the performers' whim, which in turn allows them to control the pitch and pace of whatever sonic material is recorded to the magnetic and plastic tape material.[12] The side-mounted potentiometer controls the overall speed of the player, while the face-mounted potentiometers allow for on-the-fly alterations when the related button is pressed.

The sonic material for these instruments came from the wartime recordings archive of Hwati's father Mazvimbakupa Manjenjenje, a collection which emerged from his police work in the 1990s. A member of the Central Investigation Department's music piracy team, Manjenjenje was tasked with finding, confiscating and destroying bootleg recordings in Zimbabwe's bountiful public markets; surreptitiously, he instead took the recordings home for his personal use. A selection of seven pieces was constructed into a digital playlist and recorded onto cassette, thereby linking the ephemeral, often live radio broadcasts to contemporary and past media forms. This multimedia process is audible in the sonic artefacts contained on the tape, from the distortion of the live radio broadcast, the compression of the digital files and the slight oscillations of the recorded tape.

These recordings included Chimurenga choruses such as the Zimbabwean African National Liberation Army (ZANLA) Choir's performance of 'Gwara reZanu' ('Ideology of ZANU') and Comrade Muchazotida's 'Ndiro Gidi' ('It is the Gun'), pieces which not only spread the messages and policies of the political parties but also encouraged listeners to rise up and join the fight.[13] The cassette also includes a tremendous recording of an infamous moment in which General Rex Nhongo was interrupted during his controversial explanation of the 1980 ceasefire agreement between ZANLA and Rhodesian forces; in a sonic refusal to lay down their weapons and coexist with their oppressors, young members of the army began chanting party slogans and singing Chimurenga lyrics.

Hondo, hondo, hondo kuManica!	War, war in Manica Province![14]
Aaahh yeaa yeaah aheeee, aheee yea ahehee	[Group vocables]
Chengeta Zimbabwe yababa ine madhora	Keep Zimbabwe the father land,
there is wealth in the land	
Hondo kuGaza!	War in Gaza province!
Aaahh yeaa yeaah aheeee, aheee yea ahehee	[Group vocables]
Chengeta Zimbabwe yababa ine madhora.[15]	Keep Zimbabwe the father land, there is wealth in the land.

In performance, two identical covert cassette instruments, Karingido 1 and Karingido 2, play duplicated tape recordings of the roughly 26-minute playlist. The performer utilizes the temporary speed control potentiometers and buttons to complicate the simultaneity of the re-imagined broadcasts; the tapes move in and out of phase with each other to create movement and distance, reflecting the history of transnational broadcasts and disruption that occur when other radio frequencies interrupt a signal.

Pitch manipulation emulates the embodiment of multiple listeners. Sounds can be pitched to suit the listener's voice; however, this would work against the group aesthetic of Chimurenga choirs. While the choir's leader is a solo force calling out to encourage the mass of singers, the intensity of the sonic space comes from the sheer variety of vocal ranges and performances, from deep bass voices, nasal timbres and the punctuation of ululations. Instead, the inter-mixing of identical recordings at deviating speeds and pitches allows the performer to establish new choral performances by opting to retune the recordings in dissonance or consonance.

This co-mingling of faithfully reproduced recordings and augmented soundscapes presents a constantly shifting iteration of the Chimurenga liberation choirs' own rhizomatic circuit.[16] What emerges is a non-hierarchical, multi-narrative approach to a chorus and to a sound. The exact messaging of the original Chimurenga choir recordings is purposefully blurred. This encourages the listener to enter the sonic space, hear resonant phrases or punctuations and leave without extracting a singular narrative. Instead, they get a sense of the struggle through the interchange of multiple voices speaking and signing, and the listeners called to action.

Appendix: Playlist recordings

1. 'Tinotenda' – Zimbabwe African People's Union Light Machine Gun Choir.
2. 'Gwara reZANU' – Zimbabwe African National Liberation Army Choir.
3. Ceasefire, General Solomon Mujuru (Rex Nhongo), 26 March 1980.
4. 'Ndiro Gidi' – Zimbabwe African National Union Choir.
5. 'Gwenyu Kwenyu' – Zimbabwe African National Liberation Army Choir.
6. 'Mudzimu Woye' – Zimbabwe African National Union Choir.
7. 'Tora Gidi Uzvitonge' – Zimbabwe African National Union Choir.

NOTES

1. The First Chimurenga took place in the late 1890s, when Shona and Ndebele revolutionaries fought against colonization by the British South Africa Company. The term Chimurenga comes from the legendary ancestor Murenga Musorowenzu. For more on the connections between ancestral lineage and revolutionary war in Zimbabwe, see David Lan (1985).

2. Scholars including Chikowero, Mosia et al., Ndlovu and Turino have discussed the impact of Zimbabwean radio broadcasts on the revolutionary struggle. In particular, Chikowero discusses how radio, at first a tool to colonize listeners, became an instrument of self-liberation, while Turino explains that the strength of Chimurenga choral broadcasts came in large part from the conscious use of recognizable Zimbabwean musical forms, metaphor and rhythms. See Chikowero 2015; Mosia et al. 1994; Ndlovu 2017; Turino 1998.
3. Zambia gained independence in 1964 after a war with the British colonizers, and Mozambique became independent over a decade later, when they successfully defeated the Portuguese in 1975. These countries were vital sites of pro-Zimbabwean independence and served as hubs for radio messaging until Zimbabwe achieved victory against the colonial forces in 1980.
4. Guerrillas also used pseudonyms to scramble the signal that connected them to their family ties; this protected their families at home since the colonial forces used to target the families of the fighters to force the guerrillas to yield. For more, see Pfukwa 2007.
5. Trans. Hwati.
6. Eyre describes how Mapfumo was, early on, able to avoid censorship from the colonial and post-colonial authorities by incorporating metaphor into his political critiques. See Eyre 2001.
7. While early missionaries in Zimbabwe suppressed the performance of traditional spiritual music like the Shona mbira, Turino explains that recordings of this instrument were widely distributed throughout Zimbabwe in the 1960s via colonial radio to entice Indigenous listeners. See Turino 1998: 89.
8. *Ngoma*, *jiti* and *chibhandhuru* are recreational drumming, singing and dance sessions mostly for unmarried youths. These are common in the Zvimba district. The name 'chibhandhuru' is a modification of the Shona word for bundle, and captures the idea of a loaded phenomenon that will unfold with surprise.
9. Trans. Hwati.
10. Freezit is slang for an inexpensive frozen popsicle popular with urban youth.
11. The circuit builds upon an original design by instrument maker and musician Rich Bernett.
12. This harkens to the Mellotron, an analog electric sampling instrument designed in 1963 that connects a performance keyboard to tape recordings of acoustic sounds such as string instruments, woodwinds and choirs.
13. In *African Music, Power, and Being in Colonial Zimbabwe*, Chikowero describes how, like colonial radio, the gun was first introduced as a subjugating force yet became a tool for liberation. He points to 'Ndiro Giri' as a sonic indicator of this shift. See Chikowero 2015: 252.
14. Trans. Hwati.
15. In April 2020, the Zimbabwean newspaper *The Herald* featured an extensive interview with Comrade Munosiyani Christopher Makwambeni, the young soldier who spoke out against the ceasefire. See Kachere 2020.
16. An example of these instruments in performance can be found at the following YouTube link: https://www.youtube.com/watch?v=UMHtdfRqdC4. Accessed 4 August 2022.

REFERENCES

Chikowero, Mhoze (2015), *African Music, Power, and Being in Colonial Zimbabwe*, Bloomington: Indiana University Press.

Deleuze, Gilles and Félix, Guattari (2005), *A Thousand Plateaus* (trans. B. Massumi), Minneapolis: University of Minnesota Press.

Eyre, Banning (2001), *Playing with Fire: Fear and Self-censorship in Zimbabwean Music*, Copenhagen: Freemuse.

Kachere, Phyllis (2020), 'Why we interrupted Mujuru: Ex-fighter speaks out', *The Herald*, 24 April, https://www.herald.co.zw/why-we-interrupted-mujuru-ex-fighter-speaks-out/. Accessed 20 August 2021.

Lan, David (1985), *Guns and Rain: Guerrillas and Spirit Mediums in Zimbabwe*, Berkeley: University of California Press.

Lekgoathi, Sekibakiba Peter, Moloi, Tshepo and Saúte, Saide Alda (2020), *Guerrilla Radios in Southern Africa: Broadcasters, Technology, Propaganda Wars, and the Armed Struggle*, Lanham: Rowman & Littlefield.

Mosia, Lebona, Riddle, Charles and Zaffiro, Jim (1994), 'From revolutionary to regime radio: Three decades of nationalist broadcasting in Southern Africa', *Africa Media Review*, 8:1, pp. 1–24.

Ndlovu, Everette (2017), 'Radio as a recruiting medium in Zimbabwe's liberation struggle', *Westminster Papers in Communication and Culture*, 12:2, pp. 52–58.

Nhiwatiwa, Naomi Pasiharigutwi (1979), *Women's Liberation in the Zimbabwean Revolution: Materials from the Zanu Women's Seminar, Maputo, Mozambique, May 1979*, San Francisco: John Brown Book Club.

Pfukwa, Charles (2007), 'The function and significance of war names in the Zimbabwean armed conflict (1966–1979)', dissertation, Johannesburg: University of South Africa.

Turino, Thomas (1998), 'The Mbira, worldbeat, and the international imagination', *The World of Music, Old Instruments in New Contexts*, 40:2, pp. 85–106.

PART 4

BELONGING

7

Lisbon Under Construction: The Nocturnal Stylings of *batida do gueto*

Jacqueline Georgis

Based on ethnographic fieldwork completed in Lisbon in 2019, this chapter shows how, with regard to nighttime spaces of urban sociability and collectivity, 'Noite Príncipe' and the performance of batida do gueto (ghetto beat) at Noite Príncipe have aroused new forms of musical sensibility and modified spatial relationships in downtown Lisbon. From this perspective, I approach the music venue, Musicbox, as a vibrant contact zone where, through the Noite Príncipe evenings, cultural connections take place and alternative notions of Portuguese identity are introduced and shaped.

Introduction

A sea of brightly coloured housing blocks on the outskirts of the city morphed into continuous rows of iron-wrought streetlamps as the taxi left Lisbon's Humberto Delgado Airport and sped downtown. Careening down the hills and around busy roundabouts, the car continued towards the waterfront, past the Praça Marquês de Pombal, and down the Avenida da Liberdade to the Praça do Comércio. The praça, packed with tourists, pushed its overspill onto the terraced steps leading to the river Tejo and scattered them along the Ribeira das Naus.

As the last bit of daylight faded, the city took on a different quality under a crepuscular sky that illuminated even the darkest crevices of the Cais do Sodré neighbourhood. Groups of Erasmus students, rowdy stag parties and young locals wandered through the neighbourhood's snaking streets, their anticipation of what the night might hold, palpable. Musical fragments of *kizomba*, *coladeira*, *fado* and *kuduro* sounding from various corners of the city came together to exchange their stories of glory and conquests, of life in the diaspora and of *saudade*.[1] Below the underpass on Rua do Nova Carvalho and beyond the impressive arched door frame of Musicbox through which guests of the monthly Noite Príncipe (Príncipe Night) club night shuffled in and out was another music. Guiding guests through the venue's cavernous space, the music left them at the stage upon which architects of a nocturnal sound assessed their electronic tools, rolled up their sleeves and began their work. The builders worked methodically, expertly laying down 'the heartbeat' – the foundation of the music that would sustain the party's atmosphere into the early morning hours. For regulars of Noite Príncipe, this was part of a monthly ritual aimed at diversifying the city's cultural connective tissue through a music genre known as *batida do gueto* ('ghetto beat').

Before long, the evening's darkness gave way to daybreak. The sound system was turned off, the bar cleaned and as the city started to stir, the participants of Noite Príncipe began their journey back to from where they had come. But in those few short evening hours, concertgoers entered a zone of escape. It featured a night-time atmosphere of relaxed social rules and barriers, suspended responsibilities and expanded possibilities (Garcia 2013), yet maintained its own rules and expectations. Removed from the barriers of daily life, Noite Príncipe represented a temporal space where concertgoers traded their daily routines for their

FIGURE 7.1: DJ Nigga Fox at Musicbox, 15 February 2019. Photo by Jacqueline Georgis.

'nocturnal self' (Grazian 2008) and crossed paths with other evening revellers in ways that were more casual and free, more inclusive and convivial.

Locating batida do gueto

'It's not easy to be bold', Príncipe Discos' co-manager José Moura concluded during a panel at the 2019 Lisbon International Music Network (MIL) Festival. Referring to the limited opportunities for more daring and experimental music programming at nightlife venues in Lisbon, Moura, along with co-panelist João Silva, also known as DJ Rastronaut, addressed the constraints that niche music genres face in small cities with small markets. Moura and Silva, each representing two Lisbon-based record labels, Príncipe Discos and Enchufada, respectively, openly expressed the challenges of creating a sustainable and veritable music 'scene' with limited local resources. 'There have been a lot of articles written in the past couple of years about how this new Afro-rhythms scene in Lisbon is blowing up, and it is in a way, but in another way, it's still a micro-scene', Silva expressed. 'There's still a lot to be done and a lot to fight for' (MIL panel, 28 March 2019). For the individuals behind the Príncipe Discos label, finding a home for *batida do gueto* was particularly difficult in a city where nightlife has been largely – but not exclusively – oriented around house and techno music, and where access to leisure and nightlife continues to be economically, geographically and racially determined (Nofre 2013; Calvo et al. 2016; Sedano 2018).

The story of the monthly Noite Príncipe club night and the Príncipe Discos sound that brought *batida do gueto*, an electronic dance music genre characterized by its limited vocals, melody and harmony, its prominent rhythm sections, and short, loop-based melodic lines, to the city's downtown and international dancefloors runs parallel to a period profoundly marked by an abundance of musical creativity and diversity in Lisbon. When considered alongside the underground and commercial successes of its other contemporary, urban electronic music genres such as hip-hop *tuga*[2] and progressive *kuduro*,[3] *batida do gueto*'s appearance at downtown venues, like the acclaimed live music venue Musicbox, made it one of the city's most unanticipated debuts of the 2010s. Its emergence also falls on the heels of a rise in new forms of commodified leisure activities and nightlife venues, and a cultural resignification of popular Afro-Portuguese couple dances which brought traditional African expressive forms under the guises of modernity and cosmopolitanism.

Over the course of the early 2000s and 2010s, Portugal's images, sounds and rhythms diversified as artists sought to fill the postcolonial space (Fradique 2018) with original models of cultural production. Musical crossovers (through the output of Buraka Som Sistema, Sam the Kid and Batida), a growth in local independent record labels (through dance music labels such as Enchufada and Príncipe Discos), and urbanisation (through a 'vintage-style' nightlife in the city's downtown spaces) (Nofre 2013) created opportunities for a more varied musical context that helped usher in a new chapter in Portugal's contemporary urban music (Alge 2015; Ranocchiari 2011; de La Barre 2018; Fradique 2018; Raposo and Marcon 2021).

Hip-hop music came into the cultural mainstream in Portugal during the 1990s and 2000s. As a genre that has long been mobilised by youths across the globe as a vehicle for cultural expression and a template with which to re-imagine their connection to the local and the global (George 2007; Kidula 2012; Pardue 2013), hip-hop, with its cultural and aesthetic appeal found resonance with Portugal's marginalised youth. Its sonic and thematic malleability allowed artists to transform traditional practices along localised expressive lines and produce original cultural works informed by their own frameworks of self-definition and self-expression (Shipley 2013). In Portugal, the emergence of *tuga* rap and the contributions by the country's first-generation rappers like Boss AC, Sam the Kid and Chullage, in addition to pivotal albums like *Rapública* (1994), helped to 'inaugurate a space for the empowerment of rap practices' (Fradique 2018: 67) and introduce new categories of sociability, identity and creative expression (Cidra 2002; Fradique 2003).

An early form of *kuduro*, an Angolan electronic music and dance genre, had also emerged in Lisbon during the late 1990s and early 2000s period, brought in the form of cassette tapes by migrants, students and travellers from Angola, and experienced virtually via online videos and music file-sharing platforms. Its energetic vocal animation overtop fast beats of traditional Angolan and Caribbean dance music rhythms mixed with techno music allowed it to gain popularity in Lisbon's African communities and with local dancers and DJs. Despite *kuduro's* popularity in these spaces, it struggled to be recognized as a cultural product that existed beyond the sphere of comedy and light entertainment; in other words, it failed to find a serious expression in Portugal. Kalaf Epalanga, author, music producer and member of the band Buraka Som Sistema, states in his novel, *Também os Brancos sabem Dançar*: 'Nao existe nada mais lisboeta do que o kuduro e, no entanto, a cidade levou décadas a reconhecê-lo' ('There exists nothing more Lisboetan than *kuduro*, and still, it took the city decades to recognize it') (2017: 38). By the latter part of the early 2000s, however, *kuduro* had begun to infiltrate public and private spaces in the city via genres like progressive *kuduro*, thus becoming, as La Barre (2019: 126) points out, 'enrolled in the whirlwind representations of "New Angola" and "New Africa"'.

Dj's Do Guetto *and the emergence of Príncipe Discos*

On 18 September 2006, a group of producers from various regions of the Lisbon Metropolitan Area (LMA) self-released volume one of its eponymous debut album, *Dj's Do Guetto*.[4] The album's unusual compilation of *kuduro* beats mixed with *tarraxo*, *tarraxinha, funaná* and *kizomba*, alarm sirens, voices and hand claps conjured up musical styles from the corners of Africa, Europe and the Black diaspora. *Dj's Do Guetto Vol. 1* is the brainchild of DJs Marfox, Nervoso, N. K., Pausas, Jesse and Fofuxo, most of whom were already amateur producers in their own rights. Both Nervoso and N. K. were autodidacts who DJ'd around various *bairros* ('neighbourhoods') and shared their knowledge of music production with younger producers; DJs Pausas, Fofuxo and Marfox made beats and mixes for local dance crews like Máquinas do Kuduro. With a sound that jumbled the wires of traditional Luso-African music styles with contemporary electronic dance music, Dj's Di Guetto burst onto the dance music scene and set the bar for new generations of producers.

The *batida* or 'beat' sound that grew out of Lisbon's peripheries was greatly influenced by the growth of music digitalization, digital technologies and digital distribution in the early twenty-first century. New file-sharing and peer-to-peer (p2p) platforms, music streaming services and production software increasingly shaped how music was made, disseminated and accessed. Music-sharing platforms like eMule, Napster and later SoundCloud, and software such as FL Studio promoted a 'relative democratization' (Bartmanski and Woodward 2015) of technical musical skills, production and distribution. By lowering economic and technical barriers to music production, FL Studio, in particular, appealed to young and amateur artists. The ease with which users could 'crack' (illegally copy) or download FL Studio's demo version for free made it what DJ Marfox described as 'a real emancipation tool [...] the software of the poor' (Lacaille 2019: n.pag.).

In Lisbon, these advancements in digital technologies allowed artists to transcend geographic, socio-cultural and class boundaries and gain greater visibility. The ease with which digitised music spread across different channels permitted content made in bedroom and similarly small-scale production spaces to not only reach a broad audience but also bypassed more costly and outdated forms of music media dissemination. With regard to *batida do gueto*, online instant messaging and file-sharing platforms played a central role in its early development and circulation by bridging physical distances and providing access to music cultures produced in *bairros*, kilometres away from one's own. In contexts that rendered residents in the peripheries less mobile than their urban counterparts due to low access to transportation and poor infrastructure (Pritchard et al. 2014; Santos 2016), internet-connected technologies helped bring together artists from across the greater metropolitan area of Lisbon, establish music collectives – as was the case with Dj's Di Guetto and DJs Di Puro Ritmo, for example – and broaden networks of producers and DJs.

In 2012, Príncipe Discos, an independent record label dedicated to releasing 'real contemporary dance music coming out of Lisbon, its suburbs, projects and slums' (Príncipe Discos n.d.: n.pag.) was founded by a group of Lisbon-based musicians and artists. Príncipe helped make *batida do gueto* a more visible presence by building a channel from Lisbon's peripheries to downtown music venues and supporting the development of a genre that had been previously unknown to many city residents. By late February 2012, the label had hosted its first Noite Príncipe party at Musicbox. The realization of a monthly club night that was committed to promoting African electronic dance music marked a decisive moment in the context of Lisbon's urban music and nightlife scene by demonstrating that it was indeed possible to create spaces in the city centre where urban rhythms could be celebrated and enjoyed by diverse audiences. Since its inception, Noite Príncipe has come to represent a symbol of musical and aesthetic liberation – a space where DJs are 'free to play their own music' (José Moura, personal comm., 6 February 2019).

The *bairro*: Something extraordinary out of nothing

At the heart of *batida do gueto* is the *bairro* and it is a dominant theme in the music. The term *bairros sociais* refers to government-supported housing projects found across the greater LMA. While some are located close to the city centre and are possible to reach by public transportation, most are far removed from the centre, in both a psychological and physical sense (Ranocchiari 2011). As is the case with housing projects around the globe, in this context, the *bairro* is similarly understood by the socio-economic and cultural traits of its inhabitants, its geographic isolation and the harsh 'urbanistic nature' of its environment (Campos 2018). In the Portuguese media, the *bairro* is often negatively depicted as a space rife with violence and crime; for residents, however, the *bairro* also represents a primary unit of identity (Batalha and Carling 2008) – it is in many senses, a geographically contained social territory in which their identity is rooted (Pardue 2013).

For many artists, the *bairro* and *bairro* culture are purposefully represented in a public manner, a sentiment which is apparent in the genre name itself: 'ghetto beat'. As a purely instrumental genre, there is no text with which artists may indicate to the listener any socio-cultural or spatially specific affiliations; instead, artists localise their music through their respective *bairro*. This is manifest in album and song titles, like Rinchoa Stress (RS) Produções' *Bagdad Style* (2018),[5] 'Apito do guetto' ('Whistle of the ghetto') by Nídia and DJ Marfox's '2685–2686'.[6] Or, as is

FIGURE 7.2: Mural of DJ Nervoso in Quinta do Mocho by the Portuguese artist Vhils. Photo by Jacqueline Georgis, 7 July 2019. The *bairro* of Quinta do Mocho is of particular importance in the development of *batida do gueto* as it is considered the birthplace of the music genre and is home to numerous music producers.

the case with RS Produções, the *bairro* is similarly evoked through a crew's name. In addition to informing track titles and stage names of artists, the *bairro* offers itself as a source of sonic inspiration. Artists borrow from its densely textured soundscape, drawing from the local sounds of children playing, the chatter of friends or the distant police siren.

The notion of geographic and socio-cultural isolation forms the bedrock of *batida do gueto* and is a valuable form of cultural currency. The power of an 'urban authenticity' (Zukin 2010), which here partly stems from the *bairro's* geographic peripheralization and impoverished public spaces, comes together with not only the residents' natural capacity to invent national and even globally relevant scenes with limited production technologies, but is also based in the residents' ability to claim a cultural authenticity and 'rootedness'. In the case of the actual music, its style and sonority, de La Barre (2010: 153) notes that musical authenticity may not always be derived from its sonic or stylistic attributes but will continue to be grounded in 'a local identity'. It is the 'authenticity of the place' de La Barre argues, with its necessarily political musical message (2010: 153).

Crews

It is not uncommon for amateur producers to establish informal neighbourhood-based music crews, as evidenced by the handful of groups such as Dj's Di Guetto, Piquenos DJs di Guetto, RS Produções, Blacksea Não Maya and others. Made up of anywhere from three to six members – primarily males – these groups often evolve organically and are composed of artistically like-minded members from the same geographic region, *bairro* or household.[7] Crews may be affiliated with certain music labels and find through them performance opportunities. By participating in a crew, members access an environment of open communication and support (Farrugia 2009), gain local and even international visibility and build professional reputations. Members also benefit from a space in which they may freely experiment with new configurations of cultural and sonic categories that help to re-define and re-contextualize their social worlds.

Aligning oneself with a crew establishes an affiliation with a distinct musical style (McGregor and Gibson 2009) and nurtures a sense of brotherhood as well as a broader cultural identification with *batida* music. In *batida do gueto*, this feeling is perhaps most clearly expressed through the practice of adopting the name or part of the name of a significant figure in the music's history. The legacy of DJ Marfox, one of the pioneers of Lisbon's *batida* music, is traceable through the suffix 'fox', which artists like Dario Fox, Nigga Fox, Liofox, Dadifox and others have all adopted as part of their own stage names.[8] In the same vein, the members of the former Afro-Portuguese dance music crew, Piquenos DJs do Guetto, pay tribute to their predecessor, Dj's Di Guetto. For the artist, choosing to represent the name of a musical innovator can be a meaningful act in that it displays a level of respect, while publicly expressing the artists' desired closeness and association with that figure. But beyond such acts of obeisance, crews and independent artists that work closely with one another may also show their loyalty by featuring each other's music at events. This reciprocity of symbolic support is a hallmark of established and emergent producers' behaviour and is a challenge to DJs who choose to silence or cut out an artists' ID tag during a live show.

Crews also represent a communal space where artists build alternative notions of citizenship beat by beat, layer by layer. For many, music becomes their true form of identity in a country where some are not legally considered

FIGURE 7.3: DJs Lima and Narciso of Rinchoa Stress Produções, 6 August 2019. Photo by Jacqueline Georgis.

citizens. For DJ Marfox, the São Tomean producer and DJ who was born in Portugal, *batida do gueto* has been central to shaping his own self-definition of cultural belonging:

> Before I make music, what is my identity? I am not Portuguese to Portuguese people; I am not Black to people who come from Africa. They say, you were not born in Africa. Portuguese say, you are not Portuguese, you are Black. So, this music is my Lisbon. This is my vision about Lisbon, about music, about life.
>
> (DJ Marfox, personal comm., 7 December 2019)

Through the creation of a music culture that he dubbed 'his' Lisbon, DJ Marfox navigates the social realities that he and many African immigrants of his generation experience having grown up in a liminal world. For DJ Marfox, in being perceived by others as belonging to neither Africa nor Europe, any sense of identity that failed to take root in a national space was realized through what Arenas terms one's positionality within a 'shifting multicultural urban landscape' (2010: 19).

Over the course of the last decades of the twentieth century, the idea of a distinct 'Portuguese identity' became more clearly delineated by formal and informal notions of belonging and exclusion; of what constituted Portuguese citizenship and who had access to it. In 1981, Portugal shifted its criteria for obtaining citizenship from a nationality law predicated on the principle of *jus soli* to one based on *jus sanguinis*. This legal amendment stated that a person needed to have one or more parents of Portuguese blood, meaning that at least one parent needed to have been born in the country in order for their child to be considered Portuguese by birth. What the new law meant for thousands of first-generation immigrants arriving in Portugal in the decades following the fall of the Portuguese empire was that acquiring citizenship for themselves and their children born in Portugal would be extremely difficult. Without access to Portuguese citizenship, those born in Portugal were considered illegal, a classification that stirred up feelings of social exclusion, marginalisation, segregation and an uncertainty of cultural belonging. While the law was changed in 2006 and grants citizenship to second- and third-generation immigrants born in Portugal to non-citizens, it is still largely based on the *jus sanguinis* principle. Additionally, as Lupati and Rendeiro (2020) point out, the 2006 law does not have retroactive effects, and individuals born in Portugal between 1981 and 2006 to parents of non-Portuguese blood are still considered foreigners in the country of their birth.[9]

This feeling of rejection, coupled with a longing for some sort of cultural connection, contributed to intuitive responses by youths to create their own cultural alternatives through which they might leave their own legacy. Pardue (2015) describes how Cape Verdean rappers in Lisbon utilize the power of the *Kriolu* language – its linguistic structure and particular aesthetic – to delineate space and difference through rap rhetoric in ways that indirectly shape popular discourse and politics around what it is to be Portuguese. For other youths in Lisbon, creating their own cultural alternative meant finding meaning in their musical heritage, namely the music traditions of their parents' generation. Drawing inspiration from artists from the 1970s to 1980s like Bonga, Super Mama Djombo, África Negra, producers may incorporate samples into their own music and mix them with contemporary popular African and European music genres. Through this act of sampling and mixing, artists revisit the stories of past territories and former identities and re-signify them in their present context (La Barre 2018). La Barre (2018) describes this process as a way for Afrodiasporic communities to symbolize agency through the creation of new 'possibilities of self-relocation'. Here, the paths to self-relocation are forged through the tending to of cultural breakages and ruptures (Hall 1994) of life in the diaspora and come to life through music.

Nocturnal sound design

Noite Príncipe was started at Musicbox in early 2013. For Príncipe Discos' managers and artists, the purpose behind the monthly event was two-fold: to host a musical evening where creators of experimental styles of Afro-Portuguese electronic dance music were given the creative space and freedom to share their music and to foster an environment in the city centre where African youths from the *bairros* could come to follow their DJs. This carving out of diasporic musical spaces in popular and important cultural night spaces is mirrored across Europe in venues that cater to Afro-diasporic communities. Kenny and Young's (2021) study on migrant musical spaces in Galway, Ireland's cultural venues of Áras na nGael and Róisín Dubh, is just one such example of how African migrant musicians both inhabit and expand night-time musical spaces so that they may become broader cultural spaces of encounter for Galway's citizens.

While there was precedent for music and nightlife events in Lisbon's downtown spaces outside the realm of house and techno – for example, Enchufada's bi-monthly Hard Ass Sessions[10] at Lux Frágil or 'African parties' hosted by music projects such as Celeste/Mariposa – Noite Príncipe tends to the needs of a demographic that was often overlooked, or at least, not prioritized by other events: youths of African descent. The monthly party, while serving a functional purpose, can thus be seen as an ideological representation of what social and spatial formations are believed to be possible. Noite Príncipe seeks to formalize new ways of acting and being within different cultural spaces while simultaneously offering a physical and conceptual space where a diverse audience could explore alternative nightlife possibilities together.

Finding a venue that would accommodate *batida do gueto* and configuring that space in such a way that respected and honoured its traditions was complicated. On the one hand, the musical and cultural aesthetic of *batida do gueto* seemed to be at odds with other Afro-Portuguese dance styles of music that were gaining popularity across Lisbon's European and African nightlife circuits. This made *batida do gueto* a difficult style to place, reducing possible options within an already modest number of potential venues. On the other hand, for the small number of downtown music venues that were interested to take on the challenge, this displacement of musical cultures from the peripheries to downtown that Noite Príncipe took part in reinforced a longstanding issue of privileging 'the centre' over its peripheries (Alge 2015; Arenas 2011; La Barre 2010; La Barre and Vanspauwen 2013).

Despite influential structural and social changes that in many ways facilitated Noite Príncipe's entrée into the nightlife scene, the issue of how the music fit within the scope of its other contemporary styles of Afro-Lusophone music remained. The international success of *kizomba*, a traditional Angolan partner dance, and its swift social ascent from a marginalised style to a globalized phenomenon had profound economic and social repercussions in Lisbon and to its nightlife industry. The cosmopolitan ethos associated with the world dance market of the 1980s and 1990s spoke directly to the needs of a growing Portuguese middle-class that looked for ways to participate in modernity (Sedano 2019). During this period, the country experienced interesting changes to the ways in which traditional African dance, like *kizomba*, was perceived, as it underwent a 'process of resignification in the new cosmopolitan context' (Sedano 2019: n.pag.). The 'global *kizomba* industry', albeit messy and complex in its own issues having to do with cultural capital and ownership, was quickly integrated into Lisbon's daily soundscapes and helped promote positive images of African culture associated with modernity, cosmopolitanism and sophistication (Sedano 2019).

Batida do gueto comes into tension with these renewed notions of African cosmopolitanism and sophistication. The music lacked a certain 'polish' and glamour and was undesirable for the city's 'Noites Africana' ('African nights'). DJ Nervoso remembered not being allowed to play at certain African clubs past 3:00 in the morning for fear of 'fights and disruption', recalling how he and his music would be to blame if there was violence. He further explained, 'When you leave the ghetto, you don't hear *batida do gueto* [...] Africans at the clubs don't want it to leave the ghetto. It's complicated' (DJ Nervoso, personal comm., 25 April 2019).

Sonically, the music was too aggressive, too violent, and too raw. Instead, owners sought out more commercial genres of the Afro-diaspora like R&B, afrohouse or *kizomba* – genres that spoke to a more 'aspirational' or 'bling-oriented' lifestyle, as José Moura shared. Although inhabiting a socio-cultural space far beyond that of *kizomba*, to some, *batida do gueto* threatened to undermine the more glamorous and positive images of 'African-ness' and African culture in Lisbon.

> DJs, when they tried playing their music – their own music, their own productions in their own DJs sets in those clubs – they got looked down upon [...] Their music was not welcomed because it was associated with the ghetto and because these are 'aspirational clubs', or at least they tend to represent an aspirational lifestyle.
>
> (José Moura, personal comm., 6 February 2019)

A fortuitous partnership

Movement between the peripheries and downtown for nightlife and leisure activities in Lisbon is largely unidirectional. Poor accessibility to the periphery from the centre and vice versa limits the city inhabitants' ability to access leisure activities on both sides. For local performances, then, *batida do gueto* artists travel from outside the city to the centre; very rarely is this movement reciprocated by 'downtown' fans and listeners. Príncipe Discos DJ and producer Nídia Borges speaks to this dynamic, acknowledging the city's segregated neighbourhoods:

> As we [Noite Príncipe] are in the middle of the city, it helps a lot for whites who like to listen to our music to come here [Musicbox], because it's difficult for a white person who doesn't like the peripheries to go there.
>
> (Nídia, personal comm., 3 June 2019)

José Moura echoes Nídia's sentiments, making note of these challenges:

> If you go to Musicbox on a regular night, you'll see most of the audience now is probably from the neighbourhoods [...] Unfortunately, the other way around is uncommon – people from the center going there [to the suburbs] to explore. Maybe because there are no specific reasons to go there. So, it's difficult to establish the circuit going the other way, it's really difficult. But our [Príncipe Discos'] role was more to bring people to the center. Not because it's in the center they should be[...] We wanted to break that barrier down. Unfortunately, I don't know how we would do the other way around.
>
> (José Moura, personal comm., 6 February 2019)

The motivation to host Noite Príncipe came at an opportune moment when the city's nightlife, specifically in historical neighbourhoods such as Bairro Alto and Cais do Sodré, was being re-conceptualized. Calvo et al. (2017) take note of the expansion and commodification of nightlife in the harbour neighbourhood of Bairro Alto and the privileged role international consumers, i.e., tourists and Erasmus students played in the city's urban regeneration process. The phenomena of 'night-time touristification' and 'studentification' contributed to perceptible changes. During the 1990s and 2000s, Bairro Alto, a neighbourhood valued for its authenticity and 'traditional forms of life' was reimagined as a hip, cool quarter for tourists and university students (Calvo et al. 2017). This process of urban change was similarly felt in other neighbourhoods. In the riverfront quarter of Cais do Sodré, global mass tourism took the shape of what Nofre (2013) has called a 'vintage-style nightlife' with carefully curated venues such as Pensão Amor, Bar da Velha Senhora and Sol e Pesca lining the pedestrian street of Rua Nova de Carvalho. Musicbox, too, can be seen as an early addition to this cohort of new nightlife. Strategically located in the middle of the Cais do Sodré neighbourhood, on one of the city's most popular streets for nightlife venues (Nofre et al. 2019), Musicbox attracts a diverse audience of tourists and locals. Noite Príncipe reaps the benefits of the venue's geographic positioning, pulling in curious tourists that mix with locals from the *bairros*.

This piece has shown how Noite Príncipe offers another way of hearing, encountering and experiencing migrant sounds at night, and how, together, Musicbox and Noite Príncipe have become the point of reference for *batida do gueto* culture downtown, as well as a night-time refuge for youths from the *bairros*. Reflecting on the cultural significance of these parties, Isilda Sanches expressed that Noite Príncipe 'turned out to be a monthly mass for the kids in the suburbs. Because it's that time of the month where they can come into the city and feel that's their space' (personal comm., 13 May 2019). As a result of what has been described as a 'social project', marginalized youths are given new ways to build socio-cultural relationships with the centre and gain ownership of a space in which they may celebrate their own music culture. In capitalizing on the power of monthly parties and their capacity to incite change in social life and the city's nightlife context, Noite Príncipe allows producers and consumers of *batida do gueto* to enter into a permanent cultural dialogue between the centre and peripheries.

Performers of Noite Príncipe's monthly ritual light their own paths through the nocturnal geographies that have otherwise made invisible and obscured the stories of African immigrants' contributions to Lisbon's cultural life. Operating in a sphere marked by and romanticized for its supernatural, elusive and 'strangely familiar but also otherworldly' ethos (Dunn 2016: 47), night-time music-making for these architects is the primary mode through which they present their musical creations. Rather than being the 'invisible media' (Brooks 2021), forgotten once the music is turned off and the lights raised, Noite Príncipe is a space where Lisbon's artists of *batida do gueto* centre their aesthetic qualities and virtuosic rhythms – and in so doing, shape Lisbon's social and cultural intimacies through a musical form.

NOTES

1. The sentiment of nostalgia or longing, most often associated with the Portuguese.
2. Sub-culture genre of hip-hop that formed in Portugal in the 1990s. 'Tuga' is short for Portuguese.
3. A musical genre that draws on sonic and cultural elements of Angolan *kuduro*, as well as UK derived bass music like grime, dubstep and breakbeat. Progressive *kuduro* emerged in Lisbon in the early 2000s and gained international recognition through the Portuguese music group Buraka Som Sistema (2006–16).
4. While the group's name is written as 'Dj's Do Guetto' in the original album artwork, the group would later become popularized by its creolized name, 'Dj's Di Guetto'.

5. 'Bagdad' is a nickname for the *bairro* in Rinchoa, a municipality of Sintra, located about 15 km from Lisbon.
6. '2685-2686' is a reference to the postal code of the parish of Sacavém. Sacavém, which is located in the municipality of Loures, is home to the *bairro* of Quinta do Mocho.
7. There are very few females that participate as music producers or DJs of *batida do gueto*. From the crews to the audiences at performance spaces, *batida do gueto* is a male-dominated space. There is, however, a small handful of female producers, the most well-known being the Príncipe Discos artist Nídia who has garnered national and international recognition.
8. Interestingly, DJ Marfox's own adoption of 'fox' is inspired by the Nintendo game series, *Star Fox*. FL Studio's compositional method of configuring 'colorful blocks of sound' finds parallels with video games and gaming, and has been substantively explored by music journalists and scholars such as D'Errico (2018) and Moseley (2013).
9. Despite the expansion of new forms of citizenship under the 2006 reform, the new law gives prevalence to the *jus sanguinis* principle. As such, it is important to take note of how it continued to both reinforce and favour the principles of *jus sanguinis* by creating new ways for Portuguese descendants abroad to acquire citizenship. While only sons and daughters of Portuguese emigrants had the right to Portuguese nationality under the 1981 law, under the new citizenship law, third-generation descendants of Portuguese emigrants living abroad in countries with large communities of Portuguese descendants are considered Portuguese at birth. Gil and Piçarra (2020: 1) remark that 'they just have to declare their wish to be Portuguese or to register the birth in the Portuguese register of births'. On the other hand, the *jus soli* principle is 'not an autonomous criterion for acquiring Portuguese citizenship' (Gil and Piçarra 2020: 1).
10. For seven years, Enchufada hosted the popular 'Hard Ass Sessions' club night at the downtown venue Lux Frágil. The year 2018 marked the start of the label's new club night 'Na Surra' at B.Leza.

REFERENCES

Alge, Barbara (2015), 'Lusofonia, a (R)Evolução: Discourses of Atlantic roots and routes in <<Luso World Music>>', *Norient Academic*, 6 March, https://norient.com/academic/alge2013. Accessed 15 October 2017.

Arenas, Fernando (2010), *Lusophone Africa: Beyond Independence*, Minneapolis: University of Minnesota Press.

Bartmanski, Dominik and Woodward, Ian (2015), *Vinyl: The Analogue Record in the Digital Age*, New York: Bloomsburg Academic.

Batalha, Luis and Carling, Jørgen (eds) (2008), 'Cape Verdean migration and diaspora', in *Transnational Archipelago: Perspectives on Cape Verdean Migration and Diaspora*, Amsterdam: Amsterdam University Press.

Brooks, Daphne A. (2021), *Liner Notes for the Revolution: The Intellectual Life of Black Feminist Sound*, Cambridge: Harvard University Press.

Calvo, Daniel Malet, Díaz, Ana López, Geraldes, Miguel, Martins, Carlos, Nofre, Jordi, Pereira, Patrícia, Sánchez-Fuarros, Íñigo and Soares, Isabel (2017), 'Exploring nightlife and urban change in Bairro Alto, Lisbon', *City and Community*, 16:3, pp. 330–44.

Campos, Ricardo, Nunes, Pedro and Simões, José Alberto (2016), 'Protest rap and young Afro-descendants in Portugal', in J. Sardinha and R. Campos (eds), *Transglobal Sounds: Music, Youth and Migration*, New York: Bloomsbury Academic, pp. 113–32.

Cidra, Rui (2002), '"Ser real": o rap na construção de identidades na Área Metropolitana de Lisboa', *Ethnologia*, 12:14, pp. 189–222.

D'Errico, Mike (2018), 'Technologies of play in hip-hop and electronic dance music production and performance', in S. Bennett and E. Bates (eds), *Critical Approaches to the Production of Music and Sound*, New York: Bloomsbury Publishing, pp. 138–56.

Dunn, Nick (2016), *Dark Matters: A Manifesto for the Nocturnal City*, Lanham: John Hunt Publishing.

Epalanga, Kalaf (2017), *Também Os Brancos Sabem Dançar: Um Romance Musical*, Lisboa: Caminho, SA.

Farrugia, Rebekah (2009), 'Building a women-centered DJ collective: From San Francisco to cyberspace to Sister USA', *Feminist Media Studies*, 9:3, pp. 335–51.

Fradique, Teresa (2003), *Fixar o movimento—representações da música rap em Portugal*, Lisbon: D. Quixote Publications.

Fradique, Teresa (2018), 'Spaces of representation: Identity, otherness and transformation in Portuguese hip-hop', in R. Martins and M. Canevacci (eds), *Lusophone Hip-Hop: 'Who We Are' and 'Where We Are': Identity, Urban Culture and Belonging*, Canon Pyon: Sean Kingston Publishing, pp. 61–80.

Garcia, Luis-Manuel (2013), 'Crowd solidarity on the dance floor in Paris and Berlin', in F. Holt and C. Wergin (eds), *Musical Performance and the Changing City: Post-Industrial Contexts in Europe and the United States*, New York: Routledge, pp. 227–55.

George, Brian (2007), 'Rapping at the margins: Musical constructions of identities in contemporary France', in I. Biddle and V. Knights (eds), *Music, National Identity and the Politics of Location: Between the Global and the Local*, Burlington: Ashgate, pp. 93–114.

Gil, Ana Rita and Piçarra, Nuno (2020), 'Report on citizenship law: Portugal', *Global Citizenship Observatory: Robert Schuman Centre for Advanced Studies*, Florence: European University Institute, https://cadmus.eui.eu/bitstream/handle/1814/66204/RSCAS_GLOBALCIT_CR_2020_1.pdf?sequence=1. Accessed 10 February 2021.

Grazian, David (2008), *On the Make: The Hustle of Urban Nightlife*, Chicago: University of Chicago Press.

Hall, Stuart (1994), 'Cultural identity and diaspora', in L. Chrisman and P. Williams (eds), *Colonial Discourse and Post-Colonial Theory: A Reader*, New York: Columbia University Press, pp. 227–37.

Kenny, Ailbhe and Young, Katie (2021), '"The house of the Irish": African migrant musicians and the creation of diasporic space at night', *Ethnomusicology Forum*, https://doi.org/10.1080/17411912.2021.1938623. Accessed 2 July 2021.

Kidula, Jean (2012), 'The local and global in Kenyan rap and hip hop culture', in E. Charry (ed.), *Hip Hop Africa: New African Music in a Globalizing World*, Bloomington; Indiana University Press, pp. 171–86.

La Barre, Jorge de (2010), 'Music, city, ethnicity: Exploring music scenes in Lisbon', *Migrações Journal*, 7, October, pp. 139–56.

La Barre, Jorge de (2018), 'The sampling of Lisbon: Hip-hop and the lusophone imagination', in R. Martins and M. Canevacci (eds), *Lusophone Hip-Hop: 'Who We Are' and 'Where We Are': Identity, Urban Culture and Belonging*, Canon Pyon: Sean Kingston Publishing, pp. 80–99.

La Barre, Jorge de (2019), 'Sampling Lisbon: Kuduro and the lusophone imagination', *Journal of Popular Music Studies*, 31:1, pp. 109–30.

La Barre, Jorge de and Vanspauwen, Bart (2013), 'A musical lusophonia: Music scenes and the imagination of Lisbon', *The World of Music (New Series)*, 2:2, pp. 119–46.

Lacaille, Jeanne (2019), 'Príncipe Discos: The highway to royalty', *Pan African Music*, 29 November, https://pan-african-music.com/en/Príncipe-discos-the-highway-to-royalty/?fbclid=IwAR1QsG7OsySEH2EAzh9-53-vt7OvzbswxgmutO02pSVBM04Kvg0cSnkXHUs. Accessed 13 December 2019.

Lupati, Federica and Rendeiro, Margarida (eds) (2020), 'Introduction', in *Challenging Memories and Rebuilding Identities: Literary and Artistic Voices That Undo the Lusophone Atlantic*, New York: Routledge, pp. 1–13.

McGregor, Andrew and Gibson, Chris (2009), 'Musical work in a university town: The shifting spaces and practices of DJs in Dunedin', *Asia Pacific Viewpoint*, 50:3, pp. 277–88.

Moseley, Roger (2013), 'Playing games with music (and vice versa): Ludomusicological perspectives on guitar hero and rock band', in N. Cook and R. Pettengill (eds), *Taking it to the Bridge: Music as Performance*, Ann Arbor: University of Michigan Press, pp. 279–318.

Nofre, Jordi (2013), 'Vintage nightlife: Gentrifying Lisbon downtown', *Fennia*, 191:2, pp. 106–21.

Nofre, Jordi, Martins, João C., Vaz, Domingos, Fina, Rosa, Sequera, Jorge and Vale, Patricia (2019), 'The "Pink Street" in Cais do Sodré: Urban change and liminal governance in a nightlife district of Lisbon', *Urban Research & Practice*, 12:4, pp. 332–40.

Pardue, Derek (2015), *Cape Verde, Let's Go: Creole Rappers and Citizenship in Portugal*, Urbana: University of Illinois Press.

Príncipe Discos (n.d.), Bandcamp page, https://principediscos.bandcamp.com/community. Accessed 1 December 2022.

Pritchard, John, Moura, Filipe, de Abreu e Silva, João and Martinez, M. Luis (2014), 'Spatial analysis of transportation-related social exclusion in the Lisbon metropolitan area', *Procedia: Social and Behavioral Sciences*, 111, pp. 440–49.

Ranocchiari, Dario (2011), 'Between the *bairro* and the nation: Performative identities of Afro-Lusitan rap music in Lisbon', *Music & Politics*, 5:1, pp. 65–76.

Raposo, Otávio and Marcon, Frank (2021), 'The black beat of Lisbon: Sociabilities, music and resistances', in R. Campos and J. Nofre (eds), *Exploring Ibero-American Youth Cultures in the 21st Century*, Cham: Palgrave Macmillan, pp. 175–98.

Santos, Sofia (2016), 'Who are you calling sub/urban? Socio-spatial inequality and mobility in the Lisbon metropolitan area', *Portuguese Journal of Social Science*, 15:2, pp. 387–407.

Sedano, Livia Jiménez (2019), '"From Angola to the world", from the world to Lisbon and Paris: How structural inequalities shaped the global *kizomba* dance industry', *Poetics*, 75, n.pag.

Shipley, Jesse Weaver (2013), *Living the Hiplife: Celebrity and Entrepreneurship in Ghanaian Popular Music*, Durham: Duke University Press.

Zukin, Sharon (2010), *Naked City: The Death and Life of Authentic Urban Places*, New York: Oxford University Press.

8

(Be)Longing: Irish Musicking and Place-Making in Oslo, Norway

Áine Mangaoang

In this chapter, I highlight issues of identity, belonging and place-making posed by individuals in Oslo's Irish music night scenes. I draw from narratives and stories told through semi-structured interviews and conversations with seven musicians, each of whom plays Irish music[1] of various forms, styles and genres in Oslo (see Table 8.1), along with participant observations at different musical events in the city and other ethnographic and archival methods since late 2018. Additionally, the chapter is informed by my own experiences as an Irish migrant navigating a new city through music, as I became involved in Oslo's live music scene soon after my arrival to Norway. Such stories are not representative in any statistical sense, but rather they provide useful points of departure for investigating specific sonic entanglements and social encounters between different people who call Oslo home.

The chapter aims to illustrate the ways in which migrants interact with Irish music alongside local kinds of music and musicians, and by doing so, contributes to a wider discourse on contemporary migrant experiences. I survey how various forms of musicking[2] are used in Oslo by this small community made up of Irish immigrants, migrants from other countries as well as local Norwegians, in the production of a range of complex Irish cultural identities set against ongoing theorizations of multi-culturalism in contemporary Norway.[3] I discuss the multi-faceted Nordic staging of Irishness in Oslo's nightlife and seek to give voice to a range of more 'hidden' (Finnegan 1989) experiences of Irishness in Oslo that show it to be multiple and nuanced, not least since the COVID-19 pandemic curtailed almost all formalized night-time activity between March 2020 and up to the time of writing in April 2021. This

TABLE 8.1: Overview of interlocutors interviewed in Spring 2020.

Name	Sex	Nationality/ citizenship	Age	Years in Oslo	Main instrument(s)
Anders	M	Norwegian	34	5.5	Piano accordion
Brendan	M	Irish	60	1	Uilleann pipes, flute, guitar, bouzouki
Kaja	F	Polish	31	6	Guitar, tin whistle, bodhrán
Liz	F	Irish	62	26	Voice
Michael	M	American	27	2	Fiddle
Patrick	M	German/ Irish	33	8	Guitar, banjo, voice
Snorre	M	Norwegian	45	45	Fiddle, concertina

focus on Irish music scenes in Oslo is both distinct in terms of its place within the urban landscape and given particular social etiquette surrounding Oslo's nightlife, yet in many respects, it may be scarcely unlike Irish music practices in other capital cities world over. Before turning to some thematic findings, to set the scene the following section briefly describes Irish music as defined in a Norwegian context by my interlocutors and gives an overview of the Irish music scenes in Oslo as they have come to be today.

Irish music in contemporary Oslo

> *Music is a very important part of growing up in Ireland. You absorb Irish music tradition through the breastmilk, and most of us also take it with us into adolescence and adulthood. Maybe that's why Irish rock bands usually sing more from their heart than their English counterparts?*
>
> (Gjerstad 1988: n.pag, trans. by author)

Locally and internationally, there has been a long and symbolic association between Ireland and music that often attributes to Irish people 'an inherent, if not generalized, talent in and appreciation for unspecified genres of music' (Mangaoang et al. 2020: 10). Such 'recurring myths' about the Irish and their 'natural proclivity for music and song' can be traced back to twelfth-century anthropological–colonial discourse and constructions of Irishness (McLoughlin and McLoone 2000: 181), and are perhaps bolstered by Ireland's adoption of a symbolic musical instrument – the Irish harp – as a cultural, political and financial emblem of Ireland since the early twentieth century (Mangaoang 2019). Indeed, the assumed musicality of Irish people has permeated even into Scandinavian cultural discourse. Take the above quotation from a Norwegian newspaper by Leif Gjerstad, awkwardly entitled *Morsmelk-musikk fra Irland* ('Breastmilk music from Ireland'), which takes the Norwegian metaphor of being introduced to something from birth (*å få det inn med morsmelken* ['absorbed through the breastmilk']) and applies it, however ineptly, to Irish people and their apparent genetic predisposition towards music and musicality. Nevertheless, notions of Irishness and a supposed 'inherent musicality continue to be endorsed, both implicitly and explicitly' (O'Flynn 2009: 22) across a range of platforms today.

Any contemporary definition of Irish music can and will include as many musical styles and genres as we have different countries that we call home, since such an umbrella term might include everything from radio-friendly pop and underground hip-hop that is produced in Ireland to contemporary Irish chamber ensembles and *sean-nós* (solo, ornamental, unaccompanied) singing. For my musician-interlocutors in Oslo, Irish music holds just as many meanings, definitions and connotations. For example, uillean piper, Brendan, described his understanding of Irish music in broad, quasi-abstract terms: 'Irish music is history, it is a way of life basically [...] the whole thing about Irish music is a sharing, is a cultural thing'. For Brendan, Irish music encapsulates a romanticized multitude of styles and genres that, for him, are rooted in history and a culture of sharing.

To others, Irish music conjures up a slightly narrower definition. For guitarist, Patrick, any mention of Irish music primarily calls to mind the social interaction of sessions and the musical genres of trad and folk music.

> There's the traditional music that's defined by the tunes, the themes, and the lyrics often, and the sound of it, acoustic instruments and so on. Sessions [...] I guess there's the trad track and there's the pop track, really. [But] when someone says Irish music, I think of trad mainly. Trad and folk.

Patrick's remarks chime in with the observations of numerous scholars, where rather essentialist 'notions equating "Irish traditional music" with "Irish music" appear to prevail', and suggests that while many people acknowledge such a view as being 'culturally embedded, it is not uncritically received' (O'Flynn 2009: 21).

Irish traditional music has enthusiasts around the world, in Ireland and within the many well-established diasporic Irish communities across the United States and the United Kingdom, as well as among people and places who may have little to no relationship to Ireland whatsoever. The international popularity of folk-trad groups like The Dubliners and The Chieftains in the 1960s and 1970s, followed by the global success of Irish dance shows like Riverdance (1994) and its spin-offs, gave rise to new generations of Irish music fans around the world, including Norway. Norwegian piano accordion player, Anders, who specializes in Irish traditional music, describes the problematic encounters with Irish music definitions he faces in getting gig requests as an Irish trad musician:

> One of the challenges with playing Irish music, I guess, especially outside of Ireland, [is that] compared to Norwegian music, Irish music is much more widely known. People have more an idea, or *think* they have an idea about what Irish music is and what is sounds like. What most people hear in their head when you talk about Irish music is that whole pub song, drinking song thing, with like The Dubliners. I don't have anything against that music, but that's not what I enjoy doing. I do get a few requests of: 'We are having an Irish pub night somewhere, can you come and play'. I know that they want someone to come and sing 'Seven Drunken Nights' and 'Whiskey in the Jar'. That's not what I do! There are some challenges with communication with those kinds of gigs.

While it appears that a thirst for Irish music continues within Oslo nightlife, the paid gigs tend to be the more Irish pub song acts who can deliver the well-known Irish hits like 'Whiskey in the Jar', rather than those well-versed in polkas, reels and slip-jigs from the West of Ireland. Patrick, who plays in an Irish folk-rock band inspired by The Pogues and Dropkick Murphy's, explains that the largely Norwegian audiences at his gigs come up to the band to say how much they are enjoying the music – that his band's high-energy pub gigs provide an often-welcome contrast to the typically restrained conventions of Norwegian nightlife, where cover bands like his are more of an anomaly than in Ireland, at least.

Aside from pub gigs, some interlocutors consider that the overall status of Irish folk music in Norway has waned in recent years. Anders gives his perspective on the rise and subsequent fall of Irish music in a Scandinavian context:

> Irish music isn't that popular in Norway now. I think it was very popular back in the '90s with Riverdance and all that stuff, but these days it's not super popular in the folk scene. Many festivals have a couple of Celtic acts on, but [...] Irish music just isn't super popular in the folk scene in Scandinavia, or at least not in Norway, at the moment.

Nonetheless for a beta[4] city of its size and population, with limited well-established migrant communities, and an apparent decrease in popularity of Irish folk in comparison to Norwegian and Scandinavian folk music, Oslo has a remarkable quantity and variable quality of performances of Irish culture spread across the calendar year. These range from the more spectacular annual festivities around St. Patrick's Day, Oslo Bloomsday Society festival with public readings and music inspired by James Joyce's *Ulysses*, *Nollaig na mBan* ('Women's Christmas') gatherings respite with sing-songs, to the more every day – or more accurately, every *night* – events that punctuate the working-week such as the trad *seisiún* (hereafter session) in the city's Irish pub every Tuesday and Saturday nights, the Irish community choir rehearsals on Thursday evenings, and the Irish troubadour singing cover songs at the sports bar on a Friday night. The latter three regular activities are of particular interest for this chapter, summarized as follows.

Weekly trad sessions at the Dubliner

The session is at the heart of the Irish traditional music community globally. Historically, sessions took place in the home. The pub session is a relatively recent development in the history of Irish music, having developed in the early twentieth century and popularized by Irish emigrants in London during the 1940s and 1950s (Leonard 2005; Williams 2020). As such, one of the most symbolic features of Irish music was created by Irish migrants away from 'home'. Since then, pub sessions have varied considerably in size, standard, instruments and etiquette. In that regard, Oslo is no different. Sessions are an informal gathering of trad musicians for the purpose of playing tunes and singing songs, with an occasional poem or story should any patrons feel so inclined. Dancing might also ensue, often spontaneously. While the Oslo trad sessions are informal, and there is no (paid) leader, there is a clear founder of these sessions – Northern Irish fiddler David 'Davy' Patterson Dick. Davy Dick is credited with being a crucial player in Oslo's music scene since the 1960s, for being an informal teacher and mentor for scores of aspiring Norwegian trad musicians, and for establishing the first Tuesday night trad sessions in Oslo over 35 years ago, which moved around to various locations from the 1980s until settling at its current location, The Dubliner Folk Pub. Since 1994, The Dubliner has been the centre of gravity of Oslo's Irish trad scene. Though owned by a Norwegian businessman, the bar is primarily staffed by migrant workers, especially Irish emigrants, which is noted by many patrons as adding to its 'authentic feel'. With old church pews aligning the front bar, its handmade stained-glass windows and large cosy fireplaces, the bar became a hub for Irish traditional music sessions within a year of opening and have continued to today.[5] The bar hosts trad sessions on Tuesday and Saturday evenings, and live bands – frequently flown over from Ireland – on the bar's modest stage most weekends.

Session musicians in Oslo receive no payment, though all players can avail of staff discounts on their beers, which with the price of alcohol in Oslo, is considered a rather fair incentive. Like Irish sessions the world over, musicians gather in an informal circle towards each other, for Irish trad is performed for the players' enjoyment first and foremost, rather than any audience who may or may not have gathered to listen in. Oslo's two sessions have gone through various changes over the years with an assortment of instruments and quality to be had. Two distinctly diverse sessions are now in existence, with a small handful of players consistently participating in their session of choice. The Tuesday night sessions (Figure 8.1), located in a quiet, dark corner tucked away at the back of the bar, are considered to be the more tune-focused session, instrumental rather than singing, and since the majority of regulars to these weeknight sessions are Norwegian or Scandinavian-speaking, the working language of these session tends to be Norwegian.[6] In contrast, the Saturday sessions (Figure 8.2) take place in the front bar, right next to the main entrance, and welcome a wide array of songs and session styles alongside Irish traditional music. Here, the working language is primarily English, with smatterings of Norwegian here and there, reflecting a more international – or more recently arrived – mix of migrant musicians from Ireland and beyond. Despite sharing the same venue albeit on different nights, these two musical contexts reveal how migrants experience Oslo's nightly music scenes in different ways and temporalities.

FIGURE 8.1: A Tuesday night tunes session in the back bar of the Dubliner, August 2019. Source: The Dubliner Facebook page.

FIGURE 8.2: A guitar-heavy Saturday night session in full flow in the front bar of The Dubliner Folk Pub, Rådhusgata 28, Oslo, October 2020. © Linn Schjerven.

Weekend Irish cover bands and troubadour gigs

The Dubliner is also one of the main employers of bands playing Irish folk-rock styles, with live music programmed on stage in their pub, most Thursday, Friday and Saturday nights. These musical acts include local bands with a mix of nationalities including Irish and Norwegian; more frequently, bands are invited over from Ireland and the wider Irish diaspora. International bands would usually be contracted to play a minimum of three gigs from Thursday to Saturday, or sometimes a residency of six or seven gigs over a ten-day period during particularly busy periods in Oslo's nightlife such as *Julebord* season.[7] The format of these sets would be three 45-minute sets starting from 9:30 p.m. on weekday nights, and 10:30 p.m. at the weekends, often with the tacit expectation that bands will continue playing for as long as the bar is still serving. Interlocutor Patrick, who has played at the Dubliner regularly both as a solo troubadour and as part of his band, Kearney's Dog, comments that from the bar's point of view 'they think "we sell more beer when there's music here!"' While international bands have their airfare covered, and are adequately paid with accommodation provided, the economics of such tours may not always be particularly lucrative for touring bands given the extortionate cost of living in Oslo, as well as the expense of alcohol and other aspects of the city's nightlife. One former barman at The Dubliner joked that some touring bands would end up owing more money to the pub for drinks consumed during a residency than what they were paid for the gigs themselves.

In addition to The Dubliner, a Danish-owned, international chain of Irish bars opened in nine pubs first with the name Mulligan's Irish Pub and subsequently under the name The Old Irish Pub in Norway since 2018, with three branches in Oslo (Figure 8.3). In contrast to their name, The Old Irish Pubs in Oslo operate under a rather different aesthetic to The Dubliner's snug, old-world feel, with high ceilings, neon lights and murals of leprechauns and shamrocks painted on the walls. Yet they are a key player in keeping musicians employed and entertaining local audiences. The Old Irish Pubs pride themselves in offering live music every week, stating on their website that 'Every weekend we fly in musicians from Ireland, among other places, to give you authentic musical experiences' (The Old Irish Pub 2021: n.pag., trans. by author). Conflating the importation of musicians directly 'from Ireland' with notions of authenticity through publicly signalling a link between ethnicity and citizenship, even though musicians 'from Ireland' may well encompass many ethnicities and nationalities, the bar chain also advertised for musicians from within Norway to perform at their branches in Oslo and Stavanger, with no restrictions on the musician's ethnicity. Instead, the advertisement emphasizes that they seek 'high energy solo performers, who can entertain in an Irish pub-style', as well as 'Party Bands – 80s, 90s Pop/Rock, solo, Irish-style pub entertainers, acoustic guitar and

FIGURE 8.3: The logo for 'The Old Irish Pub' chain of bars, with 'Est. 1873' embedded in the logo underneath the name; written to the side in Danish and Norwegian: 'Vi ses!' ('see you!'). Source: The Old Irish Pub website. © Linn Schjerven.

vocal, Irish style pub duos/trios all who must have at least five years' experience' (Brophy Booking 2019: n.pag.). While both pubs claim to deliver 'authentic' experiences of Irishness to Norwegian nightlife, especially through their highly visible use of Irish music and of hiring musicians from Ireland, the bars perform their version of Irishness in decidedly different ways. Of course, both pubs' claims to authenticity are highly disputable, instead raising questions about whether their perceived Irishness is more 'genuine' or whether it can be viewed as staged, manufactured or 'plastic'.

The Mná na hÉireann choir

The Mná na hÉireann ('Women of Ireland') choir, known as the Mná Singers by members, is a community choir of about 20 women with an Irish background. They specialize in learning Irish repertoire – broadly conceived as any songs produced in Ireland, by Irish people, or songs popularized by Irish artists – including a range of macaronic songs sung in Irish, English and Norwegian. An intergenerational group, the youngest member is 17, while several older members are in their 70s. Many are Irish-born women who initially migrated to Norway for love to marry Norwegian spouses several decades ago, while most of the younger members in their 20s and 30s migrated to study and/or work, having secured skilled jobs in Oslo.[8] The group emerged from an existing Mná na hÉireann network of Irish emigrants in Oslo who meet annually at *Nollaig na mBan* gatherings and other intervals including St. Patrick's Day and summer get-togethers. Interlocutor Liz founded the choir in 2016 with the explicit aim of connecting with the Irish community in Oslo, having found few opportunities to connect with other members of the Irish diaspora, stressing that the choir is informal – there are no auditions, no requirements to read musical notation – and is open to all women in the Irish community and affinity diaspora in Norway. The larger Mná network in Oslo has an active Facebook group, where they advertise choir practices and recruit new choir members, which is how I was invited to join soon after I arrived in Oslo. Initially, evening choir rehearsals were generously accommodated at the Irish Embassy offices in downtown Oslo after the diplomatic staff had finished work, aided a great deal by the fact that one of the choir members was the spouse of the then-Irish Ambassador to Norway. More recently, the choir meet for rehearsals at various venues around Oslo, depending on availability, funding and other variable factors, including in pre-booked rooms at the new Deichman Public Library, rehearsal rooms at Øvingshotellet,[9] and at times in members' homes and gardens. With a repertoire that includes Irish lullabies and nonsense songs to singles by Sinéad O'Connor and The Cranberries, the choir have performed at different public and private events within the Irish community (Figure 8.4). They also conduct outreach into

FIGURE 8.4: Members of the Mná na hÉireann choir perform with The Chieftains at Cosmopolite Scene, May 2018. Courtesy of the author.

the civic community through annual performances at cancer centres and carol singing in different Oslo neighbourhoods at Christmastime.[10]

Themes

The themes discussed here are taken from one-to-one interviews with interlocutors, five of which were held over videoconferencing, one in-person, and one written correspondence, during Spring 2021. Five interlocutors responded to an open call for participants that I posted to the Irish Sessions at The Dubliner Facebook page, followed by an additional two recruited through snowball sampling (see Table 8.1). Five men and two women were interviewed, ranging in age from 27 to 62 years old. All interlocutors self-identified as musicians and singers who performed Irish music, and all but one currently lived in Oslo – one having recently relocated from Oslo to the Norwegian countryside. With their consent, interviews were audio-recorded, fully transcribed and read multiple times to identify and code the main recurring themes.

The narratives of my interlocutors suggest that Irish musicking plays an important role in social integration at night and that such acts of cultural immersion are a two-way street. The following two key themes emerged from their narratives: '(Be)Longing: Irish music as social and cultural integration at night' and 'Rifts and ruptures: Musicking, tension and cultural difference'.

(Be)Longing: Irish music as 'home' and social integration at night

'Home' is a challenging concept to unravel, and becomes even more complex against wider discussions of globalization, transnationalism and hyper-mobility. In the context of the many migrants who participate in Irish musicking in Oslo, the concept of 'home' becomes extremely powerful for those physically distanced from it, and if we listen, this longing seems particularly potent at night. Scholars have long asserted that music is central to the affective realm of this diasporic experience and provides a sonic anchor 'linking homeland and here-land with an intricate network of sound' (Slobin 1994: 243). It is no surprise, then, that Irish music has special meaning for Irish emigrants in Oslo, who use an array of multi-sensorial, kinesthetic language to describe the feeling of listening to and performing Irish music away from the homeland. Liz depicts her response to singing Irish music at night-time sessions and rehearsals in Oslo as an evocative, emotional experience:

> It makes me feel like I'm home. Wherever I am in the whole world, and I hear Irish music, then it brings me a little bit home. It is like a smell. The sound really grounds

> me […] You can close your eyes and you can be in that place […] For me, even though I am born and raised in Limerick, I spend a lot of time in Clare, and I have a place in Clare. I mentioned The Kilfenora Céili Band earlier, and for me I can almost smell the sea when I listen to The Kilfenora Céili Band. Though I am sure they would rarely play on the beach in Kilkee!

While Liz acknowledges the at once incongruous reaction to her musical homesickness, this kind of response to music as providing an embodied sense of place is also well documented in research among Americans with Irish heritage (Dillane 2013). For an American fiddler, Michael, whose father's family moved to the United States from Ireland in the 1910s, a move to Oslo gave him the opportunity to learn a musical style that for him, felt like a connection with his Irish ancestors.

> I had been playing and discovering new types of fiddle music throughout my 20s and after moving to Oslo I took the opportunity to start learning Irish tunes and trying them out at the session.

Michael's desire to use Irish culture through Oslo's night-time trad sessions to connect with his Irish heritage mirrors that of many Americans who claim Irish ancestry (Williams 2020). He feels a certain responsibility towards at least trying out an aspect of Irishness through learning fiddle tunes, both as a homage to his Irish ancestors and in honour of his Irish names, having been named after deceased Irish family members. Meanwhile, Liz's response to listening to *céili* music at home at night, however paradoxical and knowing, and Michael's connection to playing Irish fiddle tunes at nocturnal sessions resonates with previous scholarship on notions of 'home' in the diasporic imagination, where it becomes an almost mythic place of desire (Brah 1996: 192), coupled with these occurrences happening at night, where 'things supposedly missing are keenly felt' (Dunn 2016: 14).

More surprising, perhaps, are narratives of Irish music feeling like home for more than those with Irish ancestry, however many generations ago it may be. Take, for example, the following quotations from Polish guitarist, Kaja and Norwegian concertina player, Snorre, neither of whom have any Irish heritage connection but who feel strong, emotive responses of feeling at 'home' when playing Irish music during nocturnal sessions at The Dubliner.

> I think that The Dubliner is my second home […] it's *our place* […] I'm sure I'm not the only one thinking of The Dubliner as a second home. This is our place where we play music and we know the staff and we know the place, and we know each other.
>
> (Kaja)

> The Dubliner has a reputation outside of Oslo, so there is a lot of people going if they are here for a conference or for some other thing [...] They come in and clap and dance, shout out a lot and do all the things they think they are supposed to do, and then they ask if anyone can sing 'Whiskey in the Jar' and we tell them to fuck off in a nice way. This is *our house*, not theirs, you know!
>
> (Snorre)

Kaja's feeling of being at once part of a collective when playing Irish music in 'our place' and its association with being a 'second home' for the musicians, chimes with Snorre's sense of ownership over the space when the musicians are in full flow of a session and abruptly interrupted by an innocent reveller. For Snorre, the connection between Irish music and home is further complex, as he describes his 30+ year bond with Irish music. He explains the emotional dichotomy involved when trying to reconcile his lifelong experiences of travelling to Ireland to play music, the relationships formed through music-making, yet the feeling of alienation of being *not* Irish. Snorre says:

> [T]o actually be able to put into words my relationship with Irish music and Irish culture is [...] when I go to Ireland, I feel very much at home, and I feel very much like a stranger. It's a strong duality ... I'm definitely a part of the affinity diaspora.

Both Kaja and Snorre's observations of feeling 'home' in connection to nocturnal music sessions at the Dubliner echo what music scholar Sean Williams' describes as Ireland's exceptional status as 'a kind of fictive homeland for people with no heritage connection, but who are profoundly attracted by its music' (2020: 5).

Each interlocutor further remarked on the highly social aspects of Irish musicking as being distinctly positive qualities that endeared them to the form, a theme which echoes previous scholarship on music's distinctly social qualities and abilities to create 'communities of musical practice' (Kenny 2016). In Oslo, Irish musicking facilitates intergenerational social interaction between the Irish diasporic community and those from other backgrounds. For American fiddler, Michael, Polish guitarist, Kaja and Irish uillean piper, Brendan, the night-time sessions at the Dubliner were a crucial part of developing a social network soon after they first moved to Norway, to create friendships that extended far beyond Tuesday or Saturday nights. For Norwegian musician Snorre, the significance of playing Irish music lies not only in the tunes but in the complex social interactions offered through the session, where locals can learn more than just the music from migrant musicians. As Snorre explains, the nocturnal session is fertile ground for Norwegians like him to leave behind the constraints of the day and learn the specific social subtleties of slagging and other forms of banter that are the lifeblood of many Irish sessions.

> Being in sessions in Ireland will automatically start the immersion project because you are there with Irish people doing Irish stuff. I had that from Norway, because when I joined the session, Davy Dick and other expats in the session – the language was English – and I learned about slagging in Norway from expats. It is a different tone, you know! I am a socially outgoing person, but I noticed players in sessions in Norway, Norwegians who don't grasp the social dynamics.

The art of slagging – a 'jovial or artful teasing' – is recognized as a 'favourite conversational pastime of many Irish people', of which musicians are thought to be 'particularly adept' (Williams 2020: 12). Snorre continues, stressing the vital role of Irish music as a collaborative, performative form.

> Music to me is a very social thing […] Two musicians can always make better music than one! All my best musical moments I have had with other people, with creating a common groove. When you hit the sweet spot of rhythm and style, you know, that's it! You think in the same ways and […] the sort of community feeling, that's very important in music.

This 'community feeling' of Irish sessions at night – that is perceived as unique for many musicians from other musical cultures – is what gives Irish music its value for the musicians who play it, who experience it as valuable both as an aesthetic and collaborative practice. These kinds of musical–social interactions offer novel ways for migrants, Irish and others, to integrate into Norwegian society by supporting the creation of local spaces of belonging that are largely led by members of migrant communities, and crucially, are offered *on their terms*.

Rifts and ruptures: Musicking, tension and cultural difference

Scholars have noted how the performance of Irish traditional music provided a path for Irish emigrants to connect with others and express their perceived cultural difference (Leonard 2005). For interlocutors of different nationalities, the public performance of Irish music in bars, concert venues or public spaces serves as a relaxed entry point for culturally curious locals to learn more about Irish culture and heritage. Snorre admits that to receive any outward reaction or recognition from local pub patrons during their night-time sessions is to be considered remarkable for the more reserved Norwegians.

> Because [sessions] are not a common thing in Norwegian culture as such – where people play informally – we are more used to formal music, a band or a piano-player or something like that; it has an organic feel to it as well, that you never know the dynamics and how powerful it's going to be. Some nights are quiet, and some are not. That is contagious as well [...] If it was a good night for music, people stick their head in and say thanks for the music, which is a fair step for Norwegians to take!

Some interlocutors express surprise, disappointment and even frustration at the stereotypically refined and private reactions from Norwegian audiences to hearing Irish music in informal, hidden settings, especially in contrast to clichéd connections or romanticized responses from Irish audiences. From Liz's perspective,

> Norwegians are extremely polite; they are extremely private, and they are extremely loyal and good people [...] But they are not very open, and they control their curiosity as well I think, which is unfortunate. A Norwegian is unlikely to tap you on your shoulder and say: 'I hear you. Where are you from and what are you singing?' In Ireland they would be asking you straight away your life history, and that is very different. Sometimes I appreciate that in Norwegian society, people just leave me alone and I can do my own thing [...] They are *tilbakeholden* ['restrained']. It's a resistance in many ways to connect with other people.

Other clashes emerge because of the musical format of the session, where despite the outward appearance of being an open, democratic, and even utopian space, the session is filled with a host of unwritten rules governing the proceedings. Anders describes how possible points of tension arise during the session that requires careful navigation so as not to upset the evening's flow:

> When people show up with the expectation of this jam session thing being something it's not. Like say, you show up with an instrument that isn't suited, or you think you can show up and play pop tunes. In some sessions maybe you can, you just have to use your social intelligence, but I can see a few people feeling that they maybe are being rejected [...] There are definitely no rules, so of course you could have a session where you play country songs and also pop tunes and Norwegian and Swedish folk [...] It's up to the people that shows up, but if 90 percent of the group wants to do one thing and then some people show up and insist on doing something else, that's where the tension arise, I think. There is a lot going on under the surface!

Anders reiterates the 'no rules' at sessions mantra, though for many newcomers to the sessions, it is rarely experienced as a complete free-for-all. Navigating the session's unspoken code can lead to feelings of inclusion and exclusion by interlocutors.

Reflecting on her experiences of founding a choir exclusively for Irish women, Liz questions if the social dynamics within the choir would be more balanced if the choir was open to all genders:

> The fact that we don't have any men, and a lot of woman and strong characters as well [...] maybe, had we had some men as well it would even out the tone a little bit [...] There have been times where there have been some conflicts. Women can be a little bit too direct with each other, and maybe had we had male members we might not have had that. But there is also this camaraderie, this element of like, we are all women in this together, that is also very beautiful. I think that we have appreciated this as well.

Inclusion in Oslo's Irish music scenes may not necessarily be as open or all-encompassing as its members might think. One's status, gender, age, nationality and other identity politics may work for or against one in any social setting, and Oslo's night-time Irish music scene is scarcely different in that regard (cf. Slominski 2020). Indeed, tensions, hierarchies and clashing personalities are to be found in Oslo's Irish music scene, as they may be in sessions and scenes the world over (see Kenny 2016).

Discussion: From night to day – Irish musicking in Oslo during the COVID-19 pandemic

Conducting these conversations with interlocutors during a global pandemic – when international travel to the homeland is curtailed and the city's nightlife has grounded to an abrupt halt – has coloured every aspect of this research, for better or worse. For many Irish emigrants, Irish music has come to fill the void in new ways during such unprecedented times. As Patrick remarked, Irish music comes to mean so much more during the COVID-19 pandemic as 'everyone's a little more homesick'. Listening to and playing more Irish music at home was one of the most notable changes for the musicians I spoke with. While nightly pub sessions represented an important, collective public space for the performance of Irish music, the pandemic moved these sessions to the home, and for those fortunate enough to share a home with other musicians, it remained a collective, yet more private practice. Brendan, who lives with two other musicians, describes the lockdown period as the most musically fruitful time in his life, as he got to experience in-person sessions at home on a near-nightly basis.

> I've been very fortunate in that both the two ladies that I'm living with here, we would sit on a regular basis, on a nightly basis even, and just play tunes together. Because over the years I've learned and collected so many reels, jigs, hornpipes, slip jigs, just tunes of Ireland, and songs, [so] the three of us just have a regular session ... If we're allowed more than two, three people, the weekly Saturday session people would come over to the house and during the week we would have a few tunes, nice glass of wine, have the craic and enjoy it. It's been the best time, literally, the best time of my life!

For musicians like Brendan, the pandemic has not curtailed his nightlife as much as it has blossomed. Thus, for some, the shift in sites of Irish musicking allows for more flexibility or even musical experimentation than in a pub setting, while also paying homage to the very origins of Irish sessions as being the preserve of the private home, where Irish musicking was a sit down in ones' own house.

The fleeting weeks wherein the pandemic eased in Norway and bars were allowed to re-open led to the resumption of reduced live musicking opportunities, affecting Oslo-based musicians in different ways. For Patrick, who received bookings for some Saturday-night slots at The Dubliner:

> It was different already because people weren't allowed dance, weren't allowed come up and talk to you [...] it was quite funny seeing the bar staff, because the later it was getting, they were just more and more like babysitters, like 'don't stand up, sit back down!' Basically! 'Don't go and talk to others!' [laughs] And also then quite depressing to play, because you had this huge empty space in front of you where there used to be people interacting [...] I always thought it was nice when people came up and shook your hand or came up and shouted something in your ear and say 'Great!' or 'Can you do the "Wild Rover?!"' But all those things are just ... [trails off].

Indeed, for musicians like Patrick, it was a strange, surreal, and at times, rather sad experience performing to audiences who were not allowed to leave their seats, as per government guidelines at the time. The weekly trad sessions at The Dubliner also resumed briefly, albeit with the new regulations insisting on one-metre distance between musicians, and a formal list of participants in advance of the sessions – negating the possibility of anyone dropping in as was once the case, along with ubiquitous hand sanitisers. But for Snorre and other musicians, even with the new restrictions the session still worked; there was no outbreaks or incidents, and the opportunity to play tunes together, even while seated a metre apart, was a substantial improvement from playing alone in one's apartment.

For all my interlocutors, the rare occasions when face-to-face musicking recommenced were treasured even more than usual, such as an impromptu Mná performance a few days before Christmas 2020. Remembering this 'pop up' event that took place after dark on the grounds of the Norwegian Royal Palace in downtown Oslo, Liz recalled:

> It was certainly very atmospheric [...] We all turned up and it was a good bunch of us [...] What I remember very vividly about that evening, I had an American friend with me, and she was FaceTiming with her mother in the States, and her mother is in her 90s. We were singing some Irish Christmas carols, some Norwegian, and she was listening in and crying and saying how beautiful it was. Here we are, and we are not just reaching out to Norway ... There were a lot of young soldiers outside guarding the palace, and they were listening to us, so we could see that they were quite enjoying it. We were entertaining them on their rather boring rounds. So, we were reaching out to the local community, and we were reaching out to the community in America [...] I think we were all thrilled to connect with each other through our music, during a period which has been tough for everybody, especially my community and immigrant communities as well, when they can't go home to Ireland. To be able to do this meant so much and was very special.

Under the cover of Oslo after-dark, the nocturnal urban space was transformed into an atmospheric stage, where the women felt comfortable singing nostalgic carols to a handful of strangers on the street (and to a technologically mediated audience in the United States). This low-key, somewhat hidden event on a cold winter night, empowered members of the Irish community to support each other through song – a special solidarity found in an all-female, safe space at night – during what had been an exceptionally difficult year for many.

As we have heard, depending on musicians' living situations, some have enjoyed more creative and musically engaged periods than ever during lockdowns, while others have had their entire musical world upended overnight, with sessions and gigs tours cancelled and no clear guidelines on when they can ever resume. Musicians must constantly operate within the constraints of Oslo's ever-changing pandemic guidelines that fluctuated in severity between complete lockdown and subsequent 'red level' restrictions, which saw all but essential services closed and regulated social contact to a maximum of two visitors to a private household and up to ten in public, outdoor spaces. For migrant interlocutors Brendan, Kaja, and Liz, Oslo's red-level status presented novel challenges for their musicking as they moved sessions and choir rehearsals into public parks whenever conditions allowed. Since Oslo's more severe lockdowns coincided with the colder months, and the Nordic climate after-dark is not conducive to prolonged, open-air musicking, such transitions meant that former night-time events were largely, albeit temporarily, relocated to the day; trad sessions and singing circles moved from night-time indoor venues to afternoon open-air happenings. The shift in Oslo's Irish music scene from indoors to out, and from night to day was assisted by the overwhelmingly acoustic nature of trad sessions and choirs. Yet in this transference from night to day, certain qualities of Oslo's night-time musicking were lost as daytime distractions interfered. In the bright light of day, against a backdrop of noisy traffic, general concerns of the day seem to weigh more heavily than perhaps they do at night. But the resilience of these musicians to take to the often-freezing temperatures to make music together speaks to the essential need for live, face-to-face musical communication against whatever challenging situations.

Conclusion: Integration is a sonic process

Drawing from the narratives of these seven musicians, we hear how Irish music continues to sustain and enlighten these musicians and their fellow residents of Oslo today. Their accounts express how Irish music in Oslo is 'developing into an international language for people from all over the world who know how to play and sing it' (Williams 2020: 4). It's clear that the future of Irish music – in all its guises – looks to be built around a 'shared love of sounds we will probably always call "Irish", but without the limitations of static, essentialized identity' (Slominski 2020: 174). Migrant musicians, and their local collaborators, contribute to the artistic life of Oslo through their unfailing work and creative practice. While large-scale musical presentations during the main diasporic events may draw the largest audiences, the abundance of low-key, hidden performances at civic and community events and through outreach in public parks, nursing homes and cancer centres reveal the multiple ways these musical practices engage with fellow urban residents and shape theirs and others' experiences of place. If, as Tom Western asserts, 'migration is a sonic process' (2020: 294), according to these migrant musicians in Oslo, integration is, too, a continuous sonic process – if only we care to listen.

Acknowledgements

Grateful appreciation to all the musicians who participated in this research. Additional thanks to Aileen Dillane, Marian Mangaoang, Victoria Nybråten, Linn Schjerven and David Toms for their assistance and expertise during this project.

This chapter is dedicated to the memory of David (Davy) Patterson Dick (1939–2022), the heart of Oslo's trad sessions for the past fifty years.

NOTES

1. The term 'Irish music' suggests a multitude of possible meanings, as touched upon in the second section of this chapter. However, for the purposes of this chapter, Irish music is defined here as any music composed, produced and/or performed in Ireland or by Irish people (whether they are in Ireland or in any other part of the world). This includes but is not limited to Irish traditional music (hereafter 'trad'), folk, rock, pop and a great many other musical genres produced in Ireland or by Irish people.
2. Coined as a verb by Christopher Small (1998), 'musicking' refers to any activity related to musical performance, thus places an emphasis on music as a process, rather than a product.
3. Cultural identity is understood, in this case, after Stuart Hall 'as a "production", which is never complete, always in process, and always constituted within, not outside, representation' (1990: 222).
4. Oslo is categorized as a beta world city according to the Globalization and World Cities Research Network (2020), that is a city that is not as globally connected as alpha cities such as like London, New York, Hong Kong and Tokyo. Oslo shares its beta level with other moderate economic cities such as Barcelona, Bogotá, Cape Town and Perth.
5. These sessions have continued every week until the present, corona-pandemic notwithstanding.
6. That said, all are welcome to these sessions and non-Norwegian speakers are easily accommodated, since many Norwegians – especially most of those on the trad circuit – speak English to a high degree of fluency.
7. *Julebord* is Norway's rather raucous 'Christmas party' tradition that fills the city's bars from the end of November until New Year.
8. It is worth addressing the significant shift in the Irish community in Oslo post-2008. Up until then, and still primarily, the Irish who move to Norway tend to be highly skilled, highly educated middle-class professionals, and, until 2008, were disproportionately women. However, the economic downturn following 2008 has changed this, as more agent-hired men in construction and adjacent work began moving to Oslo.
9. Øvingshotellet is a 'hotel' not for sleeping but for music rehearsing, run by the Agency for Cultural Affairs in Oslo.
10. The Mná developed a new initiative called the Singing Circle in October 2019, based on the model of an Irish traditional singing session. This monthly singer's club was hosted at the Dubliner pub, free of charge and open to any interested folk and traditional singers from all backgrounds, not only men and women from the Irish diaspora. While these sessions were gaining momentum, and attracted singers and folk music enthusiasts from

Catalonia, France, the Netherlands and Norway to join, the pandemic put an abrupt end to these sessions in March 2020.

REFERENCES

Brah, Avtar (1996), *Cartographies of Diaspora: Contesting Identities*, London: Routledge.

Brophy Bookings: The Leading Solo Agency (Official Website) (2019), 'Old Irish Pub Music Booking', http://www.brophybookings.com/index.php/en/contact/job-application/old-irish-pub. Accessed 20 December 2021 (no longer available).

Dillane, Aileen (2013), 'Nostalgic songlines and the performance of Irish identity', *Béaloideas*, 81, pp. 19–36.

Dunn, Nick (2016), *Dark Matters: A Manifesto for the Nocturnal City*, Winchester: Zero Books.

Finnegan, Ruth (1989), *The Hidden Musicians: Music-Making in an English Town*, Cambridge: Cambridge University Press.

Gjerstad, Leif (1988), 'Morsmelk-musikk fra Irland' ('Breastmilk music from Ireland'), *Bergens Tidende*, 20 November 1988, n. pag.

Hall, Stuart (1990), 'Cultural identity and diaspora', in J. Rutherford (ed.), *Identity: Community, Culture, Difference*, London: Lawrence and Wishart, pp. 222–37.

Kenny, Ailbhe (2016), *Communities of Musical Practice*, New York: Routledge.

Leonard, Marion (2005), 'Performing identities: Music and dance in the Irish communities of Coventry and Liverpool', *Social & Cultural Geography*, 6:4, pp. 515–29.

Mangaoang, Áine (2019), 'Music and tourism: Mapping popular music from St. Patrick's College', in J. Buckley and J. O'Flynn (eds), *Ceol Phádraig: Music at St Patrick's College Drumcondra, 1875–2016*, Oxford: Peter Lang, pp. 205–21.

Mangaoang, Áine, O'Flynn, John and Ó Briain, Lonán (eds) (2020), *Made in Ireland: Studies in Popular Music*, New York: Routledge.

McLoughlin, Noel and McLoone, Martin (2000), 'Hybridity and national musics: The case of Irish rock music', *Popular Music*, 19:2, pp. 181–99.

O'Flynn, John (2009), *The Irishness of Irish Music*, Farnham: Ashgate.

Slobin, Mark (1994), 'Music in diaspora: The view from Euro-America', *Diaspora*, 3:1, pp. 243–52.

Slomonski, Tes (2020), *Trad Nation: Gender, Sexuality, and Race in Irish Traditional Music*, Middletown: Wesleyan University Press.

Small, Christopher (1998), *Musicking: The Meanings of Performing and Listening*, Hanover: University Press of New England.

The Old Irish Pub (Official Website) (2021), 'Om Puben' ('About the Pub'), https://oldirishpub.no/pub/oslo/. Accessed 20 December 2019.

Western, Tom (2020), 'Listening with displacement: Sound, citizenship, and disruptive representations of migration', *Migration & Society: Advances in Research*, 3, pp. 294–309.

Williams, Sean (2020), *Focus: Irish Traditional Music*, 2nd ed., New York: Routledge.

Interlude 4

'New York Ne Dort Pas'

Brendan Kibbee

For drummers, dancers, praise singers and socialites in Senegal and its diaspora, a *tanebeer* is a type of event whose name simply means 'darkness' (from French *ténèbre*). Since the early 2010s, I've had the chance to attend a number of these events in Harlem's 'Little Senegal'. Well after midnight, in church banquet halls and restaurants, a few hundred party-goers assemble to recreate a context that regularly takes place on the streets of Dakar but only occasionally within New York's Senegalese community. The attendees include hairdressers, students, cab drivers, restaurant workers, doormen, street hawkers and a few who are able to make a living out of performances and patronage arrangements. All of these artists fuel several hours of pre-dawn excitement, most prominently highlighting the virtuosity of solo dancers, men and women, amateurs and professionals. They also praise. In eloquent sequences, singers praise patrons, drummers praise dancers (and vice versa), guests praise the host and friends praise friends. Many praises are accompanied by exchanges of cash and all of them establish the groundwork for forms of solidarity that sustain urban life, whether in New York or Dakar. This transcript represents the voices of several participants at events that I attended and recorded between 2013 and 2016. Selected and arranged from over a dozen poems and testimonials in Wolof, this translation illustrates how a prominent New York City immigrant community coalesces through languages and rhythms of pleasure, solidarity, appreciation and admiration. Mor Coumba Gueye, Mar Gueye, Kine Ndiaye and Moha Seck are prominently featured, and I would like to thank them for their hospitality at these events. I would also like to thank Saliou Ba for his help verifying the translations.

This poem contains a few Wolof interjections like 'cim!', 'ndeysaan' and 'waawaaw', and names of dance moves like 'mboro mboroxe' and 'takk ci rip'. There are also drum strokes represented by commonly used vocables that appear in the text.

> *In Wolof, double vowels are elongated. An 'i' sounds like you're saying the letter 'e.' [Try pronouncing the word 'amiin'.] Double consonants are aspirated (i.e. you 'let go' of the consonant after pronouncing it). [Try pronouncing the word 'takk'.] An 'x' is a fricative, somewhat similar to a French 'r.' ['Pax'.] A c is close to an English 'ch.' ['Cim!'.] The 'r' is trilled. ['Ram'.] A 'g' is always a hard g. ['Gin'].*
> Amiin... takk... pax... cim!... ram... gin...

First we thank God
(*La ilaha illa 'llah*)
Pray to the Prophet, peace be upon him
(*Amiin waay*)
Praise our griot heritage and everyone who supports us
(That's what I'm telling you)
Praise our elders
(Yes!)
Praise both parents
(Yes!)
Praise everyone joining in
(*Cim*!)
Praise everyone watching
(That's what I'm telling you)

We're telling Senegal
(What are you saying?)
That today we're gonna go *hard*
(It's *gotta* be hard here today)
Beat our soles on the ground til it's true
(You're telling the truth)
Jump til' it's jumpin', you see?
(Yeah!)
Do it til' it's nice.
(*Cim*!)
Put everyone watching to shame.
(*Unh*!)
Mboro Mboroxe
(You see?)
Takk ci ripp
(*Waawaaw*)

Ain't nothin' too much.

(No one could stop it!)

Harlem is gonna move

(Yeah!)

Manhattan is gonna move

(Yeah!)

Obama is gonna move

(Yeah!)

You're a good person, a great person,

(*Ndeysaan*)

You have integrity and character,

(It's true)

We share griot heritage,

(That's what I'm telling you)

When it's your event,

(Yeah?)

We drop whatever we're doing,

(What did he say?)

Come from Boston,

(It's true)

From Vermont,

(It's true)

From LA,

(It's true)

From Chicago,

(That's what I'm saying)

We come here to join in

(*La ilaha ila 'llah*)

I left my job at four,

(Uh-huh)

Took the bus six hours.

(Uh-huh)

See my drum bag here?

(Yeah)

You're worth it.

(*La ilaha ila 'llah*)

In the sabar-drum mnemonic system, 'gin', 'pin' and 'pa'/'ba'/'pax'/'bax' are open hand (LH) drum strokes, low, middle, and high pitched, respectively. [If you're keen on drumming, 'mime gin' (low), 'pin' (middle) and 'pax' (high) with your open left hand while pronouncing the syllables]. 'Ta'/'tas'/'sa' is a stick hand (RH) stroke. [Imagine holding a stick in your hand. Strike it while saying 'ta'.] 'Rwan'/'rwa'/'ram' is an accent with two strokes in rapid succession, what drum-kit players would call a 'flam'. [Try LH (open) and RH (stick) one right after the other while saying 'ram'.]
Gin... pin... pax... ta... ram

Ba-tas ***pax.****Ta... pa... rwa-sa-ram-pa-ram rwan-pin-ta-pin tam-bax...* ***gin.***

Listen! My boy says: 'Everyone here who isn't dancing, I'm talking to you'
(Ba-tas gin gin gin)
Tan...pax...rwan-pa-tan-tan-rwan rwan-pa-tan-tan-tan-pax-tan-pax... ***gin.***

He said: [in exaggerated English] 'How are you? I'm fine. I'm just going here honey honey chekicheki dabadagin këdakëda ni rwan takk ci ripp!'
Wait!

(gin-ja gin-ja)

What do you want?

(gin-ja gin-ja)

Don't you dare
Don't you dare
Don't you dare get me moving!
(Gin-sa-gin
Gin-sa-gin
Gin-sa gin-sa sa gin)
Don't you dare
Don't you dare
Don't you dare get me moving!
(Gin-sa-gin
Gin-sa-gin
Gin-sa gin-sa sa gin)

Wanna see someone good?

(Yeah!)

Come to Mor

(sa sa)

Wanna see someone good?

(Yeah!)

Come to Mor

(sa sa)

Wanna see someone good?

(Yeah!)

Come over here

(*sa sa*)

Wanna see someone good?

(Yeah)

Come over here

(sa sa)

Wait, wait, wait!

After God, no one helped us more than Kiné
I'm saying, no kindness can exceed what you've done
Everyone who knows you knows it's true

I'm so happy with you
(Really, you're a good person)
You're an example
(Really you're a good person)

You show everyone respect and openness
I pray that God pays you
I pray that God gives you peace in your heart

When you pay, you're sowing the seeds!
(Gin-ta-ta gin-ta-ta-ta-gin ta-ta-gin)
When you pay, you're sowing the seeds!
(gin-ta-ta gin-ta-ta-ta-gin ta-ta-gin)

Where do you do 'New York ne dort pas?'
(Point to your heart!)

I said, where do you do ‘New York ne dort pas?’
(Point to your heart!)
Where do you do ‘New York ne dort pas?’
(Point to your heart!)
Where do you do ‘New York ne dort pas?’

RIGHT HERE!

♫ Audio can be accessed at https://intellectdiscover.com/content/books/9781789386967.

PART 5

DISCORD

9

Urban Outcasts and the Defiant iSicathamiya Music

Sipho Sithole

This chapter explores how in an act of defiance, a subversive migrant community uses iSicathamiya[1] music as a sonic or auditory cultural process to imagine new possibilities. It investigates how the adherents of iSicathamiya have created a heightened cultural consciousness to survive urban marginality. Historically crafted in the middle of the night, far from the gaze of authorities – at the servants' quarters and men's hostels – this music has earned its name *ngoma busuku* ('night music'). A call-and-response acapella style of music, sang in four-part harmony by male choral ensembles, iSicathamiya was developed by Zulu hostel dwellers who came to the cities as reluctant migrant workers. A cultural phenomenon which first came to life through Solomon Linda's *Mbube* (*Mimoweh*) and later popularized by Ladysmith Black Mambazo, iSicathamiya represents the sounds of migration – voices from the margins. The chapter investigates how, through iSicathamiya, migrants have used their bounded and segregated spaces to re-organize themselves into a formidable creative social force. It argues how the dark of the night breaks down walls for the marginalized migrants, helping them find a voice and gain recognition in their surrounding metropolis.

It's going to be a long night

It's after 7:00 p.m., late November 2020. A few people have gathered outside Hall No. 3 at Thokoza Men's Hostel on the outskirts of Johannesburg.[2] It is the annual year-end iSicathamiya music spectacular, held just before migrant workers return home to their villages to be re-united with their families for the festive season. By the look of things, there is no sign of a show about to start; it is night music anyway, however, the night is defined here.

Apart from the distant flood lights that shine out the hidden secrets of the township enveloping the hostel, the only lights illuminating the place are those flickering inside the single men's rooms and the one inside the hall (see Figure 9.1). This is where tonight's year-end competition is taking place. Supplementing the light of the hostel precinct is that from *isibhakabhaka* – the night sky and the constellation of stars that shine like broad daylight, much to the delight of children scattered in the yard, excited about the evening.

Concerned about the night, mothers are shouting at the young ones to come inside for the last meal of the day, a bath and then straight to bed. The presence of women and children at men's hostels was unheard of during apartheid. Only African men with a work permit were allowed in the city, albeit confined to the men's hostels or at the servants' quarters. Unless granted a permit to be in the city,[3] women and children were barred from the urban areas. They remained behind in the villages, looking after the homesteads and tending to cattle and goats until their husbands returned from the city.

Well, they are here now and getting the children inside is going to be tough. Nobody is going to sleep tonight.

It's 11:38 p.m. and suddenly there are signs of life all around. Minibus taxis, carrying iSicathamiya groups, begin to trickle in. Even the hostel residents, who have been camped inside their compound, are coming out of their rooms, heading to the hall for *qhudemanikiniki* – a fierce competition that will last until daybreak.

FIGURE 9.1: Audience and groups waiting outside Thokoza Hostel Hall (east of Johannesburg) for the iSicathamiya competition. Photo by the author.

Tonight is a culmination of iSicathamiya night competitions that have taken place around the year at various men's hostels in and around Johannesburg. These participating groups tonight are vying for a top spot in this marginalized genre that has existed outside of the mainstream since it first broke out into song at the turn of the twentieth century. The evening is filled with not just a singing competition but is also preceded by the best-dressed men competition (*oswenka*) (see Figure 9.2) and the best-dressed women competition (*onobuhle)*, a precursor to the night music competition otherwise known as *ungoma busuku* ('night music'). The best-dressed competition is a display of elegance, swag, sophistication and imagined opulence by a migrant community whose meagre wages are saved for the best three-piece suit, two-tone shoes and a Dobson hat to go with a glittering gold-plated watch for the night.

Those who have entered the best-dressed competition will be adjudicated by a single judge, who has been randomly picked up from the street.[4] The same judge will also decide the winner of the singing competition later on in the programme. For the best-dressed man or woman, the judge will choose the winner for the overall presentation that in the main is based on neatness, swag and style and more so on the character of the participant. It is theatrical and a marvel to watch. Each participant has a unique and grand style of how they choose to enter the stage. One participant could simply jump onto the stage like an acrobat or walk in slow motion and like a stealth with their eyes locked straight onto the judge as if to say, 'don't miss a thing of what I am about to show you'. From the socks that match

FIGURE 9.2: A man showing off his outfit in front of the judge at the best-dressed male competition, a precursor to iSicathamiya competition. Photo by the author.

the shirt to the belt that matches the shoes, the participant ensures that the judge sees and appreciates every item, including the label of the suit and the brand of the watch on the wrist. Each item is shown singularly, in the most dramatic fashion and to a judge, always a man, and who seems unmoved, lest he let the cat out of the bag about his favourite contestant.

A tough call for the judge, because every participant is dressed to kill and with a swag in abundance – men and women alike. A huge investment for the participants who probably are wearing items worth a second-hand car or a few cows in a man's *kraal* back in the village.

At the end of it all, the judge has the last say, 'you won, you lost', and then everyone waits for the night music.

As the best-dressed competition is nearing completion, outside the hall already more than ten groups taking part in the competition have gathered in anticipation for the night. Scattered outside the yard and in various corners, these groups are warming up their voices and doing final touches and practising dance choreography and their signature footsteps, for what looks like it's going to be a long night (not that they are bothered, anyway). Knowing that they are only scheduled to perform in the wee hours of the morning, more groups will be arriving, even after midnight and will find a quiet corner to brush up on their harmonies and choreography.

Eavesdropping and trying to check who stands a chance, a group breaks into a song with some catchy lyrics 'turn around my baby, I want to see your figure' – a very familiar song back in the villages by those who have picked up some English in the city. Another group, not wanting to be seen by others in case they steal their style, is singing 'holy spirit, rain rain rain'. A cry for rain is a common denominator amongst villagers who rely on arable land to plough and graze fields for their cows. The song conjoined with vernacular voices, singing 'hhawu lami ngiyovika ngani?' ('my shield how will I protect myself?') What appeared to be Zulu warriors ready to go to war with the enemy inside the hall, turns out to be a call to Jesus, their shield, to protect them and guide them throughout the night.

I am defeated. Where are the Shaka Zulu's warriors in the music? Having heard enough outside, I decide to move into the hall in anticipation of a great night indeed.

Inside the hall, the audience is suddenly illuminated by what appears to be a group of already intoxicated iSicathamiya enthusiasts, who decide to jump on stage for an impromptu performance, to a very amused audience. Obviously, confused as to whether the official programme has begun, the audience then realizes that this was just a bunch of happily tipsy young men excited about the night. Imitating the groups that will be gracing the night, they stylishly tip-toe themselves off stage.

What happens thereafter is each competing group taking turns to come onto the stage to announce their presence to an enthusiastic audience. Each group sings a song just to greet the audience and gracefully steps out of the hall only to return later for the real deal.

Ultimately, there will be about twenty groups tonight. Finally, way after midnight, the first group enters the hall; each will have their turn to impress the judge and has been given ten minutes on stage. About 30 minutes later, the first group is still on stage. By the look of things, the night will become morning when the last group enters the hall.

Each group, an ensemble of up to twenty singers or more, organized in four-part harmony – soprano, alto, tenor and bass – are all set for an impressionable performance tonight. The leader, who also is a conductor of the group, must be animated and with gestures that could get the audience jumping with adulation (see Figure 9.3). Whether talented or not, by virtue of being the group's founder, he will lead and direct his singers in a call-and-response fashion. With careful and well-rehearsed moves, mainly through tip-toeing as if to imitate tap dance, each characterized body gesture separates one group from another and could determine who takes the trophy.

With the aesthetic and poetic display and improvised performance of the group's leader, his gesture and facial expression – what Hofmeyr (1999) calls 'carnivalesque' cultural activities – will make a great impression on the judge. Suddenly, those who cannot contain their excitement of what is going on stage

FIGURE 9.3: Mzwandile Kunene leads his group, Ladysmith Hlanganani, with character in front of the judge at iSicathamiya competition. Photo by the author.

will sporadically jump up and down, whilst the ululation of women present begins to drown those melodic and harmonious voices, much to the amusement of the audience.

It's going to be a long night; maybe, a long morning.

Tonight, the judge has been briefed and the program director has announced which group comes in first and which one will be last. When the judge finally announces the top three winners, whose decision cannot be questioned, everyone will go home at daybreak; completely fulfilled, until the next competition.

What is happening tonight dates far back to the early twentieth century when Africans were recruited to the mines in Johannesburg and took with them village songs, sung at wedding ceremonies and other cultural celebrations, only to re-imagine them in a more contemporary style. It is through these songs of migration that vocal ensembles were formed by migrants from the same villages or region and who would hold competitions with groups from other regions – a practice still prevalent today.

Till today, this night music has been deeply intertwined with the cultural and social life of migrant workers, particularly those living at the men's hostels spread across the metropolis. To them, iSicathamiya is a cultural weapon of survival, transported as village memories and interwoven with melodic lyrics telling tales of triumph, love and pain, albeit with 'hidden transcripts' (Scott 1990), that have defined the nightlife of migrants.

An interview conducted with Nqolokazi Dzanibe, the secretary of the federation iPhimbo iSicathamiya, which organizes iSicathamiya festivals, reveals how this music of migrants, passed down between generations, has managed to re-fashion a village sound for urban consumption. Dzanibe explains the existence of three structures that organize iSicathamiya festivals: at the federation, at a clubhouse level within each hostel and at the individual group level. The federation, led by a President, has its own calendar of festivals and competitions where all affiliated groups enter to compete. Clubhouses, at the hostel level, can organize their own festivals for the groups that are residents within the hostel.

To sustain itself, outside of the mainstream cultural and creative economy, each of the three levels of competitions or festivals is a revenue-generating activity. Entering a competition at the national, clubhouse or group level, each competing group pays an entrance fee which is then supplemented by ticket sales at the door. It is this entrance fee and revenue from ticket sales that make up the winner's final prize.

At these competitions or festivals, iSicathamiya is presented as a nocturnal ritual that engages the night, not as an extension of the day, but as another time that occupies urban life. The practitioners of iSicathamiya exist within two time zones, where one does not replace the other; a worker by day and an artist by night.

As Dunn attests (2016: 10): 'the city is not one but has dual character', allowing it to be experienced and sensed differently in each time zone and is reproduced into multiple versions depending on how one locates themselves in it.

But rest assured, the night is 'electric with possibilities' (Dunn 2016: 15).

Locating iSicathamiya as a nocturnal sonic agency

The chapter first posits that iSicathamiya emerges out of a feeling of displacement and alienation by village migrants who find themselves in an urban setting that was only designed as a place of work. The chapter shares the story of migrants, particularly Zulu migrants, who were compelled to seek employment and refuge in the cities (Laband 1995; McClendon 2002) due to land alienation and heavy taxation, including escaping from forced labour conscription on White farms. It relates a story of how migrants, having found themselves in an urban setting that sought to exclude them, engaged in musical practice in order to re-arrange their space and existence in the city.

Arriving in the city and racially excluded from enjoying some of the amenities, including being out at night in the city, the chapter shares how these labour migrants watched the city lights from their compounds with envy. Imagining a life beyond these walls and in the city's racially segregated clubs, bars and theatres, they sought to artistically dissolve what Brar (2021) calls 'racialized spatial constraints' in order to give 'genuine alternatives to the functioning of the city'. This chapter also discusses how returning migrants brought with them this newly formed and re-fashioned sound back to the villages, thereby introducing new ways of experiencing music at night for those based 'at home'.

iSicathamiya is located within this context and is presented as a visual and 'audible migration' (Western 2016: 296), reflecting the migrants' own 'manifesto of the nocturnal city' (Dunn 2016). It is these conventional memories that Bae Suah (2013: 5) argues are in essence 'either visual or aural, shifting eventually to those which, through their own agency, reclaim past scenes inside remembered soundscapes'. It is through this sonic process that iSicathamiya allows village migrants to carry with them a cultural memory that later becomes a conduit between home and away. Western (2016: 294) describes these mobilities as an 'access point to the agency of people on the move', where those arriving from home bring along fresh narratives through which new songs are crafted. It is when these 'mobilities assume social forms', as Brah (2022) asserts, that their transition to the city assumes a sonic auditory agency from which sounds of migration emerge.

This chapter examines iSicathamiya in relation to the night when migrants relinquish the day only to conjure and re-capture the night in what Bronfen (2008: xiv) calls 'the creation of the artistic worlds'. When the day dies, the 'aesthetically reimagined night' Bronfen (2008: xiii) takes with it a culture into a time and space where those who fraternize with the night experience the sound differently than if it were to happen in the daytime. Understanding and appreciating iSicathamiya as an art form that finds life only at night, where 'night is conceived not as a mere extension of the day, neither as its negative counterpart' (Garcia-Ruiz 2021: n.pag.), requires being present in the time and space where this culture manifests itself. For the architecture of the city to be sensed differently (Dunn 2016), it is by being present with the night and through 'connective marginality' (Osumane 2007) that we are able to feel its texture and the mood of its patrons. It is then that iSicathamiya is lived not just as a cultural spectacle of performance and celebration but one that is shaped by the environmental conditions and historical connections of its practitioners, or 'historical particularism' (Darnell 2013: 399).

The testimony from the practitioners, who feel treated as urban outcasts, tells how in the dark of the night they have used iSicathamiya to artistically break down social barriers in order to find a voice and gain recognition as voices from the margins. They share how inside these confined spaces a cultural phenomenon was crafted in the middle of the night and created their own lifestyle and a sound to be known as *ungoma busuku* or night music. This sonic signature happened in the servants' quarters, at the men's hostels, where the night concealed its creation from being detected by their bosses or by the police patrolling at night. The emergent musical genre's name – iSicathamiya – underscores the significance of going undetected, as in the Zulu language, *cathama* means to slowly tip-toe like a stealth as if not wanting to be detected. It was the slow dance movement and light footsteps which became known as *ukucothoza* – to tip-toe, hence the name iSicathamiya. Stealing time and space inside the servant's quarters, when employers were asleep, these acapella groups rehearsed songs and practised choreographed dance movements, which they called *istep* – the step. These synchronized footsteps had to be practised in complete silence so as not to make noise that would wake neighbours, or those sleeping in the main house. Afraid of being detected, even by the slightest noise from stamping on the floor, they tip-toed and, in four-part harmony, melodically sang, albeit in whispering voices, some of the coveted songs their country will be remembered for.

At night competitions, it is this footstep movement that distinguishes each group from another. The format of competitions derives from wedding ceremonies back in the village where the bride and groom party would try and outperform each other in front of a cheering crowd. Johnson (2001: 2) writes that this tip-toeing is displayed in 'slow shuffling movements, interspersed with high kicking of legs and silent tap dance movements [that] are the hallmark of iSicathamiya'. This slow and careful stepping is contrary to most traditional dance styles, which

Johnson argues 'display forceful stamping movements expressing virility' whilst 'iSicathamiya movements are graceful' (2001: 2).

Reclaiming the night

The gathering at Thokoza hostel on 30 November 2020 detailed in the introduction of this chapter is a culmination of a culture of a people 'who see themselves as social group' (Darnell 2013: 399). The night gathering reveals a determination amongst participants to lay claim to the night and to the city as its legitimate residents. In laying claims of belonging, participants draw upon a culmination of cultural currencies including fashion, dance and song. Singing, in particular, remains central to urban belonging at night, as is evidenced by the chronology of each event, with singing punctuating all other nocturnal festivities. By 'using sound as an access point to the agency of people on the move' (Western 2020: 295), they forge these 'unlikely publics' (LaBelle 2018: 15) and, like any men's hostel in the city, Thokoza becomes a place where the day is forgotten as the night takes over.

In South Africa, night culture and night economies have to be understood through these nocturnal segregated cultural spaces and places, or what Hollands (2002) terms 'divisions in the dark', where spatial and racial separation in the night takes on a different character. To the Black majority, the 'complex relationship between labour market divisions and cultural identities in the night-time economy' (Hollands 2002: 153) defines the city as a place of work, after which workers leave in droves to racially segregated townships on the outskirts of town.[5] Those that remain in town quickly disappear into the servant's quarters or dedicated men's hostels within the city.

For those who cannot remain in the city, they take the night with them back to the townships, where Black music and celebration soon find resonance. This is articulated by Coplan (1985: 2) in his scholarship on Black South Africans, whose relentless desire to gain control of their cultural practices, products and representation, created new institutions, communities and cultural forms in the struggle for urban survival. During apartheid, the city and the township were opposites, experienced differently by their inhabitants. The township was a racially segregated settlement where Blacks retreated back to when night approached, whilst the city remains intact under strict surveillance by the police who want to keep it pure from any racial contamination.

In his book, Coplan (1985) reveals how, free to engage with the night, the township became a hive of activities where the so-called *shebeens* ('taverns') became a platform for new forms of music, particularly *marabi* – a sound that fused both local and foreign forms of music. The *marabi* sound was fused with new musical styles which later became Township jazz. The night was the township and the township was the night. Coplan observes, 'increasingly shebeens customers demanded urban "modern" forms of cultural entertainment that expressed the quality and permanence of the city way of life' (1985: 114). So, by the 1950s, the shebeens became a melting pot for Black cultural nightlife. Consequentially, *marabi* music, influenced by the social conditions and experiences of the Black working class, had found its expression.

Concerned by this cultural phenomenon and how the night suddenly became the leitmotif of Black lives in the township, the night became a threat to White authorities. When the grand apartheid scheme had become institutionalized and was threatened by the rise of Black cultural production, Coplan (1985: 225) observes, 'urban black South Africa was to be torn up, root and branch'. The musicians, who continued to perform with White bands in town faced arrests if found performing in 'Whites only places' or roaming in the inner-city without a special night pass. It was common knowledge that when White police officers were about to pounce on these clubs, Black musicians would leave the stage and rush to the back of the venue where they would pretend to be dishwashers in the scullery. The famous South African jazz band, the Jazz Epistles would later release a song called 'Scullery Department' (Jazz Epistles 1960), a reference to Black musicians hiding as dishwashers to avoid arrest for being found in the City at a White club.

Back in the Black townships, shebeens continued to become spaces of convergence for the weekend night music and night revellers, fuelled by illegal liquor brewing and consumption with beautiful women who patronized these places. Regardless of the occasional night raids by the police, this cultural phenomenon sparked a night-time economy that was Black controlled and Black consumed. Bands were born and those who managed to leave the country would eventually tour the world, like Miriam Makeba, Hugh Masekela, Caiphus and Letta Mbulu, who also became migrants on foreign lands where they had taken along with them their songs of migration.

However, back in the city and in the servant's quarters or inside the single men's hostels, were those migrants who could not be in the township because of the nature of their employment conditions. At night, they created a new sonic agency and sound that would later occupy a space bigger than its humble beginnings. This migrant community's subversive vision and refusal to be treated as urban outcasts responded with what Brandon LaBelle (2018) calls 'sonic thought and imagination'. This is the music that would later be known as the sound of the five-time Grammy award-winning group, Ladysmith Black Mambazo – iSicathamiya. As Erlmann (1990: 199) testifies, 'the roots of iSicathamiya dates back to the turn of the twentieth century and constitutes one of the most compelling and complex statements about the experience of millions of Black migrants in South Africa'.

It was the creative expression of a people who found themselves trapped in the city that sought to find a meaning in this new world by creatively and artistically delving deep into hidden memories of life left back in the villages. In what (Shusterman 2000: 73) calls 'mutable but coercive facts and patterns of the material, sociohistorical world', iSicathamiya became their response through which cultural and social barriers of exclusion, alienation and exploitation were confronted. By engaging in 'resilience and creative resistance' (LaBelle 2018: 5) they crafted 'a path from the fringes toward hope, citizenship, and vibrancy' (6) and what Hannah Arendt terms 'spaces of appearance' (cited in Labelle 2018: 5) or 'social spaces of distraction' (Harvey 1989: 234). Here, a network of village migrants found purpose through sound, from which an urban night culture was formed; iSicathamiya became a raft that kept migrant workers buoyant and claimed their existence in the city.

Acapella voices: A testimony

Mkhehle Nxele (aged 31), the founder and leader of Inkululeko (see Figure 9.4), otherwise known as Omashiya kukhalwa, translated 'the group that leaves fans gasping for more', started singing when he was about 10 years old. Upon arriving in Johannesburg, the youngest leader of iSicathamiya, Nxele looked for his village folks living at one of the hostels in Soweto, where he then founded the group in 2012. To Nxele, because of what Johnson (2001: 3) refers to as the 'process of voluntary associations which helps build and reinforce values and norms of behaviour suitable to city life and provide networks of support relations', joining iSicathamiya was a natural choice upon arriving in Johannesburg. Joining a 'network of homeboys' (Harriet-Jones 1969: 297) helped Nxele to adjust to an unfamiliar environment and provided some measure of stability, where, according to Homi Bhabha (1992: 141) 'the border between home and the world becomes confused' or what he calls 'an unhomely' moment.

Nxele attributes his love for iSicathamiya, against any other genre, to the discipline the music teaches its followers. He explains that this music takes people and its followers away from the streets at night, where they are susceptible to criminal activity, mainly induced by drinking and crowded spaces. To avoid such nightly encounters, Nxele testifies that iSicathamiya keeps them at 'practice' (rehearsals), within the hostels and with their home boys. Johnson (2001: 4) also confirms that the network of 'home boys' remains an important rural-orientated foundation for the emergent cultural formation of migrants in the cities.

FIGURE 9.4: Inkululelo group at iSicathamiya Competition, led by the youngest group leader, Mkhehle Nxele. Photo by Nqolokazi Nomvalo.

Noticeable from where the interview is conducted under the tree and a few metres from the hall where the competition will be taking place throughout the night, are the groups that have started to arrive. A beautiful soundtrack accompanying the conversation with Nxele, which contextualizes the interview, comes the groups harmoniously warming up their voices, in preparation for the night to ensue. Explaining why the music is referred to as *ungoma busuku* – night music – his only explanation is that it has been like that since the days of their grandfathers, when, as mine workers, they would emerge from deep down in the belly of the earth and head straight to compound. With the only time they had at night, they would sing the night away. 'This is the music *wama nono* ['neat and nicely dressed people'], says Nxele. iSicathamiya groups are distinguished with their dress sense; suits, snow-white shirts, two-tone shoes or shiny black shoes, colourful socks and white gloves, with the leader dressed distinctly from the group. The act of discarding overalls and hard hats for three-piece western-style suits and white gloves at night signifies a transition from daytime labourer status to that of the metropolitan man in touch with urban culture. Exchanging overalls with three-piece suites, the daytime labourers become their own bosses at night. This transition is both a political and economic statement that symbolizes ownership of the night. The freedom from daytime 'menial forms of manual labour' (Johnson

2001: 77) is shown by the wearing of white gloves, confirming Nxele's statement about this music being 'neat'. Here they project 'resolute men defiantly walking the streets of the white man's city' (Elrmann 1999: 204) with an in-your-face attitude that says 'we are here now; deal with us'. Also arriving in fashionable style, to complement the evening, are those who will be participating in the best-dressed competition, without which the iSicathamiya showcase loses its flavour. No sooner has the competition finished, the music will then take over to dictate the pulse and the rhythm of the night.

Mdletshe Albert Mazibuko (aged 73) – the longest-serving and founding member of the five-time Grammy Award-winning group, Ladysmith Black Mambazo, arrived in Durban in 1964 at the age of 16 years, after having worked at a farm from the age of seven. Escaping hard labour at the farm where his parents and uncles had lived all their lives, Mazibuko had worked at an adjacent farm where his later fellow group member and long-time friend Joseph Shabalala worked till he was 18 years old.

Just like Nxele, who also left his village almost 50 years later, Mazibuko sought his rural folks when he arrived in Durban in 1964. Naturally, iSicathamiya was the obvious conduit between home and the new urban setting for Mazibuko, as it played an important role in the orientation to urban life for new arrivals.

Fleeing inhuman conditions on the farms, Mazibuko looked for and found his fellow countrymen in Clermont, a freehold African township founded in 1931. Ironically, Mazibuko had escaped from the farms in rural Natal where he had worked since the age of seven only to move to a place named after a farmer (Sir Clermont) who had sold his land to make way for a Black township – the only place in Durban where Black people were able to buy property.

In search of 'common regional origin and kinship ties' (Harries-Jones 1969: 297), Mazibuko found his 'home boy' networks; amongst whom was Joseph Shabalala, who also worked at the nearby farm back at home. They would later found Ladysmith Black Mambazo. Mazibuko explains that Joseph Shabalala had earlier founded the group eZimnyama in Durban in 1967. The name eZimnyama, meaning 'the Blacks', was only used when the group was in Durban, as a political statement and would be called the Durban Choir when Shabalala and the other members returned home on the farms for Christmas. Alternating between the two names had interesting contradictions, in that the group embraced and disowned the city at the same. In the city, they asserted themselves and their presence by assuming the name that identifies with their place of origin – eZimnyama or 'the Black ones'. Changing the name to Durban Choir, every time the group returns home, Mazibuko says this was to brag to the other young adult males, who are still stuck on the farms.

In the villages, the Durban Choir would come back and rekindle with a long-held tradition of night music and celebration, albeit taking a different shape and style. Returning migrants would come home to festivities of rituals of either the coming of age or wedding ceremonies, that start in the night and continue throughout the day. During the wedding ceremonies, the groom's party always arrives at the bride's home a night before to fetch the bride. Inside the groom's homestead, the night becomes a festivity of braggadocious songs and traditional dance between the groom and the bride's party, reminiscent of regiments preparing to go to battle. Carrying on until the middle of the night or early hours of the morning, the bride will then be taken to the groom's family where the rest of the wedding ceremony will take place during the day (see Figure 9.5).

Mazibuko explains that in the city, iSicathamiya became known as *ungoma busuku* ('night music') because Black people were not allowed to be outside the city when the night curfew was in force. This forced groups and their followers to remain in the halls till the early hours of the morning when they could now travel back to the hostels or to other racially segregated communes. When migrants returned home for visits, iSicathamiya competitions also took place at night in the villages, maintaining the nocturnal tradition of the city where iSicathamiya came from.

FIGURE 9.5: A traditional wedding ceremony at a village in Pomeroy, KwaZulu-Natal Province. Photo by Siphiwe Mhlambi.

Obhuti baseGoli – *Brothers from Johannesburg*

After a twelve-month stint in the city, migrants return home again and are reconnected with a culture and celebrations that they have missed. Here they will again be part of wedding ceremonies and other traditional celebrations from which new iSicathamiya songs have been composed. These wedding songs are composed at *umfundelo*, the preparation and practice for the ultimate wedding ceremony, where warring groups from the groom's and bride's party would square up in song and dance spectacular. At this *umfundelo*, the song is led by a front man, a showstopper with exuberance and charisma, who hypes up the ensemble of voices through his zeal, trance, boisterous and artistic techniques. It is this frontman stunt, at *umfundelo*, that is reincarnated as iSicathamiya group's front leader when the same village songs and dance movements – *istep* – are taken back to the city and modified during the night as songs of migration.

Returning home for the festive season is a big deal and quite a spectacle. This is the time for festivities, traditional weddings and coming of age ceremonies; there are feasts and villagers move from one homestead to the other as cows are slaughtered and traditional Zulu beer is in abundance. Those returning from the city also bring gifts with them for their siblings, parents and loved ones. Daytime festivities precede the night-time music competitions.

In the village, the ultimate showcase day is 26 December. This day starts with an event called *ihlahla lika Khisimuzi*, the Christmas tree event, where villagers gather under the tree during the daytime to exchange gifts and read letters from loved ones. The day transitions to the night, when migrants showcase some of the latest material acquisitions from the city, including new fashion styles and night music. Those who had remained in the villages get to experience this phenomenon before *obhuti baseGoli* – brothers from Johannesburg – return back to eGoli ('place of Gold', another name for Johannesburg). Fresh from the men's hostels and iSicathamiya competitions, they are ready to belt out one more song before the city beckons again. At night, these brothers from Johannesburg, with their newly acquired taste of city life, get to showcase the new compositions of iSicathamiya, re-fashioned from traditional music which they had taken to the city from the previous visit at home. Those who had remained in the villages or farms would hear the ways that singing had been modified from traditional songs sang at wedding ceremonies to iSicathamiya. This will be the night of *ungoma busuku* ('night music') now happening in their own backyard in the village. Similarly, returning back to the city, the migrants take along with them new songs from the weddings and ceremonies, which they later modify into iSicathamiya. As both wedding and ceremonial music and iSicathamiya music have their roots in the night, communities collectively engage in the complexities of music's own nocturnal migrations on the 26th of December.

Conclusion

This chapter has explored how iSicathamiya offers a nocturnal musical lens through which experiences of urban migrants find a purpose in their determination to re-organize their social and economic circumstances. It has sought to explain how cultural memory can be carried into unfamiliar territories only to be artistically reimagined as songs of migration. As migrants' sonic signature, iSicathamiya becomes an artistic tool used by these 'transnational villagers' (Levitt 2001) to assume a collective marginal posture in order to defy urban marginality.

The testimony from interviews above and lived experiences of iSicathamiya practitioners described in my fieldwork make clear that migrants have refused to see the night as an occasion to sit and sulk at daytime misgivings. They have used these nocturnal 'bounded and segregated spaces' (Wacquant 2008: 169), or 'invisible walls of the ghetto' (Clark 1956: 12) as spaces and time for uninterrupted creativity. It is through this uninterrupted creativity that a formidable cultural force, a night economy built on fashion, music and a sense of belonging, that iSicathamiya becomes the nocturnal sound through which a community survives the night in order to see the day.

The chapter argues that through cultural memory and collective remembering, village migrants have been able to create a society within a society; build an independent social system that displays the 'highest level of self-sufficiency relative to its environment' (Parsons 1971: 8; Hayles 1999) in their response to feelings of exclusion and alienation. Therefore, when the cock crows and all go to sleep, this art form and its pioneers will emerge from the dark and creatively occupy a space where a world imagined becomes a world realized.

NOTES

1. iSicathamiya is a type of secular acapella choral singing developed in South Africa by migrant Zulu communities. The music became widely popular outside of Africa in the late twentieth century, particularly by the Grammy Award winning group, Ladysmith Black Mambazo and was picked up and promoted by the world-music industry.
2. In the South African context, the word 'hostel' refers to a housing compound that was developed and designed for Black migrant workers in South Africa, whereby Black workers would live inside highly controlled living quarters without their families and visit home once per year.

3. Any reference to the city, unless specific, is either Johannesburg or Durban, where labor migrants from Zululand and Natal were recruited to.
4. To avoid bias and favoritism in choosing a winner in this long-held tradition of iSicathamiya competition, a team is sent out to look for someone totally unfamiliar with the occasion and the participants to be the judge.
5. From the late nineteenth century until the end of apartheid, townships in South Africa were racially segregated urban areas built on the periphery of towns and cities and reserved for Africans, Indians and the so-called coloured people.

REFERENCES

Bae, Suah (2013), *A Greater Music*, Rochester: Open Letter Books.

Bhabha, Homi (1992), 'The world and the home', *Social Text*, 31/32, pp. 141–53.

Brah, Avtar (2022), *Decolonial Imaginings: Intersectional Conversations and Contestations*, London: Goldsmiths Press.

Brar, Dhanveer Singh (2021), *Teklife, Ghettoville, Eski: The Sonic Ecologies of Black Music in the Early 21st Century*, London: Goldsmiths Press.

Bronfen, Elizabeth (2008), *Night Passages: Philosophy, Literature and Film*, New York: Columbia University Press.

Clark, Kenneth B. (1956), *Dark Ghetto: Dilemmas of Social Power*, Middletown: Wesleyan University Press.

Coplan, David B. (1985), *In Township Tonight: Three Centuries of South African Black City Music & Theatre*, Johannesburg: Longman.

Darnell, Regna (2013), 'Historical particularism', in R. J. McGee and R. L. Warms (eds), *Theory in Social and Cultural Anthropology: An Encyclopaedia, Vol. 1*, Thousand Oaks: SAGE Reference, pp. 397–401.

Dunn, Nick (2016), *Dark Matters: A Manifesto for the Nocturnal City*, Winchester: Zero Books.

Erlmann, V. (1990), 'Migration and Performance: Zulu Migrant Workers iSicathamiya Performance in South Africa, 1890–1950', *Ethnomusicology*, 34:2, pp. 99–220.

Erlmann, V. (1999), *Music, Modernity and the Global Imagination: South Africa and the West*, Oxford: Oxford University Press.

Garcia-Ruiz, Manuel (2021), 'Nocturanl ethnographies: Aesthetics and imaginary of the night', *International Night Studies Network*, 6 March, https://nightologists.hypotheses.org/489. Accessed 6 June 2021.

Harries-Jones, P. (1969), 'Home-boy ties and political organization in a Copperbelt township', in J. C. Mitchell (ed.), *Social Networks in Urban Situations*, Manchester: Manchester University Press, pp. 297–347.

Harvey, David (1989), *The Urban Experience*, Baltimore: Johns Hopkins University Press.

Hayles, N. K. (1999), *How We Became Posthuman*, Chicago: University of Chicago.

Hofmeyr, Isabel (1999), 'Making symmetrical knowledge possible: Recent trends in the field of Southern African oral performance studies', in D. Brown (ed.), *Oral Literature and Performance in Southern Africa*, Oxford: James Currey, pp. 18–27.

Hollands, Robert (2002), 'Divisions in the dark: Youth cultures, transitions and segmented consumption spaces in the night-time economy', *Journal of Youth Studies*, 5:2, pp. 153–71.

Johnson, S. L. (2001), 'Defining the migrants experience: An analysis of the poetry and performance of a contemporary Southern African genre', MA dissertation, Pietermaritzburg: University of Natal.

Laband, John (1995), *Robe of Sand: The Rise and Fall of the Zulu Kingdom in the Nineteenth Century*, Johannesburg: Jonathan Ball Publishers.

Labelle, Brandon (2018), *Sonic Agency: Sound and Emergent Forms of Resistance*, London: Goldsmiths Press.

Levitt, Peggy (2001), *The Transnational Villagers*, Berkeley: University of California Press.

McClendon, Thomas V. (2002), *Genders and Generations Apart: Labour Tenants and Customary Law in Segregation-Era South Africa, 1920s to 1040s*, London: Heinemann.

Osumare, H. (2007), *The Africanist Aesthetic in Global Hip-Hop – Power Moves*, New York: Palgrave Macmillan.

Parsons, Talcott (1971), *The System of Modern Societies*, New Jersey: Prentice-Hall.

Scott, James (1990), *Domination and the Arts of Resistance*, New Haven: Yale University Press.

Shusterman, R. (2000), *Performing Live: Aesthetic Alternatives for the Ends of Art*, Ithaca: Cornell University Press.

The Jazz Epistles (1960), *Scullery Department* (compos. Kippie Moeketsi), Johannesburg: Continental Records.

Wacquant, Loïc (2008), *Urban Outcasts: A Comparative Sociology of Advanced Marginality*, Cambridge: Polity Press.

Western, Tom (2020), 'Listening with displacement: Sound, citizenship, and disruptive representations of migration', *Migration and Society: Advances in Research*, 3, pp. 294–309.

10

Rooms for Resistance: Migration and Social Markers of Difference in Berlin's Queer Underground Electronic Music Scene

Gibran Teixeira Braga

Warm and cold

Berlin, Saturday, 2 May 2015. It was 1:30 a.m. and I was getting to the door of the club Griessmuehle. Like every first weekend of the month, that night the renowned party Cocktail D'Amore was on. Since its beginning in 2009, it has held a central place within the queer[1] electronic music scene in the city. Having arrived in the German capital exactly two months before, that would be the first of many times that I have seen and experienced such an event. I had been warned by interlocutors and friends that at Cocktail, the entry lines were very long (as is the case in almost every relevant party on the Berlin scene). However, I miscalculated the dimension of the human mass eager to enter the world of sounds and pleasures that were offered there. I had thought: 'if the party starts at midnight, by 1:30 a.m. there should be no queue'.

My mistake! As I made my way down the alley between the train line and the Neuköllner Schiffahrtskanal ('shipping canal') to the entrance of the club, I noticed not only the sound that came from the powerful equipment of the party but the length of the queue that awaited me. In a short while standing alone in the queue, I realized yet another miscalculation. It was 3 °C and the cloth sneakers that I wore were not suitable for the fledgling European spring. It didn't even occur to me, coming from a warm climate. I was born in a city that, despite the ironic name Cabo Frio (Cold Cape), is hot even during the night, as is the whole state of Rio de Janeiro and a good part of my tropical country Brazil. I had no idea of the effect of standing for two hours in the cold night air would have on my toes.

Stunned by my inexperience, I realized this was a really different scene to the one I had been used to for much of my nightlife as a DJ, researcher and partygoer. This was not a regular party of mainstream clubs like the ones I knew in Brazil, which started at midnight and ended at most just after dawn. Cocktail would go until midnight the next day, extending the nocturnal experience to reach a good part of the weekend. It made sense then that the lines were so long since people would have time to enjoy an extensive and, for many interlocutors, fulfilling club experience.

After quite a while of cold and tension, I finally entered the party. When I saw the first known face, I asked him for a hug. I needed warmth, literally, but also human warmth. I was welcomed by a Finnish guy who I had met a few weeks ago at another party. Although we only knew a little bit about each other, there was an instant connection and deep affection felt in that embrace. I came to understand that this feeling was one of the main characteristics of this nocturnal scene: the strong connections that are produced at parties, packed with drugs, music and an atmosphere of freedom.

Doubly warmed, I had a lot of fun all night. At dawn, we went out to the garden which was next to the river, where we would snuggle up around the campfire while the temperature was easing. At mid-morning, when the party was less crowded, I found myself alone again and felt another strangeness: the few acquaintances I had were no longer there; the boy with whom I exchanged kisses and caresses was gone. Experiencing this party temporality, which was new for me, I started to wonder what to do next. Go away, to another party, whose best time to arrive was precisely Sunday morning? That would mean spending more money, and I still didn't know how to handle the newness of my expenses in Euros. I decided to just sit and wait for something to happen. As time unfolded, I began to understand the logic behind long parties. Friends I hadn't seen during the night and who had left the party were now coming back. Other friends were arriving for the first time, and things started to unfold. Here is the cyclical character of such events: interleaved periods of dancing, chilling, talking, taking drugs, having sex and relaxing. As one interlocutor says, 'a good party is a party where things happen', and at Cocktail, they were happening. Or, as another interlocutor says, 'when you're wondering why to stay at a party, ask yourself: why not?'. In this chapter, I will show how the cyclical character of the parties relates to the kind of music played at them, based on a game between repetition and change that helps to create an intense experience of dancing, affection and physicality.

The queer electronic party scene of Berlin

With my own first experiences on the Berlin scene in mind, this chapter discusses the role of foreigners in the constitution of such a vibrant nightlife, based on the experiences of non-German citizens. If some of these foreigners are strong participants and help to shape the nightlife of Berlin, others face some difficulties to get into the scene, as I will show later. I draw on many fieldwork examples and stories from interlocutors that address issues regarding social markers of difference, such as gender, sexuality, ethnicity, nationality and migration. I additionally draw on my own experiences, as when I moved to Berlin as an intern at Freie Universität as part of my Ph.D. research. I was also a kind of migrant participating in parties, first as a partygoer and researcher, and later working at a few events. In 2017, 2019, 2021 and 2022, I was involved as a musician in Berlin, playing as a DJ at some parties, as well as producing an edition of Pista, the party that the collective I belong to held in São Paulo city. In 2019, I returned to Berlin to continue fieldwork, now for my current post-doctoral research.[2] After that, I was a visiting scholar at Freie Universität Berlin for twelve months, between 2021 and 2022. Throughout my time in Berlin, I worked with sixteen parties and one festival, all of which are (or were) produced by foreign people living in Berlin.[3] This attests the relevance of translocality (Appadurai 1996; Bennet and Peterson 2004; Garcia 2011) and circulation on the scene.[4]

The social relations explored in this chapter include musicians as well as partygoers. Authors such as Rapp (2010) and Peter (2014) point out how the centrality of the universe of underground electronic music in Berlin since the 2000s was reflected in the intense circulation not only of clubbers, but of artists: several musicians, producers and DJs moved to the city, attracted by the fertile environment for the scene, less pressed by the prohibitive regulations of other big cities around the world, like New York and London.

Berlin's nightlife is central to the economy of the city, being one of the main motivations for tourism. That's why clubs have a relative autonomy to negotiate their demands with the government when compared to other major cities around the world. It is through the combination of this specificity and the apport of migrant clubbers, artists and party producers that a very creative nocturnal scene establishes itself.

In Berlin, both Italian and Brazilian musicians and partygoers shape the underground electronic music scene, an aspect that is even recognized by German partygoers. In an interview, a Berlin-born interlocutor commented on this aspect, highlighting the fundamental role that the movement of people plays in the oxygenation of a scene:

> Several of the parties we mentioned are organized by people who moved here only a few years ago. And they became famous in a very short time. They are people who do not even know how to speak German, because they are from Brazil, São Paulo, Chile, Madrid, or whatever. What I learned, to a lesser extent, when I lived in Chicago, is that when you arrive in a new city, and fall in love with the city, you might learn a little about culture and enjoy the party culture, and learn about history – obviously they know about the name that Berlin has, since the 90s, techno, and how it started, the underground, and this thing of being open for days – they want to bring it back. It makes sense, if you arrive in a new city, you are more curious, more adventurous. If you live in the city, you don't even leave your neighborhood. Like, 'why should I?' In other words, you need that freshness. The parties are all held by Latinos. I think it's great, I love that people love the city so much.

Cocktail is an example of what was mentioned above. One of the most relevant parties, it is produced by two Italians, Giovanni Turco and Giacomo Garavelloni. As well as party producers, they are also a duo of electronic music producers and DJs, under the name Discodromo. After moving to Berlin in 2008, they created the party the following year. A Brazilian interlocutor defined Cocktail as 'the canon of post-Berghain parties'. Until 2009, Saturday nights were monopolized by Berghain, a huge and famous club run by Germans. Cocktail has three dancefloors. The main inside dancefloor, where the sound varies around harder techno styles, the Cosmic Hole floor, where you can listen to more experimental sounds, and the Garden floor, where during the day people can listen to sunny disco and house tunes.

Giovanni tries to explain why 'the main mixed-gay parties in Berlin are [...] mostly made by Italians. I don't really know what that has to do with BEING Italian. [...] Maybe it's the shallow openness – talking to people, being very social'. Giacomo adds:

> In Italy, the meal is traditionally one of the most important moments to socialize with the people you care about. So the family always eats together at a certain time. At dinner, it's common to just hang out, cook, enjoy the moment with your loved ones. It's very Italian, this communal experience. And probably you can transpose this to a party – it's like an intimate moment which you can share with strangers as well.
>
> (cited in Wang 2015: n.pag.)[5]

In the above excerpt, Giacomo brings the idea of communality that relates to the cyclical aspect of long parties that I mentioned in my own account above.

Another major party on the scene was Homopatik, also run by two Italians, Mr Ties and Danilo Rosato. Held at the famous left-wing club About Blank, it ran from 2010 to 2016, when the partnership ended. In its end, Homopatik was criticized for attracting a large heterosexual attendance, which earned it the ironic nickname Heteropatik. Danilo then went on to start Buttons, which take place every third weekend of each month at the same venue until 2021, when they left the club. Buttons managed to maintain the previous success of its predecessor and has been praised by participants in the scene: the party recovered the underground and gay spirit of Homopatik's first years. One of the initiatives that seems to have contributed to this was the installation of a dark room. Through the use of a curtain that separates part of the ground floor lounge, it creates an environment conducive to sexual practices. Another initiative is the effort to affirm a proposal that goes beyond the frequent protagonism of gay men, reflected in queer speeches and aesthetics, mixing male and female signs and images of bodies outside standard beauty patterns.

The idea that immigrants should be integrated is common in the official German discourse. However, the same charge is not made to Germans in the sense of respecting cultural differences. About this matter, we can highlight the presentation of the singer and DJ Aerea Negrot at an edition of Buttons, in the summer of 2017.[6] During her performance, the Venezuelan artist spoke of her experience as a Latin American transgender woman living in Germany. She uttered slogans such as 'integration is a two-way street!', alluding to the debates about immigration.

In addition to the Italians, Brazilians are also relevant protagonists within the scene. For example, in 2013, Raquel Fedato, Chris Phillips and Diego Garcia created the party Pornceptual (with Raquel and Chris producing the event, and Diego as its main resident DJ, under the name Project Gestalten). Pornceptual mixes house and techno music with a sexual and fetish environment and is presented as a platform for people to express sexuality in a creative way. The event was born as the physical extension of the project of an online gallery of erotic art. In an interview, Raquel recalled the proposal for Pornceptual in the following terms:

> [it's a] concept of criticism of porn industry, which is hypermasculine [...] it's not human, it's not realistic, it's plastic, it's something that does not make me horny. So, it was always a matter of exploring gender, exploring what art is, and how art comes into sex and nudity.

As well as Pornceptual, there was also Trashera, a project led by the Brazilian producer Geovane Pedro de Bortoli, which has for many years featured the Portuguese Bráulio Bandeira AKA Deepneue as its main resident DJ. In Figure 10.1, we can see a representation of the open area in one edition of Trashera. Another of Geovane's parties is Riot, a partnership with producer and DJ Mauro Feola, who is also from Brazil. Figure 10.2 reproduces the artwork of Riot's poster, created by Brazilian artist Leandro Cunha. Mauro Feola had two more parties, which bring Brazilian gay references in their names. Beitola is a wordplay with the German term

FIGURE 10.1: Trashera's open area. Photo by Ema Discordant. Courtesy of Trashera.

FIGURE 10.2: Leandro Cunha, illustration for Riot's poster. Courtesy of the artist.

Bei and the Brazilian word *baitola*, which means faggot. The other party was called Boyola, matching the word boy with another Brazilian slang for faggot, *boiola*.

All these parties play a relevant role on the scene, according to many interlocutors. The migrant background of their Brazilian producers is seen as central in the accomplishment of parties that are very appreciated by the partygoers that live and visit Berlin and experience its nocturnal musical scene.

In an interview with DJ Mauro Feola, he told me about his first impressions on Berlin's nightlife, including his position as a foreign DJ and the role of foreigners in the musical scene of the city:

> My first contact with Berlin's nightlife was very much connected to a more superficial Berlin, not so underground; I was still a tourist. In 2007, I met Berghain. When I moved in 2009, I was attending an indie music party in Prenzlauer Berg. Then I got a sense of how different Berlin was on the gay scene – I think that by this time queer was still starting to be born as a more prevalent concept in the community. It was a different environment, there was a more alternative group of people, not so much '*padé* and champagne'[7] as in the Brazil scene of the 2000s. I used to go to Vegas, to Glória a lot.[8] The Berlin scene that we know started to emerge in 2009, when Cocktail, Horse Meat Disco appeared. I arrived with these changes, which when you arrived were already sort of established, you know? In other words, it was all still very German, although this indie party was made by Brazilians. [...] As a DJ, I believe it is there, my Brazilian identity is there, but there is no general Brazilian identity. It is complicated to say that the Brazilian perceives music in a certain way, each person perceives it in a different way. And, since what we play is produced by musicians of different nationalities, there is a mixture, there are encounters. Foreigners have a definite role in the history of the Berlin electronic music scene, due to the presence of DJs here, of all possible nationalities. They bring their influences, which determine new trends in music here, so I can't say that Berlin's music is German music, it would be ridiculous to say that. Foreigners have transformed this world of electronic music from the queer scene that surpasses a party that is entirely German. If we think about it, the big parties are from Brazilians and Italians. They are those who have a more nomadic idea that is perhaps more connected to the underground and less to the mainstream.

It is interesting to note here how Mauro mobilizes the notion of nomadism to define the dynamic character of a scene that defies conventional social norms. We can refer to this notion in the figure of the nomad, introduced by Deleuze and Guattari (1987), where deterritorialization tends to resist the powers of the state. In the following section, I look at how the music played at these parties can relate to their cyclical character and intensify the experience of clubbing.

Electronic dance music structure and process pleasure

Certain aspects of electronic dance music (EDM) are fundamental to the physical experience of clubbers, such as the musical structure of the tracks. One of the main characteristics of EDM is that it is almost always organized around the loop. Loop is the sequence of sound elements that are repeated in the construction of a musical piece, sometimes identically, sometimes with the addition and/or subtraction of certain elements, as well as the increasing and/or decreasing of their emphasis. The elements that make up the loops are called, in turn, riffs – short musical phrases. The compositions are produced from synthesizers and drum machines, among other equipment. Currently, sophisticated music production software allow for the coming together of a multitude of sounds. To these sounds can be added samples of other recordings or even live recorded instruments.

Authors such as Ferreira (2006) and Garcia (2011) point out that the frequencies released by the high and low spectra of music are fundamental for the sensation produced by listening to EDM. Especially in spaces such as clubs, powerful sound systems multiply physical sensations that go beyond simple hearing. Such sensations are provoked in the public through three techniques, according to Ferreira (2008). These techniques are used by music producers when they are composing and by DJs when they are manipulating the tracks on the dancefloor. They are intensity effects (decibels), manipulating the sound volume (including effects of different frequency ranges, or hertz), differentiating between sounds that collide with the body (high) and those that penetrate it (bass), and speed effects (beats per minute, stimulating different rhythms in the dance). The mixer, indispensable equipment for the DJ, serves to manipulate these devices by controlling the volume, BPM and frequencies, which are divided into highs, mids and lows. Through equalizer controls, these can be rearranged in the track according to the desired effect.

Repetition is also a fundamental element in the enjoyment of EDM, creating an intense and growing form of engagement. Garcia (2005) sought to theoretically translate the achievement of pleasure into the enjoyment of this musical subgenre through repetition. The author draws on practice and experience to argue that repetition can be pleasurable. Garcia presents the concept of process pleasure, as a form of pleasure that generates itself during the action, not at the end of it. Through musical theory references, the author locates in the loop the locus from which the process pleasure is obtained, both in listening and in dancing to this type of music. Looping designates the technique of creating a rhythmic effect by layering loops. This practice thus produces the paradoxical effect of a constantly changing 'same'.

We can apply Garcia's model not just to individual tracks, but extend it to electronic music sets played on the dancefloor. The technique of mixing tracks, creating an uninterrupted sequence of sounds and rhythm, is fundamental to creating the atmosphere of the genre's dancefloors. Emerged in the mid 1970s in the context of disco music, the practice of mixing tracks became the norm in house and techno parties in the following decades and it is central to establishing a specific way of presenting music and dancing.

On the one hand, disco music innovated by being presented without interruption between one track and another, which produces a more intense experience on the dancefloor. On the other hand, the disco music scene was one of the first spaces of social dancing in which the dance was not performed necessarily by pairs of opposite-gender dancers. One could dance alone, with a pair from any gender or with three or more partners. It was also a scene marked by a mix of straight and LGBT people, as well by the protagonism of Latin and Black communities in New York City.

House and techno scenes emerged in the cities of Chicago and Detroit, respectively, as developments of the disco scene. These new genres of electronic music go beyond in dance innovations because there are no more pre-established dance steps. That allowed more people to engage on the dancefloor, intensifying the participation of the partygoers. It also impacted gender and sexuality dynamics on the dancefloor. Straight men started to enter the dancefloor to dance, not only to court women. This gave women more freedom to enjoy a party without being harassed by men when compared to different nocturnal spaces of sociability. The increased mix of straight and LGBT people also created unprecedented interaction opportunities between these two groups of people. All of that characterizes Berlin's EDM scene since its beginnings, in the late 1980s.

Circulation of people and sounds marks EDM scenes, and translocality is at their roots. It was through the connections between the emerging sounds of techno coming from Detroit and the correlated music being developed in Berlin that the scene of the German capital grew. Before being broadly recognized in the United States, the music produced by Underground Resistance (UR), a Black collective from Detroit, was well received in Berlin. In 1991, they signed with Tresor's label. Tresor was the first techno club of the city. This relationship became known as the 'Berlin-Detroit alliance'. The alliance brought an interesting political connection regarding feelings of enthusiasm for this new sound and a promise of future for both the Black youth of Detroit and the youth from the West and the East of the newly reunited Berlin. About this unusual arrangement of social markers of difference such as race, generation and nationality, DJ Robert Hood from UR, testifies:

> The enthusiasm we met in Berlin was surreal. But at the same time, it was sort of familiar. We had a common bond, and we knew that the bond was there, that we were on the same page. What was surreal was that we came from such different

> backgrounds. It seemed that they wanted to escape their past. And we wanted to escape our past, too, the one so full of racism. Escape and move on. Remember the past, but look for a better world. That, I believe, was the common thread. We were all looking to these futuristic, experimental sounds as an escape vehicle, as a spaceship with which to get away, to transport ourselves into the future where we're all one, where divisions of race and religion and culture are torn down just like the Berlin wall.
>
> (cited in Dunk and Von Thülen 2014: 154–55).

Coming back to Garcia's concept, to understand parties as a social phenomenon, I propose to extend the idea of process pleasure even further, applying it to the broader experience of the type of party I research. Thinking of pleasure as an open and continuous process offers a way to grasp the transforming potential that surpasses the ephemeral nature of the events themselves. The nights of these parties are lived as intense moments of interactions that impact participants in many ways.

The collective use of certain drugs like MDMA, a substance that has empathogenic effects, is seen as an enabler for the relaxation of social barriers of gender and sexuality. New ways to relate to body and pleasure emerge, destabilizing norms and conventions naturalized in broader society. Ketamine and amphetamines help to develop a new time-use regime, especially in long parties, in which cycles of dancing, conversations, erotic practices, rest and collective consumption of substances (drugs, drinks and food) alternate and are repeated for many hours, creating a modality of experience that could be described as an 'inhabiting' of the party. This opens up space for the appreciation of a party that is not productive in the standard sense of the term, to use an idea that Garcia mobilizes in his conception of process pleasure. My experience presented at the beginning of this chapter is an example of that multiple meaning of repetition and cycles, which applies to both the music and the inhabiting of the party. Therefore, there is a specific aspect of temporality present in the night and in the looped music produced and consumed by people that circulate through different scenes, cities and countries.

Door policy, inequalities and reactions

Despite all the examples above, there are some ambiguities around the atmosphere of acceptance and diversity of the scene. Such ambivalence has to do with the door policy, a practice common to almost every party and club in Berlin, of selecting who is going to get in or not. Most of my interlocutors justify this practice by claiming that those safe spaces for freedom, drug use, nudity and unusual sex practices have to be preserved from uptight people, curious people and random tourists – people who could intimidate or disturb the partygoers.

That's the paradox – the parties are spaces of ambivalence and contradiction, whose egalitarian atmosphere does not mean that they are inclusive spaces. These are events that are concerned with promoting an environment free of hierarchies *within* the clubs, but they are not concerned with overcoming certain discrimination existing *outside* them, in the broader social dynamics, and sometimes even reinforcing them.

Rodgers, who did research in Berlin clubs, shows how the scene circulates a 'diversity discourse' about the parties. According to Rodgers (2015: 2), this discourse positions the parties as representing 'diversity, acceptance, equality and tolerance: spaces within which social divisions are suspended, difference is overcome and people are united'. The author argues that, despite this idealization, the access to these clubs is based on the possession of social privilege, and undertakes an intersectional investigation that seeks to contextualize the discourse of diversity with a focus on perceptions about race, ethnicity, sexuality and gender.

Rodgers points out the relative absence of people of Turkish and Arab ethnicities in general at underground parties when compared to the percentage of people of this origin living in the city. The idea that these parties are not attractive to this audience is coupled with a certain prejudiced conception that Turks and Arabs, especially men, would be more prone to having homophobic and sexist attitudes. According to the author, this stereotype partially explains the low frequency of these people: door policies would be tougher for them, systematically denying them entry. This could generate a circular effect: since this profile is 'framed', many would not even try to enter. It is difficult then to define which of these factors prevails, and when the cut works: whether at the door or even before this.

Julian[9] is a German interlocutor who, in addition to being a clubber, is a leftist militant, in his own words. He has been linked to political movements since he was a teenager and approached the theme himself during an interview when he asked me about the racial issue in Berlin. As a graduate student in the Humanities area, Julian drew a parallel between the question of Turks and German Turks on Berlin's scene and the broader picture of the relationship of White German society with the Turkish community, the main group of immigrants since the 1970s in the country:

> The Turks, who have lived here for 30, 40 years, do not go to these places. Because people often say that the problem is Turks, that they are closed communities, that Turks do not want integration, but I think it has two sides. I think the biggest problem is the Germans, it is the German state, the German society that, outside Berlin, does not have this culture of integrating foreigners. And it is always the goal to divide the Turks and the Germans. In my city there are many Turks, and you can see in the architecture and how the city is, it is clearly divided, the Turkish and German neighborhoods. I think it is important to always remember that too, that it's not just

> because the Turks don't want to integrate. Because here, in this underground scene, foreigners have a very good impression of Germany. Because they see how things are in Berlin, many times the image of people in Berlin is very limited.

The interlocutor points out how an image of current harmony in Berlin can blur certain symbolic barriers typical of German society that persist even in the less hierarchical environment of Berlin's underground scene. On the other hand, he says that, when it comes to Black people, the situation is different. Since no alternative party wants to be labelled racist, they tend to let Black people in more than White people, proportionally. Those ambivalences could be thought through the difference between two categories regarding people living abroad: 'expats' and 'migrants'. The scene seems to be more open to the first, that usually choose to be in Berlin and share certain middle-class, cosmopolitan logic. I include myself in this category, being a party producer, a DJ and an academic researching the city's nightlife. Otherwise, the term 'migrants' usually refers to people that come from poor backgrounds and were not supposed to integrate, by the mainstream German standard.

However, some initiatives tried to address the issue. I worked at two parties whose motto was 'Refugees Welcome' – at these events, the entrance fee was going directly to refugees who had recently arrived in Berlin. At one of those events, it was interesting to see how a group of straight Syrian men, brought by a social worker, interacted with the regular mixed LGBT public of the club. That happened at the traditional queer club SchwuZ, which was created as a mutual support group for LGBT people and offers a kind of welcome letter (circulated within the club) explaining the politics of space:

> Since opening in 1977, SchwuZ strives to create a non-discriminatory forum for homosexuals and queers. Today, more than 30 years later, we still benefit from the courage of those who fought in the name of a gay movement that faced radical political and social repressions. Nevertheless, are discrimination and outlawing (e.g. through sexist or racist behavior) also still part of our community: our own experiences of discrimination do not necessarily prevent us from discriminating against someone else. Particularly black people, queers of color, trans* and inter* people, people with handicaps, women and female-identified people, those who do not correspond to dominant beauty aesthetics, those who are considered to be too old or too young or those who are expected to have a migration background, are frequently exposed to discriminatory responses. We do not tolerate any kind of derogatory practices at SchwuZ. You are at a location that seeks to be a place for joint development, where fascist or racist symbols and clothing (e.g. swastika) are not tolerated, where sexual harassment or sexual violence are not tolerated and where we hope our DJs,

> artists and hosts respect our values with their selected content. We want to create a space that is exempt from discrimination, where people are considerate and pay attention to one another, and where everyone is comfortable and feels supported. If you share the ideas conveyed in this self-conception and want to support us in being a non-discriminatory forum as well as a protective space for everybody, we are looking forward to welcoming you as our guest. If you experience any kind of verbal or physical abuse, homo/trans*fobic behavior, subliminal or overt sexism, racism or ableism, please do not hesitate to immediately contact our night manager or door staff.

This particular club, in recent years, became a kind of a hub for young queer migrants. With increasing migration in the city from 2015 to 2019, I noticed a shift in the atmosphere and the demographics of the club. The crowd was becoming younger and more mixed in terms of ethnicity and nationality. That was also reflected in a change in the focus of the music. Mainstream pop music, especially from the United States, was gaining more prominence in the programme of the club parties.

Other initiatives emerge, such as the collective Room for Resistance (R4R), a 'queer femme/non-binary forward collective [that] runs intersectional and body/sex positive queer raves [...] to promote women, gender queers, non-binary, trans, inter, black and POC [people of color] artists' (n.d.: n.pag.). R4R works with an academic/militant approach, addressing not only gender and sexuality issues but also those of ethnicity and nationality, serving as a space that welcomes immigrant and refugee artists. Moving beyond the fund-raising focus, the idea of the collective is to explicitly embrace refugees. Since 2016, Luz Diaz, one of its founders, has been reaching out to a queer refugee centre, inviting folks to go to their party. One attendee, Ola, declared: 'when I go there, I feel like I'm at home. I'm with friends and friends of friends, I just feel really comfortable in that atmosphere. Everyone is really nice and awesome. I have so much fun'.[10] It is interesting to note here how this nocturnal scene happens in cycles, not only through the course of a night but also through the years. The increasing debates about the inclusion of migrants and refugees favours an extension of the atmosphere of freedom that characterizes the scene.

Final considerations

To conclude, I would like to present Jackson's view of the clubber experience, which he calls clubbing. The author uses Bourdieu's concept of *habitus* – a process by which social structures are embodied by actors, and argues that

> [t]he sensual intensity of clubbing generates an alternative body in which the structuring framework of habitus is temporally erased and this erasure underpins the modified social world you encounter through clubbing. Obviously, this is not the reason why people club, they're not sitting at home thinking: 'Right, I'm off to erase my habitus'. It is an unintended consequence of the drugs, the dancing and the crowds. It is an experience that impacts incrementally on people as the body of clubbing begins to challenge the body bequeathed to them by their own culture, thereby changing the way in which they negotiate their passage through their social realm and relate to the symbolic and ideological frameworks, which govern that realm. This can be a problematic process – with its dangers, confusions and blind alleys – yet my informants all agreed that the risks they sometimes took while clubbing were worth because clubbing had added something to their lives they valued.
>
> (Jackson 2004: 5).

I came across very similar statements made by several of my interlocutors. Thus, clubbing, more than a momentary relief from everyday hardships, seems to be a true clubber existence, by transforming their lives to a greater or lesser degree. I agree with Jackson when he defines it as 'a form of knowledge' and 'a way of occupying the world'. And, in this dwelling, displacements about the way of being in the world occur beyond the hours of the party. The interlocutor Virginia,[11] an American Black woman who moved to Berlin accompanying her German husband (who works as a bouncer in a famous club), summed up her clubber experience, associating her with a certain libertarian vocation that inhabits the imaginary about the city:

> Perhaps it's not a coincidence that I started to like the city when I started to know the club scene. It was on the club scene where I didn't feel rejected in the city for the first time, where I felt at home for the first time. People were so free, so permissive. It was so incredible to have a gay mayor.[12] I love the fact that here it was no big deal that he was gay, so I loved the gay mayor. And I loved parties where people really did whatever shit they wanted, but the point was to live and let live, which for me, has always been the basis of my policy: my personal policy, my 'political' policy: if is anything that doesn't hurt you or others, ok. [...] Berlin's party scene for me has always been about freedom. Not about acceptance – I don't need to be accepted, or walking around making best friends – I just want to be free.

In the above excerpt, we can see how the interlocutor extends the clubber's way of life to her position in the wider world and locates in clubbing the process by which she found herself in a city that was not hers, in a country that was not hers. Returning to Jackson's aforementioned definition, for Virginia, it is clear that there is 'something valued' that clubbing has added to her life.

Therefore, we can think of the scene discussed in this piece as a complex space of ambivalence. On the one hand, it offers an environment of freedom stimulated by the type of music played, marked by a structure that increases people's engagement on the dancefloor, through techniques of intensification of sound and the interplay between repetition and change. The parties are spaces where people can experiment with various arrangements of social markers of difference such as gender, sexuality in new ways of living their time and their bodies; and the participation of foreigners and migrants has been crucial to the constitution of this scene, as seen above. On the other hand, there are still remaining tensions from broader social dynamics regarding those social markers of difference, including ethnicity, nationality and the issue of migration.

NOTES

1. This classification is at dispute: some participants contest the use of the term queer, pointing out that several normativities would persist in the scene, such as the predominance of bodies that follow the dominant beauty pattern, male protagonism and the invisibility of lesbian women. However, I choose to keep the term because most of the interlocutors thus define the scene. As we will see, recent initiatives are trying to fight this imbalance.
2. My Ph.D. thesis is called 'O fervo e a luta: políticas do corpo e do prazer em festas de São Paulo e Berlim' ('Party for your rights: Politics of body and pleasure at parties in São Paulo and Berlin') and my post-doctoral research is 'O musicar clubber: corpo e subjetividade em cenas de música eletrônica underground de São Paulo e Berlim' ('Clubber musicking: Body and subjectivity in underground electronic music scenes of São Paulo and Berlin'). Both research projects are funded by FAPESP (processes 2013/04891-7 and 2018/10332-4).
3. See more in Braga (2018).
4. Garcia, who also did fieldwork on Berlin's nightlife, defines translocal musical scenes as 'geographically specific spaces of musical activity articulated through translocal circuits (of people, music, information) to similar translocal scenes in other locales' (2011: 14).
5. Interview available at https://groove.de/2015/11/06/discodromo-interviewed-by-daniel-wang/. Accessed 7 April 2021.
6. https://soundcloud.com/aereanegrot/buttonslive2017. Accessed 14 April 2021.
7. *Padé* is a term for cocaine in Brazilian LGBT slang. The expression '*padé* and champagne' refers ironically to fancy gay spaces.
8. Vegas and Gloria were clubs of São Paulo that used to be seen as more mainstream.
9. Fictitious name.
10. See more in https://ra.co/features/2771. Accessed 4 April 2021.
11. Fictitious name.
12. The openly gay Klaus Wowereit was the mayor of Berlin from 2001 to 2014.

REFERENCES

Appadurai, Arjun (1996), 'The production of locality', in *Modernity at Large: Cultural Dimensions of Globalization*, Minneapolis: University of Minnesota Press, pp. 178–99.

Bennet, Andy and Peterson, A. Richard (eds) (2004), *Music Scenes: Local, Trans-Local and Virtual*, Nashville: University of Vanderbilt Press.

Braga, Gibran Teixeira (2018), '"O fervo e a luta": políticas do corpo e do prazer em festas em São Paulo e Berlim', doctoral thesis, São Paulo: Universidade de São Paulo.

Deleuze, Gilles and Guattari, Felix (1987), *A Thousand Plateaus. Capitalism and Schizophrenia*, Minneapolis: University of Minnesota Press.

Dunk, Felix and Von Thülen, Sven (2014), *Der Klang der Familie: Berlin, Techno and the Fall of the Wall*, Norderstedt: BoD.

Ferreira, Pedro Peixoto (2006), 'Música eletrônica e xamanismo: técnicas contemporâneas do êxtase', doctoral thesis, Campinas: Unicamp.

Ferreira, Pedro Peixoto (2008), 'Transe maquínico: quando som e movimento se encontram na música eletrônica de pista', *Horizontes Antropológicos*, 14:29, pp. 189–215.

Garcia, Luís-Manuel (2005), 'On and on: Repetition as process and pleasure in electronic dance music', *Music Theory Online*, 11:4, pp. 1–14.

Garcia, Luís-Manuel (2011), '"Can you feel it, too?": intimacy and affect at electronic dance music events in Paris, Chicago and Berlin', Ph.D. thesis, Chicago: University of Chicago.

Jackson, Phil (2004), *Inside Clubbing: Sensual Experiments in the Art of Being Human*, Oxford, New York: Berg.

Rodgers, Naomi Alice (2015), '"House and techno broke them barriers down": Exploring exclusion through diversity in Berlin's electronic dance music nightclubs', MA dissertation, Linköping: Linköping University.

Room for Resistance (R4R) (n.d.), home page, https://room4resistance.net/. Accessed 4 April 2021.

Interlude 5

Sounding In, Sounding Out: Remembrance and Resistance at the Border

Emilie Amrein and André de Quadros

I.

We approached the border at sundown, the air thick with electricity. The traffic slowed slightly as we crossed into Mexico, and after a few traffic lights, we were sucked into the gravitational pull of a Tijuana roundabout, a chaotic and disordered miracle of human intuition. Holding my breath, I tracked the brake lights and protruding mirrors of the cars in my proximity, my ears attuned to the honk of horns punctuating the hot night sky. In the distance, a siren sings a mournful tune, and without warning, I was transported back to Chicago in the winter of 2009.

I remember closely following the ambulance, lights flashing, from our small regional hospital into the city, her little infant body under close monitor just 36 hours post-partum. What a terrifying sensation to have this new-born, this tiny creature who had recently resided within my own body, strapped into an incubator transport unit in a tangle of monitor wires and feeding tubes! The doctors and nurses whisked her away into an ambulance, and we were told to follow as best we were able in the icy, winter weather.

Looking back, I remember the backwards logic of new motherhood. How could it be that I did not feel, in my own body, the pain she endured as she was poked with sharp needles and prodded by metal instruments in gloved hands? How disorienting and surreal to understand that her body was not an extension of mine! She was not me.

Though the journey through the winter night felt a million miles away from that roundabout in Tijuana, I was not able to move the needle in my mind's eye out of the groove of that memory. Only in the last few years have I understood the fiery power of that moment in my life, forging me into some new being, part satellite, part empty vessel, fear filling the space she once occupied. That night in Tijuana, I felt distance and time, and every fibre of my identity, bend in the crossing.

II.

The wall, long, tall, forbidding, with holes and cracks, places and spaces for falling tears and unmet kisses – this is the wall that the governments boast about, a place of pilgrimage, hope and mourning. I put my fingers in the crevices, my nose pressed against it, and stared at the bodies on the other side – the Mexicans on one side and the Americans on the other. I was neither.

I allowed my eyes to run along the wall to the water, and there it was. A child's shoe (Figure I5.2), half-buried in the sand. When I was a boy, a smuggler had picked me up in his hard hands in the dead of night and put me in a rowboat. They chose the darkest night for the crossing. Not a word, barely a breath. And when he put me soundlessly in the boat, my sandal fell in the water. I remember the way it floated on the surface of the water, like a toy, unbothered by danger and fear.

For many years, my parents referred to this period as being 'stranded in Goa', for that is where we were – stranded in a Portuguese colony in India, tucked away along the coast, separate from independent India – on what was to be a family holiday. I can still see my father weeping, wondering what would happen next. The smugglers took us over the border in that rowboat, and soon we were back in India. We hid for weeks. Other children went to school, but I didn't. Others could play outside but we couldn't. We lived in the shadows of exile, until it was safe.[1]

Decades later, I recognize the boy in the boat in my adult body, moving between countries, with relative ease. The gentle lapping of the waves at the Tijuana wall was strangely like the waters of the Arabian Sea, on the Bombay coast. As I stared into the distance, the sound of the water brought me back to the wall. I reached through, wondering if my long and bony fingers would find a human connection. My body holds the wounds of my own life journey, my grief and my guilt. Standing at the wall, that monument to colonial brutality, I was reminded of the paradox of colonization; I have been both the violated and the violator. I have inherited, indeed benefited from the pyramid construction of caste and class. I carried both truths in my fingers, as I reached through the iron rebar. The shame of borders! I wept for the boy in the boat and for the man whom that boy would become.

FIGURE I5.1: The Mexico–US border wall, 2019. Photo by Emilie Amrein.

FIGURE I5.2: A shoe on the beach at the Mexico–US border wall, 2019. Photo by Emilie Amrein.

III.

We had made a big, beautiful mess of the common space on the ground floor of Espacio Migrante.[2] Papier-mâché masks with brightly coloured markings were stashed in corners and on tabletops.

Bright blue painter's tape attached one end of a paper bridge to a desk and the other to a plaster wall. Abandoned scissors and crayons were stationed next to mountains of clothing and toiletries donated by the community to be distributed to our new friends whenever they had need. The entire place took on the sweet smell of sawdust and laundry detergent, a familiar perfume that reminded me of new beginnings.

That night, under the cover of darkness, we sat in a circle on the floor with our new friends from Ecuador, Guatemala, Cameroon, Haiti and Cuba, telling stories and sharing songs from home. We had come to listen and play, to cry and laugh and sing together in the safety of the shelter common room. We transformed the shelter into a stage, inhabiting one another's memories and dreams for a few moments that night.

Like a child, I climbed up the iron staircase with Maria to the new storage loft that looked down on the larger room.[3] At that moment, I was transported to the top of the stairs in my childhood home. I remember sneaking out of bed with a blanket and pillow, making a nest for myself on the staircase landing, pulling at the edges of the carpet where it met the baseboard of the wall. I would lean into the bannister rails, peering at my mother who would spend her nights folding

FIGURE I5.3: Papier-mâché masks at Espacio Migrante. Photo by: Emilie Amrein.

FIGURE I5.4: A group from Common Ground Voices / La Frontera meeting at Espacio Migrante, 2019. Photo by Mariana Jones.

FIGURE I5.5: Emilie and workshop participants at Espacio Migrante, 2019. Photo by Mariana Jones.

laundry, tidying up toys, or paying bills in the room below. We were a holy trio – my sister, my mother and me. How she managed, I'll never know.

Back in the shelter, I sat in the loft with Maria, as she described breastfeeding her young daughter in the open boxcar of La Bestia.[4] She spoke of the impossible decisions she was forced to make, the fear she felt in her bones. Her grief was palpable but matched by a profound strength. As we wept together, holding hands, we looked down at the mess of the room, children and adults huddled together talking and listening. From the vantage point of that storage loft, I suddenly understood how a shelter becomes a sanctuary, how sacrifice is born of deep love, and how stories and songs can bind us to one another in powerful ways.

IV.

On the night of the performance, the community[5] divided itself into two, singing the story of this place with our voices as a witness. We sang to each other, eyes fixed, bodies transformed passing the song from one to another through arms, torso, toes, breath and more. 'Dos cuerpos' – two bodies. We built a sonic world, a consoling signature of the stars falling at night. Cascading voices draped over the deep undulating bass line, grounding Julio's song.[6]

With eyes wide, I saw the bodies on the other side of the stage animating, together moving like a multi-limbed organism. Here was the wall and no wall at the same time. *Para mí, estábamos separadas y no.* The cries from another piece earlier in the concert, 'inmigrante' and 'deportada' were ringing in my ears. I could no longer sing.

Why was I so profoundly shaken at that moment? Was it Julio's interpretation of the poem?[7] Was it the image of the bodies facing each other? Was it the gaze, eyes to eyes? Or was it the reminder of the brutal wall that did me in? The sounded word opened the wounds of past lives, and I wondered about the precarious future that Maria and her family faced. What would become of the countless others who are fleeing and banished?

Though we had stood face to face on stage, and at the wall, we would eventually turn away. We crossed back into San Ysidro, not fully knowing the wings of our privilege. Could the poet not see the way this world is fractured? Maria and the other migrants and I are *not* two bodies facing, *not* two stars falling together. I left Tijuana with a new understanding of my own subjectivity, as well as a series of deeply unsettling questions. We carry our stories with us, and with each new experience, we re-story ourselves in this world. What was the soundprint that we left behind for Maria and the other forced migrants? Would they carry our stories in their bodies the way I carry

FIGURE I5.6: Common Ground Voices / La Frontera at the border wall, 2019. Photo by Luke Leidiger.

theirs in mine? How might we fix our gaze on the border, so that we might face one another on the journey ahead? As we remember those nights of singing and playing, always witnessing, what signature did we leave behind?

NOTES

1. For further information on this dark time in my family's history, see de Quadros (2020).
2. Espacio Migrante is a refugee shelter and community space in Tijuana, BC, México.
3. Maria's name has been changed to protect her confidentiality. For more information about her journey, see Chapters 3 and 5 of de Quadros and Amrein (2022).
4. La Bestia, sometimes referred to as 'the death train' is a freight train that runs from the south to the north of Mexico, carrying forced migrants.
5. The community referred to here is Common Ground Voices / La Frontera. For more information on Common Ground Voices / La Frontera, see https://www.cgvlafrontera.org. Accessed 4 August 2022.
6. Julio Morales's song is 'Dos cuerpos', a setting of Octavio Paz's poem. https://www.youtube.com/watch?v=hQQrbck1DyE. Accessed 4 August 2022.
7. The poem referred to here is Octavio Paz's 'Dos cuerpos'.

REFERENCES

De Quadros, André (2020), 'From boy in a boat to searching for song', in K. T. Vu and A. de Quadros (eds), *My Body was Left on the Street: Music Education and Displacement*, Leiden: Brill, pp. 11–15.

De Quadros, André and Amrein, Emilie (2022), *Empowering Song: Music Education from the Margins*, Abingdon: Routledge.

Morales, Julio (2012), 'Dos cuerpos', score, Xalapa: Julio Morales.

Paz, Octavio (2003), *Libertad bajo palabra: obra poética (1935–1957)*, México: Fondo de Cultura Económica.

Contributors

EMILIE AMREIN is an Associate Professor of Music and Chair of the Department of Music at the University of San Diego where she teaches courses on the intersection of music and social justice movements, community music and changemaking. In 2022, she co-authored *Empowering Song: Music Education from the Margins* (Routledge). As a speaker, she has presented her work for numerous professional organizations, including the National Collegiate Choral Organization, Chorus America, the American Choral Directors Association and the College Music Society.

* * * * *

GIBRAN TEIXEIRA BRAGA is a Brazilian anthropologist, DJ and producer of electronic music parties. He is a researcher at NUMAS (Center for Studies on Social Markers of Difference) and at PAM (Research in Musical Anthropology), a Postdoctoral Fellow at University of São Paulo and a Visiting Postdoc at Freie Universität Berlin. The scholar is currently engaged in research about São Paulo and Berlin scenes of independent electronic music, focusing on issues about gender, sexuality, race, class, politics and the creation of safe spaces and communities in these scenes.

* * * * *

POL ESTEVE CASTELLÓ is an architect, researcher and teacher. His work explores the relationship between space, technology and body with special attention to anonymous and collective histories of architecture. His work has been shown in the context of architecture and fine arts in CA2M (2022), Theatrum Mundi (2021), La Casa Encendida (2021), Architectural Review (2020), Matadero Madrid (2020), Arch+ (2020), Yale Paprika (2019), Cruising Pavilion in ArkDes Stockholm (2019), Vitra Design Museum (2018), among others. He is cofounder of the architectural studio GOIG, and is a Studio Master in the Architectural Association, and a Ph.D. candidate in The Bartlett (UCL).

*****

ANDRÉ DE QUADROS is an artist and human rights activist with work in over 40 countries in diverse settings including professional ensembles, projects with prisons, psychosocial rehabilitation, refugees, and victims of torture and trauma. His work crosses race and mass incarceration, peacebuilding, forced migration and Islamophobia. He is a Professor of Music at Boston University with affiliations in African, African American, Asian, Jewish and Muslim Studies, Prison Education and Antiracist Research. He directs choirs and choral projects in Indonesia, Sri Lanka, the United States, Israel and the Arab world, and the Mexico-US border. In 2019, he was a Distinguished Academic Visitor at the University of Cambridge. https://www.andredequadros.com/

*****

NICK DUNN is Executive Director of ImaginationLancaster, an open and exploratory design and architecture research lab at Lancaster University in the UK, where he is also Professor of Urban Design. He is the founding Director of the Dark Design Lab, exploring the impacts of nocturnal activity on humans and non-humans. Nick is author of *Dark Matters: A Manifesto for the Nocturnal City* (Zero, 2016) and co-editor of *Rethinking Darkness: Cultures, Histories, Practices* (Routledge, 2020).

*****

JILLIAN FULTON-MELANSON is a Course Director in the Department of Anthropology at York University and has training in ethnomusicology, education and music performance. Her current research is an ethnographic account of queer, subaltern youth who participate in a niche community of industrial techno and noise music in Montreal and Casablanca, and whose music and branding speak to social issues such as nationalism and violence. Outside of academia, she actively performs at underground electronic music events and collaborates/plays with Arabic folk musicians.

*****

JACQUELINE GEORGIS is currently a Visiting Assistant Professor of Music at College of the Holy Cross (2022–23). She received her Ph.D. in Ethnomusicology from Yale University in May 2022. Her research interests include global music history,

Lusophone popular music, African popular music, electronic dance music, and migration and diasporic studies. Her doctoral dissertation 'Batida of the diaspora: Afro-Portuguese electronic dance music in Lisbon' examines ideas of cultural hybridity and transnational exchange within the Lusophone-Atlantic.

* * * * *

MASIMBA HWATI works across sculpture, sound, performance, video and text. He holds an MFA from the University of Michigan, Ann Arbor, MI and is a Ph.D. candidate in Art Practice at the Academy of Fine Art, Vienna. Hwati is a Skowhegan School of Painting and Sculpture alumni, class of 2019, and he studied and taught sculpture at Harare Polytechnic Art School. His work is included in collections such as University of Michigan Museum of Art (UMMA), Iziko, South African National Gallery, Montreal Museum of Fine Arts, Scott White Contemporary Art Inc. in San Diego, Jorge M. Perez Collection in Miami, George R. N'Namdi Collection in Detroit, National Gallery of Zimbabwe and the Gervanne & Matthias Leridon Collection. In 2015, Hwati showed at the Zimbabwean Pavilion at the Venice Biennale 56th edition. He is an honorary research fellow at Rhodes University Fine Arts Department in Grahamstown, South Africa.

* * * * *

AILBHE KENNY is Associate Professor of Music Education at Mary Immaculate College, University of Limerick, Ireland. She is author of *Communities of Musical Practice* (Routledge, 2016) and co-editor of *Musician-Teacher Collaborations: Altering the Chord* (Routledge, 2018). She is a Fulbright Scholar, EURIAS fellow, Irish Research Council Laureate and holds a Ph.D. from the University of Cambridge. Ailbhe was a PI on the HERA-funded project 'Night Spaces: Migration, Culture and Integration in Europe' (2019–22) and is currently PI on the IRC-funded 'Music in the Intercultural School: Uncovering Spaces for Agency and Belonging' (2022–26).

* * * * *

SEGER KERSBERGEN is affiliated to the Leiden University Centre for the Arts in Society (Leiden, The Netherlands). His Ph.D. study was part of 'Night spaces: Migration, culture and IntegraTion in Europe', a collaborative research project funded by HERA. Drawing on his previous work on spatial practice and landscape, his research focused on the Cape-Verdean community in Rotterdam, investigating how Cape Verdean migrants (have) navigate(d) and imagine(d) the city of Rotterdam, producing both spaces of belonging and resistance. His main focus is on spaces of music-making and music-sharing.

*****

BRENDAN KIBBEE is a Lecturer at John Jay College of the City University of New York. He received a Ph.D. in Music at the CUNY Graduate Center, analyzing music as a form of African urbanism in Dakar, Senegal. A pianist and percussionist, he has also worked with musicians in New York's Senegalese diaspora community for much of the past decade. Recent publications include articles in *African Studies Review* and *Current Musicology* and a chapter on 'Music and Islam in Africa' in the *Palgrave Handbook of Islam in Africa* (2020).

*****

ÁINE MANGAOANG is a musicologist at the University of Oslo and recent recipient of the Norwegian Research Council's Young Research Talent award. She is author of *Dangerous Mediations: Pop Music in a Philippine Prison Video* (Bloomsbury, 2019); winner of IASPM-US Woody Guthrie Book Prize. Recent research on music, (dis)ability, place and prison politics appear in *Musicæ Scientiæ* (SAGE, 2021), *Beyoncé: At Work, On Screen and Online* (Indiana University Press, 2020) and the *Journal of World Popular Music* (2019). Her co-edited book, *Made in Ireland: Studies in Popular Music* (Routledge, 2020), is a comprehensive introduction to the history, sociology and musicology of Irish popular music.

*****

DEREK PARDUE is Associate Professor and Coordinator of the Brazilian Studies Program inside the Global Studies Department at Aarhus University in Denmark. He works on issues of urbanism, migration and expressive culture throughout the Black Atlantic. Currently, he is a Principal Investigator in the HERA-funded 'Night spaces: Migration, culture and integration in Europe' project. His latest book is a collection of ethnographic short stories inspired by the lyrics of a famous Brazilian rap recording.

*****

NICK PRIOR is Professor of Cultural Sociology at the University of Edinburgh. With interests that span urban soundscapes, social theory and the sociology of music, his work explores the myriad ways technologies are sunk into everyday cultural practices and entangled within social formations. He is author of a series of articles that explore digital mediations of popular music culture in the post-1980s period, culminating in a monograph, *Popular Music, Digital Technology and Society* (SAGE, 2018). He also works with sound and how sound recordings and music composition might be used to enliven our understandings of multi-sensorial assemblages.

*****

AUSTIN T. RICHEY is a musician, multimedia artist and Ph.D. candidate in Ethnomusicology at Eastman School of Music. His dissertation research is based in Detroit, MI, where he explores the resonances between diasporic African musical, dance and visual arts and Detroit-specific genres such as Motown and techno. Richey has published original research in *Opioid Aesthetics: Expressive Culture in an Age of Addiction* (West Virginia University Press, 2020) has contributed research to the Public Broadcasting Service digital series Sound Field and has a forthcoming essay in the *Routledge Handbook of Music in the New African Diaspora.*

*****

WILLIANS SANTOS is an actor, DJ, musical curator and podcaster. He is also a doctoral candidate in Social Sciences at the University of Campinas (Unicamp) with funding from the CNPq agency in Brazil. His project is entitled: 'Africa in Brazil: Encounters and tension in the trajectories of African musicians in the Brazilian scene.' Santos has published material in *Le Monde, Diplomatique Brasil*, *Brasil de Fato*, *Ponte Jornalismo*, *Migra Mundo* and *Hits Perdidos.*

*****

SIPHO SITHOLE is a Research Fellow at the Johannesburg Institute for Advanced Study (University of Johannesburg). He holds a Ph.D. in Anthropology from the University of the Witwatersrand. His research interests are on culture and the creative economy, language and identity, marginality and belonging, culture and celebration, social mobility and songs of migration. He is also a cultural and creative economy strategy consultant.

*****

KATIE YOUNG holds a Ph.D. in Music and is currently a Postdoctoral Research Fellow at Brock University, Canada and Editorial Assistant for *Ethnomusicology Forum* journal. Katie has conducted research in Ghana, Ireland and Canada, and has published in a range of journals and edited volumes.

Index

ill refers to an illustration; *n* to a note

www.ingramcontent.com/pod-product-compliance
Lightning Source LLC
LaVergne TN
LVHW060728310826
846742LV00016B/51
* 9 7 8 1 7 8 9 3 8 6 9 9 8 *